Chronicling California

A Primary Source Reader

Edited by Päivi Hoikkala and Eileen V. Wallis

California State Polytechnic University - Pomona

Bassim Hamadeh, CEO and Publisher
Kassie Graves, Director of Acquisitions
Jamie Giganti, Senior Managing Editor
Jess Estrella, Senior Graphic Designer
Gem Rabanera, Project Editor
Alexa Lucido and Elizabeth Rowe, Licensing Coordinators
Allie Kiekhofer and Chelsey Schmid, Associate Editors

Printed in the United States of America

ISBN: 978-1-63487-969-9 (pbk) / 978-1-63487-970-5 (br)

CONTENTS

GUIDE TO FIGURES AND TABLES

HOW TO ANALYZE A PRIMARY SOURCE

What Are Primary Sources?

Primary sources are the evidence left behind by participants and observers of a given event or during a particular period of time. Primary sources allow us to make personal connections to the past. They are the evidence historians build upon to create an interpretation of the past. There is no more effective way to get a sense of past events than to examine documents directly related to them and from the perspective of those present. The more effectively you can use primary sources to support your arguments, the more effective a student of history you will be.

What Kinds of Primary Sources Are There?

There are many different types of primary sources in history, depending on the era and culture you are studying. They can be original documents, such as diaries, speeches, letters, official government documents, newspaper articles from the time, manuscripts, interviews, autobiographies, among other things. Artifacts of the past are also primary sources: pottery, clothing, buildings are some examples. Creative works of art, like plays, novels, music and art can also be used as primary source documentation. Can you think of any other types of primary sources?

How Should I Read a Primary Source?

Each historian approaches primary sources from a different perspective. This perspective may be influenced by political views, social class and the questions we are asking of the source. But each historian, including you, must carefully read and interpret primary sources. It can sometimes be challenging to stand in someone else's shoes and try to understand how they view the world. This is even more challenging when you are trying to understand someone from another historical era.

Working with a primary source is different from reading a textbook or a novel. You should approach every source as a scholarly investigator, not just as a reader. To be able to do this, you need information about two things: the time period you are studying and the source you are analyzing. Textbooks and course lectures can help with the first task; the other requires you to analyze, or better understand, the source. It is important to note that analyzing a primary source is not the same as agreeing with it. Your goal as a scholar is to understand the author's motives and arguments. There are some important questions you therefore need to ask of the source as part of your analysis.

Questions about the author:

- Who was the author?
- What do you know about the author's race, sex, class, religion, political views? Does any of this matter? How?

Questions about the purpose of document:

- Why did the author create the source?
- Did the creator have first-hand knowledge of the events described in the source? If so, how do you know? If not, why not and with what consequences for understanding the event?
- When did the author create the document?

Questions about the audience:

- Who was the intended audience?
- Was the intended audience private or public? What impact does this have on the source?

Questions about language and message:

- What is the message/main points in this document?
- How does the author try to get the message across?

- What biases or hidden agendas did the authorr have?
- Is the document meant to persuade or inform?
- How does the language work in this document? What are important symbols and metaphors used? What about the author's choice of words?
- What about the silences in the document (what the author chooses not to address)?

How Should I Use This Book?

As you read through and analyze the primary sources in this book, think about each of the questions above, what your answer to each one might be, and why. We suggest that you take notes, perhaps even in the margins next to the source itself.

Once you have completed these steps, you will be in a much stronger position to effectively respond to questions about each source. You will then be able to use primary sources to build effective historical arguments.

PREFACE

EVERY YEAR, FOURTH GRADERS ACROSS California study the state's history. Most prepare a report on one of the California missions. As part of the assignment, students may build missions out of cardboard, balsa wood, or sugar cubes. Pre-made mission kits are now even available for purchase. Other major turning points in the state's history, such as the gold rush, might also receive some attention in the class. For many Californians, this fourth-grade experience marks both the first and the last time they study the history of their state. Yet, however little most of us know about this history, there are few states that loom as large in the popular imagination of Americans and of people around the globe. Whether they claim to love the state or to hate it, few lack an opinion on California.

To help better understand the power of the Golden State in the global imagination, take a moment to ask yourself this question: "How would I describe California to someone who knew nothing about it?" For you, the word "California" might conjure up images of the bright blue Pacific Ocean; of palm trees, the Golden Gate Bridge, and Hollywood glamor. Even its nickname, the Golden State, speaks to an idea of abundance. But it might also conjure up images of drought, political dysfunction, and social unrest; of taxpayer revolt, underfunded public services, and a gridlocked state house; of two major urban riots, pollution, and growing income inequality. Which is the real California?

In *Chronicling California: A Primary Source Reader*, we argue that California is all of the above, and much, much more. It has always been a state of contestation, of debate, and of change. This reader relates stories from the history of California in order to help us better understand modern, multi-ethnic California in all of its complexity. Organized chronologically, this volume begins with indigenous California, before the arrival of Europeans, and ends in the early twenty-first century.

Instead of covering all of California history, we chose to highlight four major themes in the state's past. First, we focus on racial and ethnic diversity in the region across time. California today is the most ethnically diverse state in the country. This diversity, we argue, is not a modern development but, rather, a direct product of the state's complex history.

Second, we examine the evolution of state politics and the ties between state concerns and federal as well as international politics. California has always played an outsized role in both federal and international politics. As early as the late eighteenth century, California found itself at the center of an intense geopolitical competition between nations. Today, it has the power to drive the national economy and to swing presidential elections. Thus, the interplay of state, federal, and international politics constitutes the second theme in this reader.

Third, we discuss the interplay between the environment and California's economic growth. This allows for the exploration of economic events that were integral to California's development, such as the extraction of gold in the nineteenth century. But it also provides us with the opportunity for analysis of more abstract influences of the state's environment on its economic growth. California's multimillion dollar tourism industry, for example, capitalizes directly on California's environment to promote an international image of the state as a land of sunshine, blue skies, and blue oceans. It is not a coincidence that Californians are also pioneers of, and major players in, the debates over modern American environmentalism.

Finally, we explore the contrasts and connections between historical California and the California of popular imagination. It is critical that we understand California's powerful influence on shaping the understanding of the state through mass media, be it film, television, or music. History, we argue, has always shaped the stories California chooses to tell about itself.

We believe that there is no better way to understand history than by examining the documents previous generations have handed down to us. Thus, *Chronicling California* collects a wide range of primary sources into one volume. Letters, newspaper articles, historical images, maps, and graphs all provide rich starting points for student analysis and classroom discussion.

The first chapter, "Early California," focuses on the estimated three hundred thousand to one million Native men, women, and children who lived in California before contact with Europeans. Native peoples across the region effectively and efficiently managed their environments in order to sustain their populations. The reader then explores the catastrophic impact of Spanish colonialism along the Pacific Coast, which culminated in the rise of the mission system. Documents explore the profound influence of the new population of California-born individuals of Spanish or Mexican descent, known as Californios and Californianas, on the California frontier society in the early nineteenth century.

The story continues in Chapter 2, "American Expansionism and the Mexican-American War," introducing Europeans and Americans into Mexican California in the 1830s and 1840s. Driven by both economic and political motives, these new arrivals exhibited a variety of responses to life in Mexican California. Some became trading and marriage partners with Californio families. Others coveted the area's rich agricultural lands and natural resources but resented the presence of both the Californios and what remained of Native peoples. The push of Manifest Destiny and American expansionism in this era laid the groundwork for the Mexican-American War, an event that forever changed the future of the region.

Chapter 3, "California Gold Rush and the New Economy," provides perspective on one of California's most celebrated historical events. Rather than merely recounting the chronology of the period, the documents in this chapter emphasize how race and gender shaped historical experiences during the gold rush. Man or woman; American, Chilean, or Chinese—how one experienced the Rush, we argue, was very much a product of who one was and where one came from. This chapter also tackles the transformative impact of this period on the state's future, including how it accelerated California on a path to statehood far ahead of the rest of the Southwestern United States.

California in Chapter 4, "Conflict and Identity in a New State," is a young state, reeling from trying to absorb the events of the gold rush and accelerated statehood. This chapter emphasizes how racism emerged as a key issue in the 1860s through the 1880s, with both Native Americans and the Chinese often bearing the brunt of racialized violence at both the individual and state level. This period also served as a prelude to the Progressive Era of roughly 1890 to 1920, addressed in Chapter 5, "The Paradox of Progressivism." Perhaps more than any other historical period, the Progressive years gave shape to California politics. Introducing political reforms such as the initiative, the referendum, and the recall, and pushing to use the government to solve political and social problems, California Progressives put in place governmental structures that continue to affect the daily lives of Californians well into the twenty-first century.

In Chapter 6, "Myth and Modernity," we visit the 1910s and 1920s. This chapter focuses on the influence of mass media and modernity on the popular understanding of the Golden State. Here we see how California carved out a unique identity for itself with the creation of the Spanish Fantasy Past. The rise of the motion picture industry, we argue, reflects the rise of California as an increasingly powerful influence on modern American popular culture. As increasing numbers of Americans went to the movies, and more and more movies were made in California, the state was able to set national and sometimes international trends. From cars to clothes, what Americans saw on the screen often reflected what the Californians who made those films wanted them to see. This power was only amplified with the introduction of television and, later, the Internet. On a darker note, the restrictive federal immigration policies in the 1920s are contextualized in this chapter as in large part the fruits of anti-immigrant sentiment deeply rooted in the state's history.

Chapter 7, "The Great Depression and New Deal," and Chapter 8, "World War II," cover the key decades of the 1930s and 1940s. The Great Depression struck California slightly later than it did the East Coast, but it was no less devastating. Unemployment and racial strife helped turn Californian against Californian. World War II, on the other hand, saw the state's population struggling to pull together as part of a massive war effort. World War II significantly shaped the state's economy for years to come. But it also once again revealed the deep racial, ethnic, gender, and class divides that separated Californians from each other. This was most notable in the internment across the American West of some one hundred twenty thousand men, women, and children of Japanese ancestry. Many were Californians; two-thirds were United States citizens.

In Chapter 9, "Postwar California and the Problem of Growth," we again see the state trying to catch up to the profound changes generated by world events. Postwar economic development and the rise of the aerospace industry provided good-paying jobs for thousands of returning military personnel and their families. Massive population growth, fueled by both the baby boom and by migration to the state, created new suburban communities. Other documents in this chapter touch on issues of education and anti-Communism. California in this era once again became the focus of American popular culture. Hollywood films and television shows promoted the image of California as a carefree land where every teen could surf and everyone drove a convertible.

In many ways this was a continuation of the myth making about the state that had begun at the turn of the century. It was, however, an image in some ways dangerously far removed from reality.

The 1960s brought along the collapse of the postwar consensus, addressed in Chapter 10, "Conflicted California." This decade witnessed both the emergence of modern California liberalism and of modern California conservativism. Many of the tumultuous events highlighted here, such as the Berkeley Free Speech protests and the 1965 Watts Riots, had national as well as statewide impact. The debate over Proposition 14 (1964) again highlighted the complexities of race, as did the rise of the Oakland-based Black Panther Party. In this era, California conservatism grew to maturity, culminating in the election of Ronald Reagan in 1966 to two terms as governor of the state.

Chapter 11, "New Economy, New Immigrants," tackles the 1970s and highlights statewide economic changes and the impact of new technologies and new immigrant groups. Also included are documents related to the rise of the environmental movement and to the tax payer revolt that culminated in the creation of Proposition 13 (1978). Finally, Chapter 12, "California Enters the New Millennium," finds California, now on the cusp of a new millennium, still facing challenges. Topics covered here include the 1992 Los Angeles riots, the debate over illegal immigration to California, and the introduction of Indian gaming to the state's economy.

The intent of this document reader is to reinforce for students both the contestation over and the continuities embedded within California history. Thus, at the end of each chapter you will find questions for study. These questions are designed to provoke a deeper analysis of the sources in written assignments and/or classroom discussion.

We would like to extend our thanks to the editorial staff at Cognella, Inc., particularly our editor, Gem Rabanera. We are grateful to our student assistant David Baeza, who helped locate many of the sources in this volume. We also wish to thank the California State Polytechnic University, Pomona, Faculty Center for Professional Development for the grant that made it possible to hire him as our student assistant. The generous and supportive faculty and staff in the History Department at our university created an atmosphere conducive to working on this volume. Finally, many, many thanks to all our friends and family.

PH
EVW

01 Early California

INTRODUCTION

Historians are in general agreement that the first people to arrive in North America followed big game across the Beringia ice bridge from Asia to North America as early as fifty thousand years ago. Archeological evidence suggests that the land we now call California has been inhabited for twelve to fifteen thousand years, or even longer. Native peoples of California believe they originated here. Their traditional creation stories tell of a creator or creators whose powers brought forth the universe and everything in it. Each group considered themselves as the center of this creation, with a spiritual connection to their particular place of emergence as a people. The stories were passed on to next generations through oral tradition, connecting the people to their past and to their environment in intimate ways. As American Indian cultures appeared on the brink of extinction by 1900, ethnologists, anthropologists, and others began documenting

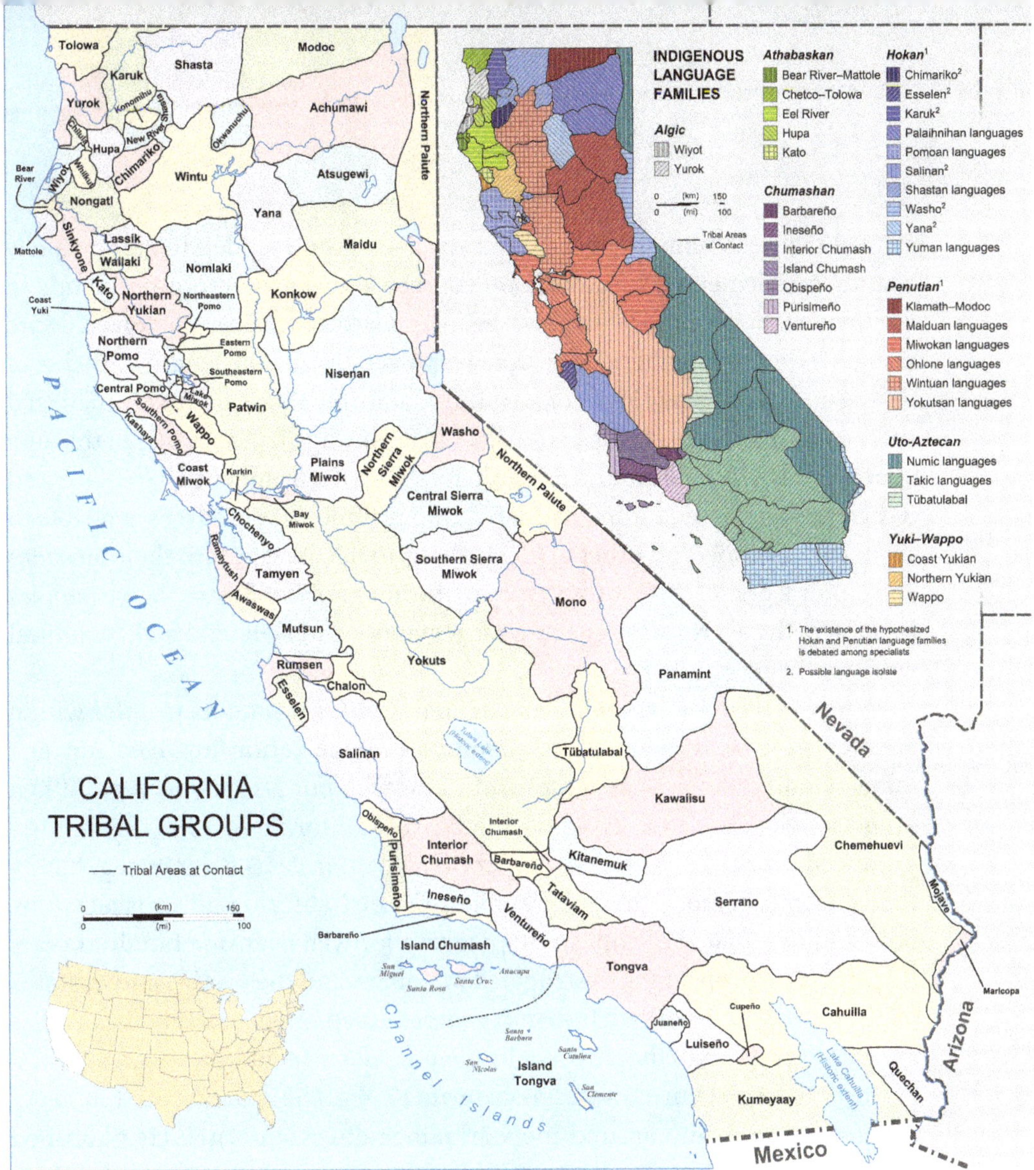

FIGURE 1.1. Map of California Tribal Areas and Languages at the Time of Contact

Native cultures and oral traditions. Novelist Constance Goddard Du Bois, for example in the first reading, had a deep interest in Southern California Indians. Between 1897 and 1907, she spent many of her summers assisting the Luiseño and Diegueño people. She also collected their oral traditions, including the "San Luiseño Creation Myth," told to her through an interpreter, José, an educated Indian fluent in both reading and writing English.

On the eve of contact with Europeans, at least three hundred thousand and perhaps as many as one million people lived in California, making it the most densely populated area in what is now the United States. The some one hundred California indigenous language groups lived mostly in small villages of one to five hundred people as autonomous tribelets with well-defined territorial boundaries (Figure 1.1). The diverse ecological zones of California shaped their economies and food quests. Each group tended to rely on a few staples, supplemented by other food sources. Acorns figured prominently in the diets of most California Native peoples. Gathering acorns involved entire villages, while women tended to take responsibility for the lengthy process of drying and processing them (Figure 1.5). California Indians actively managed their environment to increase the yield from the available resources through controlled burns and other such practices. The environment also influenced indigenous material culture, as each group utilized the resources available to them to craft tools and other artifacts that provide insight into their lifestyles and cultural practices. Contradictory to the image of California Native peoples as simple, these artifacts reflect great ingenuity and skill, and a rich cultural tradition (Figures 1.2–1.4).

When Europeans arrived, they had to fit California and its peoples within their existing world view. This cognitive reorganization involved not just understanding the new geography of the world, but also its peoples. When Francisco de Ulloa first explored the Bay of California in 1539, his reports produced maps with a correct depiction of California as a peninsula, but by the sixteenth century the geographic myth of California as an island took hold and dominated European mapmaking for well over one hundred years (Figure 1.6). Europeans also struggled to understand the origins and customs of the people they called Indians, generally depicting indigenous peoples and cultures through their own cultural lens. German-Russian naturalist and explorer Georg Heinrich von Langsdorff (1774–1852) participated in expeditions that took him around the world, including California. He published narratives of his travels, illustrated by engravings of his original drawings (Figure 1.7).

Many of the early observations and musings on California Native peoples came from the Spanish friars, who became agents of Spanish colonization with the establishment of the mission system. The first mission in Alta California was established in 1769 in the Native village of Cosoy, which the Spaniards called San Diego. Eventually, twenty-one Franciscan missions dotted the landscape of Alta California as the dominant symbol of the Spanish rule. Friar Geronimo Boscana headed the San Juan Capistrano mission from 1812 to 1826. During his tenure, Boscana wrote an ethnographic account of the culture and beliefs of the Native peoples near the mission, describing them in great detail and thus providing the only first-hand account of the mission-era people in this region (see "Of What Race of People Are These Indians?" translated by Alfred Robinson in 1846). In writing his account, Boscana wanted to provide other friars with the necessary knowledge "to remove [the Indians'] erroneous beliefs, and give them an understanding of the true Religion," or, Catholicism. His account thus aligned with the ultimate goal of the mission system: to convert local Indian populations to Catholicism and ultimately turn them into productive Hispanic citizens. Indian converts, or neophytes, lived and worked in the missions, susceptible to the harsh discipline of the padres and disease epidemics with appallingly high death rates. While there are various accounts of the missions from the perspective of European and other observers, the only indigenous account of early nineteenth-century California comes from Pablo Tac (1822–1841). A Luiseño, born and raised at Mission San Luis Rey near San Diego, Tac traveled to Rome, where he studied Latin and other subjects. While there, he produced writings on the language and culture of his people as well as the mission experience (see "Conversion of the San Luiseños of Alta California"). He also penned some drawings that give us insight into their cultural practices (Figure 1.8).

Presidios were established at the same time as the missions. They served as forts that housed soldiers with the responsibility of protecting the missions, controlling the Native population, and defending California against imperial rivals (Figure 1.9). The missions and the presidios coexisted, sometimes peaceably and cooperatively, sometimes at odds with each other. Spanish soldiers at the presidios led a hard life with poor pay. They often enslaved Indian men and mistreated Indian women, drawing criticism from the mission priests. Tensions between the two became part of the pattern of Spanish expansion into the north, illustrated in the reading, "Father Luís Jayme criticizes the treatment of Indians by Spanish soldiers." Father Jayme (1740–1775) arrived in New Spain in 1770 and, after participating in a special training course to prepare for the conditions on the mission frontier, set out for California. He was assigned to Mission San Diego, where he died in an Indian uprising in November 1775.

Civilian towns, or pueblos, made up the third arm of Spanish colonization. Spanish authorities carefully planned their location to provide the presidios with agricultural products. Laid out on a standardized plan, pueblos consisted of the plaza as the center of village life, surrounded by house lots and the outer commons. The actual farms were assigned from the land best fitted for agricultural production, and beyond them pasture and timber lands stretched out the municipal boundaries. Many of the first settlers, or pobladores, were farmers, miners, and traders of various ethnic backgrounds from Mexico (Table 1.1). They received land, tools, cattle, and horses from Spain in return for establishing settlements and growing food for the presidio soldiers. Many also employed Native Californians to work for them in various tasks.

Additionally, viceroys of New Spain could grant individuals rancho grants with the goal of encouraging agriculture and industry, and to reward soldiers for their service. Of the total of over eight hundred rancho grants, the Spanish government granted only approximately thirty, with the remainder granted in the Mexican period. Rancho lands comprised about ten million acres of land. The growth of the ranchos also placed increasing pressure on mission lands, contributing to their secularization in the 1830s and 1840s. Additional factors in secularization were the anticlericalism that carried over from the war for independence from Spain, and the mounting Indian resistance to the missions (see "An Act of Secularization of the Missions of California").

In Mexican California, the rancho replaced the mission as the defining economic and social institution. A small group of ranchero families, mostly born in California, emerged as the new elite, their wealth based on the raising of huge herds of cattle for the hide and tallow trade with the Eastern Seaboard and London. Mariano Guadalupe Vallejo (1807–1890) was one of this elite. In June 1834, Governor Jose Figueroa awarded Vallejo, then commandant of the Presidio of San Francisco, a land grant in Petaluma to further encourage his efforts to settle the area north of San Francisco. Figueroa, in fact, made him Military Commander and Director of Colonization of the Northern Frontier. By early 1846, Vallejo held title to approximately one hundred seventy-five thousand acres of land in the area. Under American rule, operating the rancho in the "old way" became increasingly difficult. Plagued by financial, legal, and other difficulties, and faced with increasing numbers of squatters on the land, Vallejo sold off his holdings. In "Ranch and Mission Days of California," Vallejo's nephew Guadalupe Vallejo offers a romantic and nostalgic remembrance of life at the height of the rancho period.

NATIVE ORAL TRADITION

READING 1, CONSTANCE GODDARD DU BOIS

"San Luiseño Creation Myth"

1906

IN THE BEGINNING ALL WAS EMPTY SPACE. KÉ-VISH-A-ták-vish was the only being. This period was called Óm-ai-yá-mal signifying emptiness, nobody there. Then came the time called Há-ruh-rúy, upheaval, things coming into shape. Then a time called Chu-tu-taí, the falling of things downward; and after this, Yu-vaí-to-vaí, things working in darkness without the light of sun or moon. Then came the period Tul-múl Pu-shún, signifying that deep down in the heart or core of earth things were working together.

Then came Why-yaí Pee-vaí, a gray glimmering like the whiteness of hoar frost; and then, Mit-aí Kwai-raí, the dimness of twilight. Then came a period of cessation, Na-kaí Ho-wai-yaí, meaning things at a standstill.

Then Ké-vish-a-ták-vish made a man, Túk-mit, the Sky; and a woman, To-maí-yo-vit, the Earth. There was no light, but in the darkness these two became conscious of each other.

"Who are you?" asked the man.

"I am To-maí-yo-vit. And you?"

"I am Túk-mit."

"Then you are my brother."

"You are my sister."

. . . .

By her brother the Sky the Earth conceived and became the Mother of all things. Her first-born children were, in the order of their birth, See-vat and Pá-ve-ut, Ush-la and Pik-la, Ná-na-chel and Patch'-ha-yel, Tópal and Tam'-yush.

Then came forth all other things, people, animals, trees, rocks, and rivers, but not as we see them now. All things then were people.

But at first they were heavy and helpless and could not move about, and they were in darkness, for there was no light. But when the Sun was born he gave a tremendous light which struck the people into unconsciousness, or caused them to roll upon the ground in agony; so that the Earth-Mother, seeing this, caught him up and hid him away for a season; so then there was darkness again.

After the Sun was born there came forth another being called Chung-itch'-nish, a being of power, whose voice sounded as soon as he was born, while all the others rolled helplessly upon the ground, unable to utter a word. The others were so terrified by his appearance that the Earth-Mother hid him away, and ever since he has remained invisible.

The rattlesnake was born at this time, a monster without arms or legs.

When all her children were born, the Earth-Mother left the place and went to Ech'-a-mo Nóy-a-mo. The people rolled, for like newborn babies they could not walk. They began then to crawl on hands and knees, and they talked this way: Chák-o-lá-le, Wá-wa, Tá-ta. This was all that they could say. For food they ate clay. From there they moved to Kak-wé-mai Po-lá-la, then to Po-és-kak Po-lá-lak.

They were growing large now and began to recognize each other. Then the Earth-Mother made the sea so that her children could bathe in it, and so that the breeze from the sea might fill their lungs, for until this time they had not breathed.

Then they moved farther to a place called Na-ché-vo Po-mé-sa-vo, a sort of a cañon which was too small for their abiding-place; so they returned to a place called Tem-ech'-va Tem-eck'-o, and this place people now call Temecula, for the Mexicans changed the Indian name to that.

Here they settled while everything was still in darkness. All this time they had been travelling about without any light.

The Earth-Mother had kept the sun hidden away, but now that the people were grown large enough and could know each other she took the Sun out of his hiding-place, and immediately there was light. They could all see each other; and while the Sun was standing there among them they discussed the matter and decided that he must go east and west and give light all over the world; so all of them raised their arms to the sky three times, and three times cried out Cha-cha-cha (unspellable guttural), and he rose from among them and went up to his place in the sky.

After this they remained at Temecula, but the world was not big enough for them, and they talked about it and concluded that it must be made larger. So this was done, and they lived there as before.

It was at Temecula that the Earth-Mother taught her children to worship Chung-itch'-nish. Although he could not be seen, he appointed the Raven to be his messenger, flying over the heads of the people to watch for any who had offended against him. Whenever the Raven flew overhead, they would have a big fiesta and dance.

The bear and the rattlesnake were the chosen avengers for Chung-itch'-nish; and any who failed to obey would suffer from their bite. When a man was bitten by a rattlesnake it was known that he had offended Chung-itch'-n ish, and a dance would be performed with religious ceremonies to beg his forgiveness.

The stone bowls, Tam'-yush, were sacred to his worship; so were the to-loache and mock-orange plants. All the dances are made for his worship, and all the sacred objects, stone pipes, eagle feathers, tobacco, etc., were used in this connection.

The North Star and the Rattlesnake

While they were living at Temecula, the rattlesnake was there, and because he had no arms or legs the others would make fun of him. The North Star, especially, who was then a person, was the leader in this abuse. He would fling dirt in his face, throw him down, and drag him about by the hair. So the rattle-snake went to the Earth-Mother and complained of this treatment, wishing to avenge himself on Túk-músh-wút, the North Star. So the Earth-Mother gave the rattlesnake two sharp-pointed sticks with which he might defend himself against any who disturbed him. So the next time when the North Star came and began to torment him, the rattlesnake used the sticks (his fangs) and bit off one of his fingers as you may still see in the sky.

The Earth-Mother further contrived that, in order to make the bite of the rattlesnake effective, it should be followed by three intensely hot days; and at the present time, when three hot days come in succession, you may know that some man has been bitten by a rattlesnake.

The Story of Ouiot

There was a village and all the people were together there, and Ouiot was living there with the people. This man became a great teacher and knew more than all the rest of the people. He called all men and women his children. All were naked then, no one wore clothes. At that time there was a woman named Wa-há:-wut, who was very handsome. She was of a light complexion, and Ouiot was very proud of her. He called her his daughter. There was a pond where all the people used to go to bathe; and Ouiot was there, and this handsome woman was there bathing, and Ouiot saw that her figure was not handsome. Her back was flat and without flesh.

All the people then were like witches; and this woman could read his thoughts, so she knew that Ouiot thought ill of her. So this woman killed him. She took the spittle of Ouiot and put it in her mouth, and took a frog and hung it up. (This part is obscure.)

Ouiot at once got sick and thin. He knew what was the matter with him, and that this woman was killing him; so he called all the people together, and told them to send for some of the people from the north to help him. So they came. They were the stone bowls (Tam'-yush), and they were people then. They came to see him and to doctor him. They knew what was the matter with him, but they could do nothing to help him.

So then he sent east for some others. They are the stars, Nu-kú-lish, and Yung-á-vish,[1] people then. They came to see what was the matter with him, but they could not help him.

Then he sent south, and some people came from the south (now the oak and the live oak), and they tried to doctor him, but did no good. Then from the west, the tule and the pine-tree (people then) came, and tried to cure him, but in vain.

He was sick for a long time, and he called all these people, and all who were then living around him. He did not know in which month he should die, but he lingered through all the months.[2] In the eighth month he called them all about him, and told them that he was the one who made death. No one had ever died before, but after his death all would die too. Death would come for all. So the month was called Soym'-a-mul (or Som'-o-y-mal), Soym or Som meaning "all." It is applied to a man who in eating takes the whole of a thing into his mouth.

While Ouiot was dying, Coyote was trying to eat him. He was weeping, and Coyote licked his tears. After Ouiot died, Coyote wanted to eat the body, but the people took clubs and would not let him come near. They told him to go north to get fire. He ran a little way and came back. Then they sent him in the same way east, west, and south; but when he looked back he saw the smoke already rising. The big blue-fly, Sar-é-wut, had made fire with the whirling-stick. That is the reason flies rub their hands together. When Coyote came back, the body was burned all but the heart. He began to cry out that he wanted to see his father, but the people clubbed him to drive him away. He still shows the marks of the clubs on his body. But he got the heart and ate it.

Just before Ouiot died, he told his people that they could kill and eat the deer. They had never killed anything before this time. And when they had killed the deer, they must take the small bones of the leg for awls to make baskets with. This was the beginning of basket-making. Spider was a woman, and it was she who must make the baskets.[3]

So they made awls out of the bones, and gave them to Spider, and she made a basket. The first basket was made to put the bones of Ouiot in, and they buried it and had. a big fiesta. That was the beginning of the fiestas for the dead. As they burned Ouiot, so they burn clothes and other things.

The eagle was a big man and a very great captain, and Ouiot had told them that when they made this fiesta they were to kill the eagle; and so they do. They kill the eagle, and burn the possessions of the man, and then begin to sing.

Before Ouiot died, he commanded that when they sing they should use a rattle made out of shells of turtles.[4]

A man (now the kingbird) was his best friend, and a very good man, and before he died Ouiot told him that he would soon return.

So kingbird got on the highest mountain near San Bernardino, and began to tell the people that Ouiot was coming back. You can still hear him saying this on the top of a tree in the early morning. He sings, "Ouiot is coming Ouiot is coming."

When the people heard him saying this, they all went out to look, and to their surprise they saw him. He came up in the shape of the Moon. After he came in the morning he went west. Kingbird alone saw him in the east. Then all the others, and Coyote first among them, saw him in the west; and Coyote said, "Moyla has come."

Notes

1. Antares and Altair.
2. The series is given as above.
3. Others say that a cicada-like insect that sings on summer evenings was the first basket-maker.
4. The most primitive form of rattle, mentioned by Boscana, is still in use. It is made of two hollow land-turtle shells, the top and bottom of which are joined by finely woven milkweed twine, the two shells being fastened upon a stick for a handle, and having small pebbles within.

MATERIAL CULTURE OF NATIVE CALIFORNIANS

FIGURE 1.2. Miwok Abalone Necklace

FIGURE 1.3. Pomo Cooking Basket

FIGURE 1.4. Maidu Fish Trap

FIGURE 1.5. Woman with Mortar and Pestle

EUROPEAN PERCEPTIONS

FIGURE 1.6. Geographic Myth of California as an Island

FIGURE 1.7. Georg Heinrich von Langsdorff, "An Indian Dance at the Mission of San José in California," (c. 1806)

READING 2, FRIAR GERONIMO BOSCANA

"Of What Race of People Are These Indians?"

translated by Alfred Robinson (1846)

TO COMMENCE THIS RELATION, IT MAY BE PROPER, IN the first place, to search after the origin, or lineage of these Indians of New California. But it is impossible to find any account of where they originated; as those of this mission, (St. Juan Capistrano) and indeed those of all the missions in the province, have no tradition, and are entirely ignorant of their descent. Without examining into the opinion of others, as to their being descendants of the Jews, Carthagenians or Phœnicians, I shall confine myself to the class that came to populate the Mexican Territory, and from these have doubtless descended the natives of California.

The tribes that populated the Mexican Territory at different epochs, according to the writings of Father Torquemada in his "Monarquia Indiana," were four; and as follows: "Tulticas," "Chichimecas," "Aculnas," and "Mexicanos." Of these distinct tribes, my opinion is, that the race of California proceeded from the Chichimecas, because, from the Tulticas they could not have originated, as is manifest from their characters, and inclinations; for "Tultica" signifies Art, and these Indians do not manifest the least industry or ingenuity. They are, in every respect, like the Chichimecas, according to the description given of them by Father Torquemada. "Near the northern boundary of Mexico there was a province, the principal city of which was called Amaqueme; its inhabitants, Chichimecas, were people entirely naked, fierce in appearance, and great warriors. Their arms the bow and arrows; their ordinary sustenance game and wild fruits, and their habitations were caves, or huts made of straw. As it was their manner of life habitually to roam about among the mountains, in search of game, they paid but little or no attention to the art of building." This is the picture given by Father Torquemada of the Chichimecas, and comparing them with the natives of California, they are found the same in every respect.

Although the habitations of the said Chichimecas formed a kind of village, still they had no police, nor acknowledged any higher power than that of "Capitan" or chief, and toward him was observed but little respect; indeed, hardly sufficient to designate him from the rest. They did not live permanently in one place, but roamed about, from spot to spot, as the scarcity of game compelled them. Of medicine they had no knowledge; consequently, no means of curing the sick, and the bodies of their dead were immediately burnt. Idolatry prevailed among them, but not a belief in a plurality of gods; neither did they sacrifice, as was the custom among the Mexican Indians.

Having thus described the Chichimecas, we see precisely the character of the Californians, with the exception, that the last mentioned lived in villages, and were governed by a chief, whom they entitled "Not," signifying lord, or master; he possessed but little influence over his subjects, and they in return entertained no respect for his authority, as we shall see hereafter. The name, Chichimeca, signifies a "sucker." Their principal sustenance was the flesh of animals taken in hunting excursions, and which was generally consumed in a raw state, after sucking all the blood; and from this, arose the term Chichimeca.

The Californian, often made his repast from the uncooked animal, and at the present day, flesh, very slightly cooked, is quite common among them. They also extract the blood in like manner, and I have seen many instances of their taking a rabbit, and sucking its blood with eagerness, previous to consuming the flesh in a crude state. The diversities of language, and other pecularities, render it extremely difficult to ascertain to a certainty, if all the inhabitants of Alta California descended from the Chichimecas. Those between Monterey and the extreme northern boundary of the Mexican domain, shave their heads close; while those to the south, between Santa Barbara and towards St. Lucas, wear their hair long, and take pride in cultivating its length as a mark of beauty. Those between Santa Barbara and Monterey, differ considerably from these, as regards their habits; being much more industrious, and appear an entirely distinct race. They formed, from shells, a kind of money, which passed current among them, and they constructed, out of logs, very swift and excellent canoes for fishing. Their dead, they interred in places appropriated to that purpose. The diversity of language is so great, in California, that almost every 15 or 20 leagues, you find a distinct dialect; so different, that in no way does one resemble the other. It is natural to suppose, that the Chichimeca nation, would have had but one language, notwithstanding, it might have varied a little, from one place to another, as is seen in other parts of the world, where are to be met with certain provincialisms, which are not to be found in the original tongue. But here, it is not so; for the natives of St. Diego cannot understand a word of the language used in this mission, and in like manner, those in the neighborhood of St. Barbara, and farther north. If it should be suggested, that people thus separated, could have corrupted the original language, in all its phraseology, and manner of pronunciation, I would reply, that such might be the case; but still, there would be some connection,

FIGURE 1.8. Pablo Tac Depicts His People

or similarity, so that they could understand each other. This has placed me somewhat in perplexity; and I am without means of discovering the cause of such dissimilarity in a spot, confined like California; and I shall leave the subject to some of my brother missionaries, or to those who may peruse these writings, to explain.

READING 3, PABLO TAC

"Conversion of the San Luiseños of Alta California"

1835

AFTER THE JESUIT FATHERS OF CALIFORNIA HAD BEEN barred form the missions, there came the Fathers of the Orders of St. Francis and of St. Dominic, the first for Alta California, the second for Baja California. California is one, divided into two parts, that is to say, Baja California and Alta California, thus called by the Señor Don Cortez, who was the first who discovered it. Baja California extends from the Mission of San Lucas to the Mission of San Diego, Alta California from the Mission of San Diego up to Monte Rey. It is known from history that the first of the missionaries who came to California were the Jesuit Fathers, and the first among them was Father Salvaterra Juan, renowned in the history of California for his works of piety.[18]

The Dominicans came to Baja California, and the Franciscans came to Alta California. The Franciscan Fathers of whom I speak are called Padres Fernandinos in Mexico, because their college or convent is called the Convent of San Fernando Rey de España. These Fathers came to Alta California, and one of them came to our country which we call Quechla, and because of this we called ourselves Quechnajuichom, that is to say, inhabitants of Quechla, when we were at peace, because always there was war, always strife day and night with those who spoke in another language.

Before the Missionaries Came

It seems that our enemies were those that now are called Diegueños by the Spanish, and Quichamcauichom by us, which means "those of the South." Before going to war they used to paint themselves in order to be terrible to the enemy, and they would surprise the enemy either when he was sleeping or when the men were leaving the house, the women remaining alone; and they would kill the women, old people and children. This done, they burned the camp, fleeing to their homes.

The weapons were bows, arrows and certain swords of wood and lances of wood in our language called vacatom. The bows were made of strong wood that could not easily be broken. In length they reached to the shoulders of the man, one finger and a half thick in the middle, three fingers broad. The arrows were of reed thick as a finger, four hands long. At the tip a little stick one and a half hands long was inserted. The feathering was of three feathers of any bird. The sword was four hands long, three fingers broad, and it began to curve at the third hand. The lance was eight hands long, four fingers thick, and it had a sharp point. To carry the arrows they had at the back of the shoulders a skin of coyote or other animal. The swords were thrown at the enemy, or the head of the enemy was struck off. The swords when they were thrown carried more than five hundred paces of a big man.

With these arms, which we still have, they used to go to war. The life of that time was very miserable, because there was always strife. The god who was adored at that time was the sun and the fire. Thus we lived among the woods until merciful God freed us of these miseries through Father Antonio Peyri, a Catalan, who arrived in our country in the afternoon with seven Spanish soldiers.

Arrival of the Spaniards

When the missionary arrived in our country with a small troop, our captain and also the others were astonished, seeing them from afar, but they did not run away or seize arms to kill them, but having sat down, they watched them.[19] But when they drew near, then the captain got up (for he was seated with the others) and met them. They halted, and the missionary then began to speak, the captain saying perhaps in his language "What is it that you seek here? Get out of our country!" But they did not understand him, and they answered him in Spanish, and the captain began with signs, and the Fernandino, understanding him, gave him gifts and in this manner made him his friend. The captain, turning to his people (as I suppose) found the whites all right, and so they let them sleep here. There was not then a stone house, but all were camps (as they say). This was that happy day in which we saw white people, by us called Sosabitom.[20] O merciful God, why didst Thou leave us for many centuries, years, months and days in utter darkness after Thou earnest to the world? Blessed he Thou from this day through future centuries.

Building of the Mission

The Fernandino Father remains in our country with the little troop that he brought. A camp was made, and here he lived for many days. In the morning he said Mass, and then he planned how he would baptize them, where he would put his house, the church, and as there were five thousand souls (who were all the Indians there were), how he would sustain them, and seeing how it could be done. Having the captain for his friend, he was afraid of nothing. It was a great mercy that the Indians did not kill the Spanish when they arrived, and very admirable, because they have never wanted another people to live with them, and until those days they were always fighting. But thus willed He who alone can will. I do not know if he baptized them before making the church or after having made it, but I think he baptized them before making it. He was already a good friend of the captain, and also dear to the neophytes. They could understand him somewhat when he, as their father, ordered them to carry stone from the sea (which is not far) for the foundations, to make bricks, roof tiles, to cut beams, reeds and what was necessary.[21] They did it with the masters who were helping them, and within a few years they finished working. They made a church with three altars for all the neophytes[22] (the great altar is nearly all gilded), two chapels, two sacristies, two choirs, a flower garden for the church, a high tower with five bells, two small[23] and three large, the cemetery with a crucifix in the middle for all those who die here....

The garden is extensive, full of fruit trees, pears, apples or perones, as the Mexicans say, peaches, quinces, pears, sweet pomegranates, watermelons, melons, vegetables, cabbages, lettuces, radishes, mints, parsley and others which I don't remember. The pears, apples, peaches, quinces, pomegranates, watermelons and melons are for the neophytes, the others that remain, for the missionary. The gardener must bring something each day. None of the neophytes can go to the garden or enter to gather the fruit. But if he wants some he asks the missionary who immediately will give him what he wants, for the missionary is their father. The neophyte might encounter the gardener walking and cutting the fruits, who then follows him to punish him, until he leaves the walls of the garden, jumping as they know how (like deer in the mountains).... The Mission of San Luis Rey de Francia, thus the Fernandina Father named it after having completed all the house, because our patron is St. Louis the King.

"Quechla"—San Luis Rey

But we call it Quechla in our language. Thus our grandparents called it, because in this country there was a kind of stone that was called quechlam in the plural, and in the singular quechla, and we inhabitants of Quechla call ourselves Quechnajuichom in the plural, Quechnajuis in the singular, meaning inhabitants of Quechla. In Quechla not long ago there were 5,000 souls, with all their neighboring lands. Through a sickness that came to California 2,000 souls died, and 3,000 were left.

Administration of the Mission

The Fernandino Father, as he was alone and very accustomed to the usages of the Spanish soldiers, seeing that it would be very difficult for him alone to give orders to that people, and, moreover, people that had left the woods just a few years before, therefore appointed alcaldes from the people themselves that knew how to speak Spanish more than the others and were better than the others in their customs. There were seven of these alcaldes, with rods as a symbol that they could judge the others. The captain dressed like the Spanish, always remaining captain, but not ordering his people about as of old, when they were still gentiles. The chief of the alcaldes was called the general. He knew the name of each one, and when he took something he then named each person by his name. In the afternoon, the alcaldes gather at the house of the missionary. They bring the news of that day, and if the missionary tells them something that all the people of the country ought to know, they return to the villages shouting, "Tomorrow morning ..." ...

With the laborers goes a Spanish majordomo and others, neophyte alcaldes, to see how the work is done, to hurry them if they are lazy, so that they will soon finish what was ordered, and to punish the guilty or lazy one who leaves his plow and quits the field keeping on with his laziness. They work all day, but not always. At noon they leave work, and then they bring them posole.

(Posole is what the Spaniards of California call maize in hot water) They eat it with gusto, and they remain sated until afternoon when they return to their villages. The shoemakers work making chairs, leather knapsacks, reins and shoes for the cowboys, neophytes, majordomos and Spanish soldiers, and when they have finished, they bring and deliver them to the missionary to give to the cowboys. The blacksmiths make bridle kits, keys, bosses for bridles, nails for the church, and all work for all....

The Fernandino Father

In the Mission of San Luis Rey de Francia the Fernandino Father is like a king. He has his pages, alcaldes, majordomos, musicians, soldiers, gardens, ranchos, livestock, horses by the thousand, cows, bulls by the thousand, oxen, mules, asses, 12,000 lambs, 200 goats, etc. The pages are for him and for the Spanish and Mexican, English and Anglo-American travelers. The alcaldes to help him govern all the people of the Mission of San Luis Rey de Francia. The majordomos are in the distant districts, almost all Spaniards. The musicians of the Mission for the holy days and all the Sundays and holidays of the year, with them the singers, all Indian neophytes. Soldiers so that nobody does injury to Spaniard or to Indian; there are ten of them and they go on horseback. There are five gardens that are for all, very large. The Fernandino Father drinks little, and as almost all the gardens produce wine, he who knows the customs of the neophytes well does not wish to give any wine to any of them, but sells it to the English or Anglo-Americans; not for money, but for clothing for the neophytes, linen for the church, hats, muskets, plates, coffee, tea, sugar and other things. The products of the Mission are butter, tallow, hides, chamois leather, bear skins, wine, white wine, brandy, oil, maize, wheat, beans and also bull horns which the English take by the thousand to Boston....

Of the Dance of the Indians

Each Indian people has its dances, different from other dances. In Europe they dance for joy, for a feast, for any fortunate news. But the Indians of California dance not only for a feast, but also before starting a war, for grief, because they have lost the victory, and in memory of grandparents, aunts and uncles, parents already dead.[32] Now that we are Christians we dance for ceremony.

The dance of the Yumas is almost always sad, and thus the song; the same of the Diegueños.[33] But we Luiseños have three principal kinds for men alone,[34] because the women have others, and they can never dance with the men. Three principal ones, two for many, and the other for one, which is more difficult. Many can dance in these two, and in this kind it is possible to dance day and night, and in the other only at night....

Notes

18. The Jesuit missions did not extend north of the present border of the Mexican State of Baja California. The first missions in what is now the State of California, U.S.A., were established by the Franciscans, beginning with Mission San Diego de Alcalá in 1769. Tac here also reverses and misspells the name of Father Juan Salvatierra, S.J., the famous missionary of Baja California.
19. Another leaf of the Tac MS contains a slightly different version of this passage. Tagliavini, "L'Evangelizzazione e i costumi degli Indi Luiseños," pp. 638-639, note 24.
20. Sosabitom was the term for Spaniards only. The Anglo-Americans were called momñawechom, from momat (ocean), i.e., "ocean people." A.E. Kroeber, Shoshonean Dialects of California (Berkeley, 1907), p. 73.
21. Here another leaf of the MS gives a variant version with the following additional information: "Our country, before the Fernandino came, was a woods. He ordered them to cut the trees and make in this fasion a clearing." Tagliavini, "L'Evangelizzazione e i costumi degli Indi Luiseños," p. 639, note 28.
22. Here the variant reads: "...with altars, one in the middle and the other two on the sides. On the main altar there are statues of many saints, and in the middle, St. Louis, King of France; lower, that of the Virgin Mary, of wood. On the right side of the main altar there is a second altar and the statues which are as follows: the statue of St. Joachim, [and] of [St.] Joseph. The altar placed on the left is of St. Anthony of Padua."
23. The word "small" (chicas) has been added in the handwriting of Cardinal Mezzofanti. (T)

[...]

32. The variant pages of the MS supply the following additional remark: "...for good harvest." Since the Luiseño did not practice agriculture before the coming of the missionaries, this may refer to the harvest of wild plant-foods, such as acorns.
33. The variant reads: "The Apaches, another tribe, also have their dance. The Christian Diegueños have their dance. The Sanluiseños, which we are, have many for men, and the women have other kinds. Also the Sanjuaneños, the Gabrielinos, the Fernandinos [i.e. the Fernandinos of Mission San Fernando Rey de España] and those of Monterey—they also have their dances, different one from another."

PUEBLOS, MISSIONS, AND RANCHOS

Felix Ant[oni]o Villavicencio	Español	45	Villa De Chiguagua
Ma[ria] de los Santos Soberinia	India	30	
Ma[ria] Ant[oni]a Josefa		8	
Antonio Mesa	Negro	36	Los Alamos
Ana Gertrudis Lopez	Mulata	27	
Maria Paula		10	
Antonia Maria		8	
Jose Lara	Esp.	50	Puerto de Cadiz
Maria Antonia Campos	India Ladina	20	
Juana de Jesus		6	
Jose Julian		4	
Maria Facestina		1	
Jose Barnegas [Vanegas ?]	Indio	28	R. de Volaños
Mariana Agulas	India	20	
Cosme Damian [hijo]		1	
Pablo Rodrigues	Indio	25	R. de Volaños
Ma[ria] Rosalio Noriega	India	26	
Maria Antonia		1	
Manuel Camero	Mulato	30	Chamatta [?]
Maria Tomasa	Mulata	24	
Jose Nabarro [Navarro ?]	Mestizo	42	del Rosario
Ma[ria] Refina Doratea	Mulata	47	
Jose Mana		10	
Jose Clemente		9	
Maria Josefa		4	
Jose Moreno	Mulato	22	Rosario
Ma[ria] Guadalupe	Mulata	19	
Bacilio Rosas	Indio	67	Villa de Nombre de Dios Durango
Ma[ria] Manuela Calistra	Mulata	43	
Jose Maximo		15	
Carlos		12	
Maria Josefa		8	
Antonio Rosalino		7	
Jose Marcelina		4	
Esteban		2	
Alejandro Rosas	Indio	19	Rosario
Juana Rodrigues	Coyota	20	
Antonio Rodrigues	Chino	50	Vindo, Manila
Juana Maria [hija]		8	
Luis Quintero	Negro	65	Guadalajara
Maria Petra Rubio	Mulata	40	
Maria Gertrudis		16	
Ma[ria] Concep[cion]		9	
Tomas		7	
Rafaeta		6	
Jose Clemente		3	

TABLE 1.1. First Census of Los Angeles, 1781, Pueblo de la Reyna de los Angeles, 31 de Diciembre 1781, Pr. St. Pa. B. Mil xvii 22.

FIGURE 1.9. View of the Presidio, San Francisco

READING 4, FATHER LUIS JAYME

Father Luís Jayme Criticizes the Treatment of Indians by Spanish Soldiers

1772

WITH REFERENCE TO THE INDIANS, I WISH TO SAY THAT great progress would be made if there was anything to eat and the soldiers would set a good example. We cannot give them anything to eat because what Don Pedro has given is not enough to last half a year for the Indians from the Californias who are here. Thus little progress will be made under present conditions. As for the example to be set by the soldiers, no doubt some of them are good exemplars and deserve to be treated accordingly, but very many of them deserve to be hanged on account of the continuous outrages which they are committing in seizing and raping the women. There is not a single mission where all the gentiles have not been scandalized, and even on the roads, so I have been told. Surely, as the gentiles themselves state, they are committing a thousand evils, particularly those of a sexual nature. The fathers have petitioned Don Pedro concerning these points, but he has paid very little attention to them. He has punished some, but as soon as they promised him that they would work at the presidio, he turned them loose.

That is what he did last year, but now he does not even punish them or say anything to them on this point. I suppose that some ministers will write you, each concerning his own mission, and therefore I shall not tell you about the cases which have occurred at other missions. I shall speak only of Mission San Diego.

At one of these Indian villages near this mission of San Diego, which said village is very large, and which is on the road that goes to Monterey, the gentiles therein many times have been on the point of coming here to kill us all, and the reason for this is that some soldiers went there and raped their women, and other soldiers who were carrying the mail to Monterey turned their animals into their fields and they ate up their crops. Three other Indian villages about a league or a league and a half from here have reported the some thing to me several times. For this reason on several occasions when Father Francisco Dumetz or I have gone to see these Indian villages, as soon as they saw us they fled from their villages and fled to the woods or other remote places, and the only ones who remained in the villages were some men and some very old women. The Christians here have told me that many of the gentiles of the aforesaid villages leave their huts and the crops which they gather from the lands around their villages, and go to the woods and experience hunger. They do this so that the soldiers will not rape their women as they have already done so many times in the past.

No wonder the Indians here were bad when the mission was first founded. To begin with, they did not know why they [the Spaniards] had come, unless they intended to take their lands away from them. Now they all want to be Christians because they know that there is a God who created the heavens and earth and all things, that there is a Hell, and Glory, that they have souls, etc., but when the mission was first founded they did not know these things; instead, they thought they were like animals, and when the vessels came at first, they saw that most of the crews died; they were very loathe to pray, and they did not want to be Christians at all; instead, they said that it was bad to become a Christian and then they would die immediately. No wonder they said so when they saw how most of the sailors and California Indians died, but now, thanks be to the Lord, God has converted them from Sauls to Pauls. They all know the natural law, which, so I am informed, they have observed as well or better than many Christians elsewhere. They do not have any idols; they do not go on drinking sprees; they do not marry relatives; and they have but one wife. The married men sleep with their wives only. The bachelors sleep together, and apart from the women and married couples. If a man plays with any woman who is not his wife, he is scolded and punished by his captains. Concerning those from the Californias I have heard it said that they are given to sexual vices, but among those here I have not been able to discover a single fault of that nature. Some of the first adults whom we baptized, when we pointed out to them that it was wrong to have sexual intercourse with a woman to whom they were not married, told me that they already knew that, and that among them it was considered to be very bad, and so they do not do so at all. "The soldiers," they told me, "are Christians and, although they know that God will punish them in Hell, do so, having sexual intercourse with our wives. We," they said, "although we did not know that God would punish us for that in Hell, considered it to be very bad, and we did not do it, and even less now that we know that God will punish us if we do so." When I heard this, I burst into tears to see how these gentiles were setting an example for us Christians.

READING 5

An Act of the Secularization of the Missions of California

1833

THE GOVT WILL PROCEED TO SECULARIZE THE MISSIONS of Upper and Lower California.

In each mission shall be established a parish under a priest of the secular clergy, with a salary of from $2,000 to $2,500, as the govt may determine.

These curates can collect no fee for marriages, baptisms, burials, or any other service. As to fees of pomp, they may receive such as may be expressly allowed in the tariff to be formed with the least possible delay for that purpose by the bishop of the diocese and approved by the sup. govt.

1. To the parishes are given the churches of each mission, with the sacred vessels, vestments, and other appurtenances now possessed by each; and also such rooms adjoining the church as in the judgment of the govt may be deemed necessary for the most fitting service of the parish.
2. For each parish the govt will provide a burial-ground outside the settlement.

3. $500 per year are assigned as an endowment for public worship and for servitors in each parish.
4. Of the buildings belonging to each mission, there shall be assigned the most appropriate as a dwelling for the curate, with land not exceeding 200 varas square; and the other buildings shall be used as an ayuntamiento-house, primary schools, public establishments, and workshops.
5. In order to provide promptly and effectually for the spiritual needs of the Californians, there is to be established a vicar-generalship at the capital of Alta Cal., with jurisdiction over both territories; and the diocesan will confer the corresponding powers, as complete as possible.
6. As an endowment of this vicarship $3,000 are assigned, from which all expenses of the office must be paid, no fees being allowed on any pretext.
7. If for any reason the curate of the capital or of any other parish shall hold the vicarship, he will receive $1,500 in addition to his allowance as curate.
8. No custom can be introduced obliging the inhabitants of Cal. To make oblations, however pious they may be or necessary they may be declared; and neither time nor consent of the citizens can give them any force or virtue.
9. The govt will see to it that the diocesan do his part in carrying out the objects of this law.
10. When the new curates have been named, the govt will gratuitously furnish a passage for them and their families by sea; and besides may give to each for the journey by land from $400 to $800, according to the distance and number of family.
11. The govt will pay the passage of returning missionaries; and in order that they may return comfortably by land to their college or convent, may give to each from $200 to $300, and at discretion whatever may be necessary in order that those who have not sworn the independence may leave the republic.
12. The sup. govt will meet the expenses authorized by this law from the product of the estates, capital, and revenues at present recognize as the pious found of Cal. missions.

READING 6, GUADALUPE VALLEJO

"Ranch and Mission Days of California"

1890

IT SEEMS TO ME THAT THERE NEVER WAS A MORE PEACEful or happy people on the face of the earth than the Spanish, Mexican, and Indian population of Alta California before the American conquest. We were the pioneers of the Pacific coast, building towns and Missions while General Washington was carrying on the war of the Revolution, and we often talk together of the days when a few hundred large Spanish ranches and Mission tracts occupied the whole country from the Pacific to the San Joaquin. No class of American citizens is more loyal than the Spanish Californians, but we shall always be especially proud of the traditions and memories of the long pastoral age before 1840. Indeed, our social life still tends to keep alive a spirit of love for the simple, homely, outdoor life of our Spanish ancestors on this coast, and we try, as best we may, to honor the founders of our ancient families, and the saints and heroes of our history since the days when Father Junipero [Serra] planted the cross at Monterey. The leading features of old Spanish life at the Missions, and on the large ranches of the last century, have been described in many books of travel, and with many contradictions. I shall confine myself to those details and illustrations of the past that no modern writer can possibly obtain except vaguely, from hearsay, since they exist in no manuscript, but only in the memories of a generation that is fast passing away. My mother has told me much, and I am still more indebted to my illustrious uncle, General Vallejo, of Sonoma, many of whose recollections are incorporated in this article.

When I was a child there were fewer than fifty Spanish families in the region about the bay of San Francisco, and these were closely connected by ties of blood or intermarriage. My father and his brother, the late General Vallejo, saw, and were a part of, the most important events in the history of Spanish California, the revolution and the conquest. My grandfather, Don Ygnacio Vallejo, was equally prominent in his day, in the exploration and settlement of the province. The traditions and records of the family thus cover the entire period of the annals of early California, from San Diego to Sonoma.

No one need suppose that the Spanish pioneers of California suffered many hardships or privations, although it was a new country. They came slowly, and were well prepared to become settlers. All that was necessary for the maintenance and enjoyment of life according to the simple and healthful standards of those days was brought; with them. They had seeds, trees, vines, cattle, household goods, and servants, and in a few years their orchards yielded abundantly and their gardens were full of vegetables. Poultry was raised by the Indians, and sold very cheaply; a fat capon cost only twelve and a half cents. Beef and mutton were to be had for the killing, and wild game was very abundant. At many of the Missions there were large flocks of tame pigeons. At the Mission San José the fathers' doves consumed a cental of wheat daily, besides what they gathered in the village. The doves were of many colors, and they made a beautiful appearance on the red tiles of the church and the tops of the dark garden walls.

It was between 1792 and 1795, as I have heard, that the governor brought a number of artisans from Mexico, and every Mission wanted them, but there were not enough to go around. There were masons, millwrights, tanners, shoemakers, saddlers, potters, a ribbon maker, and several weavers. The blankets and the coarse cloth I have spoken of were first woven in the southern Missions, San Gabriel, San Juan Capistrano, and others. About 1797 cotton cloth was also made in a few cases, and the cotton plant was found to grow very well. Hemp was woven at Monterey. Pottery was made at Mission Dolores, San Francisco. Soap was made in 1798, and afterwards at all the Missions and on many large ranches. The settlers themselves were obliged to learn trades and teach them to their servants, so that an educated young gentlemen was well skilled in many arts and handicrafts. He could ride, of course, as well as the best cowboy of the Southwest, and with more grace; and he could throw the lasso so expertly that I never heard of any American who was able to equal it. He could also make soap, pottery, and bricks, burn lime, tan hides, cut out and put together a pair of shoes, make candles, roll cigars and do a great number of things that belong to different trades.

The California Indians were full of rude superstitions of every sort when the Franciscan fathers first began to teach them. It is hard to collect old Indian stories in these days, because they have become mixed up with what the fathers taught them. But the wild Indians a hundred years ago told the priests what they believed, and it was difficult to persuade them to give it up.

The Indians who were personal attendants of the fathers were chosen with much care for their obedience and quickness of perception. Some of them seemed to have reached the very perfection of silent careful, unselfish service.

They could be trusted with the most important matters, and they were strictly honest. Each father had his own private barber, who enjoyed the honor of a seat at the table with him, and generally accompanied him in journeys to other Missions. When the Missions were secularized, this custom, like many others, was abolished, and one Indian barber, named Telequis, felt the change in his position so much that when he was ordered out to the field with the others he committed suicide by eating the root of a poisonous wild plant, a species of celery.

The Indian vaqueros, who lived much of the time on the more distant cattle ranges, were a wild set of men. I remember one of them, named Martin, who was stationed in Amador Valley and became a leader of the hill vaqueros, who were very different from the vaqueros of the large valley near the Missions. He and his friends killed and ate three or four hundred young heifers belonging to the Mission, but when Easter approached he felt that he must confess his sins, so he went to Father Narciso and told all about it. The father forgave him, but ordered him to come in from the hills to the Mission and attend school until he could read. The rules were very strict; whoever failed twice in a lesson was always whipped. Martin was utterly unable to learn his letters, and he was whipped every day for a month; but he never complained. He was then dismissed, and went back to the hills. It was the custom at all the Missions, during the rules of the Franciscan missionaries, to keep the young unmarried Indians separate. The Young girls and the young widows at the Mission San José occupied a large adobe building, with a yard behind it, inclosed by high adobe walls. In this yard some trees were planed, and a zanja, or]water-ditch supplied a large bathing-pond. The women were kept busy at various occupations, in the building, under the trees, or on the wide porch; they were taught spinning, knitting, the weaving of Indian baskets from grasses, willow rods and roots, and more especially plain sewing. The treatment and occupation of the unmarried women was similar at the other Missions. When heathen Indian women came in, or were brought by their friends, or by the soldiers, they were put in these houses, and under the charge of older women, who taught them what to do.

The Indian mothers were frequently told about the proper care of children, and cleanliness of the person was strongly inculcated. In fact, the Mission Indians, large and small, were wonderfully clean, their faces and hair fairly shining with soap and water. In several cases where an Indian woman was so slovenly and neglectful of her infant that it died she was punished by being compelled to carry in her arms in church, and at all meals and public assemblies, a log of wood about the size of a nine-months'-old child. This was a very effectual punishment, for the Indian women are naturally most affectionate creatures, and in every case they soon began to suffer greatly, and others with them, so that once a whole Indian village begged the father in charge to forgive the poor woman.

Father Majin Catala was one of the most genial and kindly men of the missionaries, and he surprised all those who had thought that every one of the fathers was severe. He saw no harm in walking out among the young people, and saying friendly things to them all. He was often known to go with young men on moonlight rides, lassoing grizzly bears, or chasing deer on the plain. His own horse, one of the best ever seen in the valley, was richly caparisoned, and the father wore a scarlet silk sash around his waist under the Franciscan habit. When older and graver priests reproached him, he used to say with a smile that he was only a Mexican Franciscan, and that he was brought up in a saddle. He was certainly a superb rider.

The principal sources of revenue which the Missions enjoyed were the sales of hides and tallow, fresh beef, fruits, wheat, and other things to ships, and in occasional sales of horses to trappers or traders. The Russians at Fort Ross, north of San Francisco, on Bodega Bay, bought a good deal from the Missions. Then too the Indians were sent out to trade with other Indians, and so the Missions often secured many valuable furs, such as otter and beaver, together with skins of bears and deer killed by their own hunters.

At the time that the Americans began to arrive in numbers the Spanish people were just commencing to project larger mill enterprises and irrigation ditches for their own needs. The difficulties with land titles put an end to most of these plans, and some of them were afterward carried out by Americans when the ranches were broken up.

One of the greatest of the early irrigation projects was that of my grandfather, Don Ygnacio Vallejo, who spent much labor and money in supplying San Luis Obispo Mission with water. This was begun in 1776, and completed the following year. He so planned to carry the water of the Carmel River to Monterey; this has since been done by the Southern Pacific Railway Company. My father, Don J. J. Vallejo, about fifty years ago made a stone aqueduct and several irrigation and mill ditches from the Alameda Creek, on which stream he built an adobe flour-mill, whose millstones were brought from Spain.

In the old days every one seemed to live out-doors. There was much gaiety and social life, even though people were widely scattered. We traveled as much as possible on horseback. Only old people or invalids cared to use the slow cart, or carreta. Young men would ride from one ranch to another for parties, and whoever found his horse tired would let him go and catch another. In 1806 there were so many horses in the valleys about San José that seven or eight thousand were killed. Nearly as many were driven into the sea at Santa Barbara in 1801, and the same thing was done at Monterey in 1810. Horses were given to the runaway sailors, and to trappers and hunters who came over the mountains, for common horses were very plenty, but fast and beautiful horses were never more prized in any country than in California, and each young man had his favorites. A kind of mustang, that is now seldom or never seen on the Pacific coast, was a peculiar light cream-colored horse, with silver-white mane and tail. Such an animal, of speed and bottom, often sold for more than a horse of any other color. Other much admired colors were dapple-gray and chestnut. The fathers of the Mission sometimes rode on horseback, but they generally had a somewhat modern carriage called a volante. It was always drawn by mules, of which there were hundreds in the Mission pastures, and white was the color often preferred.

A number of trappers and hunters came into Southern California and settled down in various towns. There was a party of Kentuckians, beaver-trappers, who went along the Gila and Colorado rivers about 1827, and then south into Baja California to the Mission of Santa Catalina. Then they came to San Diego, where the whole country was much excited over their hunter clothes, their rifles, their traps, and the strange stories they told of the deserts, and fierce Indians, and things that no one in California had ever seen.

In those times one of the leading American squatters came to my father, Don J.J. Vallejo, and said, "There is a large piece of your land where the cattle run loose, and your vaqueros have gone to the gold fields. I will fence the field for you at my expense if you will give me half." He liked the idea, and assented, but when the tract was inclosed the American had it entered as government land in his own name, and kept all of it. In many similar cases American settlers in their dealings with the rancheros took advantage of the laws which they understood, but which were new to the Spaniards, so robbed the latter of their lands. Notes and bonds were considered unnecessary by a Spanish gentleman in a business transaction, as his word was always sufficient security.

Perhaps the most exasperating feature of the coming-in of the Americans was owing to the mines, which drew away most of the servants, so that our cattle were stolen by thousands. Men who are now prosperous farmers and merchants were guilty of shooting and selling Spanish beef "without looking at the brand," as the phrase went. My father had about ten thousand head of cattle, and some he was able to send back into the hills until there were better laws and officers, but he lost the larger part. On one occasion I remember some vigilantes caught two cattle-thieves and sent for my father to appear against them, but he said that although he wanted them punished he did not wish to have them hanged, and so he would not testify, and they were set free. One of them afterward sent conscience money to us from New York, where he is living in good circumstances. The Vallejos have on several occasions received conscience money from different parts of the country. The latest case occurred last year (1899), when a woman wrote that her husband, since dead, had taken a steer worth twenty-five dollars, and she sent the money.

Family life among the old Spanish pioneers was an affair of dignity and ceremony, but it did not lack in affection. Children were brought up with great respect for their elders. It was the privilege of any elderly person to correct young people by words, or even by whipping them, and it was never told that any one thus chastised made a complaint. Each one of the old families taught their children the history of the family, and reverence toward religion. A few books, some in manuscript, were treasured in the household, but children were not allowed to read novels until were grown. They saw little of other children, except their near relatives, but they had many enjoyments unknown to children now, and they grew up with remarkable strength and healthfulness.

In these days of trade, bustle, and confusion, when many thousands of people live in the Californian valleys, which formerly were occupied by only a few Spanish families, the quiet and happy domestic life of the past seem like a dream. We, who loved it, often speak of those days, and especially of the duties of the large Spanish households, where so many, dependents were to be cared for, and everything was d*one in a simple and primitive way.*

QUESTIONS FOR STUDY

1. The historical record is limited when it comes to information about pre-contact California. What types of sources do historians rely on when studying indigenous Californians? How do these sources help illuminate the lives of Native Californians? What are their limitations?
2. What kind of a picture emerges of early historical California when studying the sources in this chapter? What factors do we need to take into consideration when examining the images and the writings?
3. Compare and contrast the ways in which Pablo Tac discusses Native culture with the writings of the Franciscan friars. Do you detect differences? What are they and what do they tell us about the authors? What do we learn about the relationships between the Spaniards and the Indians of California?
4. What kind of a picture does Vallejo paint of the rancho period? How useful is his account? How does it compare with the oral tradition of the Luiseños? Which one would you consider more reliable and why?

CREDITS

8. Fig. 1.7: G.H. von Lansdorff, "Georg Heinrich von Langsdorff, 'An Indian Dance at the Mission of San José in California,' (c. 1806)," http://content.cdlib.org/ark:/13030/tf4k4007wg/?layout=metadata&brand=calisphere. Copyright in the Public Domain.
9. Friar Geronimo Boscana; trans. Alfred Robinson, "Of What Race of People are These Indians?," *Chinigchinich: A Historical Account of the Origin, Customs, and Traditions of the Indians at the Missionary Establishment of St. Juan Capistrano, Alta-California*, pp. 1-3. Copyright in the Public Domain.
10. Pablo Tac, "Conversion of the San Luiseños of Alta California (1835)," *The Americas*, vol. 9, no. 1, ed. and trans. Minna Hewes and Gordon Hewes. Copyright © 1952 by The Catholic University of America Press. Reprinted with permission.
11. Fig. 1.8: "Pablo Tac Depicts His People," http://en.wikipedia.org/wiki/File:Luiseno_drawing_early_1800s.jpg. Copyright in the Public Domain.
12. Table 1.1: "First Census of Los Angeles (1781)," http://www.sfgenealogy.com/spanish/cen1781.htm. Copyright in the Public Domain.
13. Fig. 1.9: Louis Choris, "Vue de Presidio, San Francisco," http://digitalcollections.nypl.org/items/510d47d9-7b6e-a3d9-e040-e00a18064a99. Copyright in the Public Domain.
14. Luis Jayme, "Father Luis Jayme Criticizes the Behavior of Spanish Soldiers," *Letter of Luis Jayme, O.F.M.*, ed. and trans. Maynard Geiger, pp. 38-42. Copyright © 1970 by San Diego Public Library. Reprinted with permission.
15. Hubert Howe Bancroft, "An Act of Secularization of the Missions of California," *History of California*, vol. III, pp. 336-337. Copyright in the Public Domain.
16. Guadalupe Vallejo, "Ranch and Mission Days in Alta California," *The Century Magazine*, vol. XLI, no. 2. Copyright in the Public Domain.

02

American Expansionism and the Mexican-American War

INTRODUCTION

Mexico won its independence from Spain in 1821. As a result, Mexico gained control of former Spanish territories in North America, including both Baja and Alta California. Unlike Spain, Mexico welcomed traders from all over the world to Alta California. A brisk trade, centered on hides and tallow from California cattle, soon linked the region with Boston, London, and ports of sail around the world. Individuals of Spanish descent living in California—who increasingly identified themselves as Californios or Californianas—capitalized on this trade and on Mexico's land grant system to develop vast family ranches. Pio Pico (1801–1894), for example, was one of several sons in a prominent Californio family. He owned over half a million acres of land in California in the 1850s (Figure 2.1). Like many Californios, Pico turned his family's wealth and influence into a career in politics. He eventually served as the last governor of Alta California under Mexican rule.

American and European traders first came to California by ship. Soon men and women from all over the world lived, worked, and traded in Alta California. Pueblos like Los Angeles, Santa Barbara, and San Jose grew into small towns. Many American and European men further solidified these commercial ties by marrying Californianas from prominent rancho families. Some even adopted Mexican citizenship and became landowners themselves. Abel Stearns (1798–1871) was one such new arrival. He was originally from New England, but moved to the pueblo of Los Angeles in 1829. The Californios nicknamed him Cara de Caballo, or Horse Face, because of the unusually long shape of his head. Stearns became one of the town's wealthiest and most influential citizens and land owners, and served as a delegate to the 1849 California Constitutional Convention. His wife, Arcadia Bandini Stearns de Baker (1826–1912), was born in San Diego, one of several daughters of prosperous rancher Don Juan Bandini. At the age of fourteen Arcadia married forty-three-year-old Abel Stearns. She ruled over Los Angeles society in the 1850s and 1860s. All but one of her sisters also married an American or a European man. When Arcadia died in 1912 the Los Angeles Times noted that she was still the wealthiest women in the city (Figures 2.2–2.3).

At the same time that traders like Stearns were establishing themselves in California, other Americans began to arrive by wagon, following overland trails. They utilized routes through the Sierra Nevadas pioneered by fur traders in the 1820s and 1830s. Unlike those Americans who came to trade, many of these overland migrants were farmers who wanted land. These settlers were much less likely to forge economic, social, or political ties with the Californios than the traders and businessmen had been. They were also much more likely to support the idea that the United States should wrest control of California away from Mexico.

The 1830s and 1840s were decades of expansion for the United States. Many American politicians eagerly looked West towards the Pacific as a way to increase the young nation's power. Some Americans even argued that it was God's will for the United States to eventually stretch from the Atlantic to the Pacific—a concept that came to be known as Manifest Destiny. Settlers like William Robert Garner speculated openly about what an American takeover of the region would mean for the people living there. Garner was an English ex-whaler who had arrived in California in 1824 and had married a Californiana, María Francisca Butrón of Monterey. But he still saw annexation by the United States as the best of several possible options for California. Indeed, there were many different opinions, but very little consensus, about what would be best for the region's future (see section "American Views of California").

One of the most vocal proponents of an American annexation of California was John C. Frémont (1813–1890). Frémont was a member of the US Army and an explorer. During his third expedition exploring the American West in 1845 and 1846, he met with American settlers in the Sacramento Valley. Historians still debate whether or not Frémont actively encouraged the settlers to rebel against Mexican authorities, in the episode known as the Bear Flag revolt (Figure 2.4). In 1848 Frémont was tried and convicted for mutiny, disobedience of a superior officer, and military misconduct. US President James K. Polk commuted the sentence to a dishonorable discharge, and Frémont went on to have a long career in American politics (see section "The Bear Flag Revolt").

War between the United States and Mexico came in 1848. Following a violent confrontation in Texas, President Polk seized on the events as grounds for a declaration of war against Mexico. Californios, even those who initially supported the idea of an American takeover of California, were soon embittered by an American military occupation of the region. Some Californios even took up arms against the Americans. Few battles of the Mexican-American War took place in California. One worth noting was the Battle of San Pasqual, which took place December 6 to 7, 1846, outside of San Diego. It was a confrontation between Californios, led by Pio Pico's younger brother Andrés Pico, and the US Army. On horseback and armed with lances, the Californios killed eighteen Americans and wounded thirteen. There were no fatalities on the Californio side, but twelve men were wounded (Figure 2.5).

The armed conflict between the United States and Mexico concluded with the signing of the Treaty of Guadalupe Hidalgo. In the treaty, the two nations attempted to settle questions of citizenship and legal rights for the thousands of Mexican citizens who became Mexican Americans as the US border shifted southward (see reading "The Treaty of Guadalupe Hidalgo"). One of the messiest issues the United States attempted to settle after the war involved determining issues of land ownership in California and the Southwest (see reading "The Land Act of 1851"). It brought about a conflict between two very different legal traditions of determining land ownership. Spain and Mexico had produced diseños, a type of hand-drawn map, for California land grants (Figure 2.6). In some cases, rancho families had not been issued a diseño, or had lost it over the generations. Americans found the diseño inadequate at best and ignorable at worst. They instead had followed a very different tradition of mapmaking though land surveys (Figure 2.7). This clash of legal cultures put Mexican American land owners in an extremely difficult position when they entered American courts to try and resolve ownership issues. The transition of the region from Mexican to American control thus raised new questions about political power, individual rights, and the future of California.

CALIFORNIOS

FIGURE 2.1. Pio Pico Family (1850). Marianita Alvarado (niece), Señora Pico, Pio Pico, Trinidad Ortega (niece)

FIGURE 2.2. Arcadia Bandini Sterns de Baker

FIGURE 2.3. Abel Sterns

AMERICAN VIEWS OF CALIFORNIA

READING 7

William Garner Promotes Annexation of California

February 24, 1847

IN THE NAME OF WONDER, WHAT IS THE MEANING OF all this fuss and bustle about us here in California; or in what is it going to result? Will this country be annexed to the United States of America, or will it not? Some doubts appear to remain, and the question is undecided. Seven-eighths of the inhabitants of California this day believe with me, that it is as easy for the American flag to come down in the city of Washington, as it is that it should ever come down in California; but then we only believe so because we, like most other people, are apt to believe what we wish to be the case; the more especially, as we have good reason to dread the consequences, should the Mexicans ever regain their sovereignty here, which almost all in California are ready to say, *and do say, God forbid.*

There is another strong reason why the U. States is in the present case bound to perform what she has undertaken. She has said, I must have California. The words were hardly spoken before we the inhabitants of California heard them, and on hearing them could not refrain from demonstrating our joy, in the hope of being by her freed from the rapacity and caprices of a few individuals who held us in bondage. Should she now abandon us, that joy would be turned into bitter lamentation; because it will not for one moment be supposed by any who are acquainted with the vindictive spirit of our former masters, that they would hesitate or make any scruple about assassinating all those individuals who had expressed the slightest wish to shake off the fetters with which they have been bound for the last twelve years.

Nothing can prevent this disaster but the retention of California by the United States, and the prompt establishment of a settled government under her sanction, and a strict execution of law. Such is the daily and hourly wish of all those persons who hold property. Those who have nothing are the only persons from whom any future dissensions may be expected. But as California has afforded to every man who wished to acquire it, a means of supporting himself and family in an independent manner, those who do not do so may be considered, with a very few exceptions, as a set of worthless men, whose only desire is to support themselves by plundering and cheating the industrious.

As plunder and fraud will not be permitted under the government of the United States with impunity, the result will be one of two things. By a strict execution of justice these delinquents will fall under the iron hand of the law, or they will have to become what they never have been, honest and industrious citizens.

The Californians are naturally very docile. Generally speaking, they are very apt to act on the impulse of the moment, without any heed to the future; but the reason is, they have never been taught to look forward for their own benefit. They have been brought up under the government and tuition of vicious and corrupt men, and nothing but example will make them see their folly. Precept will not do it; but as soon as one, two, or three of the worst malefactors have undergone capital punishment, the whole country will be at peace.

THE BEAR FLAG REVOLT

READING 8

"Excerpts from the Fremont Court Martial Trial"

***The Californian*, 1848**

MR. EDITOR:

By the politeness of a friend, I have been furnished with a copy of the "memorial with the testimony taken," as reported by the Committee on Military affairs, concerning California claims. I would solicit the indulgence of your columns for the purpose of presenting various extracts, for the information of the public, and principally those interested.

Fremont says, in his memorial addressed to the Senate and House of Representatives—"That, in June of the year 1846, being then a brevet captain

FIGURE 2.4. Bear Flag of the Republic of California (c. 1846)

of topographical engineers, in the service of the United States, and employed as such in California, he engaged in military operations with the people of the country, for the establishment of the independence of California, before the existence of war between the United States and Mexico was known, and was successful in said undertaking…

"That after the conquest," under the flag of the U. States, "a temporary government was formed; the expenses of which, like those incurred for military operations, are mostly yet unpaid"…That he "believes that half a million of dollars would pay all the just claims in California, of every kind, and defray all the expenses of a Commissioner to verify them,…avers that the people of California, served the United States faithfully and patriotically, and deserve to be fairly and promptly paid for their services, sacrifices, and supplies; and he declares it his sacred duty (independently of his personal liabilities on account of the government,) to bring their case fully before Congress, and use his best endeavors not only to have them paid, but paid in a way that will save their claims from passing for trifles into the hands of agents and speculators."

It appears from the testimony taken, that the intrigues of the British government here, were entirely overthrown by the prompt and energetic measures adopted by Fremont. – The raising of the flag of independence, within view to protect American settlers, from the murderous designs of the Californian authorities, produced hostilities which resulted not only in the conquest of the Territory on the north side of San Francisco Bay, but put an end to English intrigue, by breaking off the negotiations with Macnamara, an Irish Priest, under the influence of England, for the grant of an extensive tract of land, for a colony, with a view to counteract the designs of the American government. It appears, also, that many other grants, were very hurriedly made of the mission properties, to English subjects or residents, for the purpose of creating English interest, to which the country was to appeal for protection. As some of our people are now interested in some of these claims by purchase, it will not be amiss to give the information Fremont obtained while here, and to which he deposed in reference to the subject.

Q. "Did you know, or understand from credible report, that the Californian authorities were granting or selling the national domain or missions, and on what terms—and what effect if any, the revolutionary movements had in stopping those grants or sales?

A. I did understand from credible report that the Californian authorities were granting and selling the missions and other public domains. In some cases these lands were so conveyed simply as grants, in others as reward for services rendered to the government, and in others for amounts of money that had been advanced, or were to be paid to the government. I understood that in this way nearly all the missions south of San Louis Obispo, the mission of San Raphael, in Sonoma, and some of the large islands on the coast, were granted. I understood that many of these grants were hastily made, without the usual legal forms, and wanting the usual formalities; and I understood from citizens of the country, such as Don Abel Stearns, of the Pueblo de los Angeles, that these mission grants were illegally made, and ought not to be considered valid. I saw in the public archives, deeds and letters of some of the lands which were so conveyed away by the government of the Territory. Among them were the following, viz:

1. The *Mission of Sea Gabriel*, granted on the 8th of June, 1846, to Julian Workman and Hugo Reid, (English subjects).
2. *Mission of San Raphael*, to Julian Workman and Francisco Plinio Temple, on the 8th of June, 1846.
3. *The Island of San Clemente*, granted about the middle of May, 1846, to Julian Workman and Andreas Pico.
4. *Bird Island*, granted on the 3rd of June, 1846, to Julian Workman.
5. *San Mateo*, (part of the mission Dolores), granted in the month of May to Cayetano Arenas.
6. *Mission of San Louis Rey*, granted (I believe) in the month of June, 1846 to Senor Cot.

I submit the following extract from a deed given by Governor Pico, under date of June 8th, 1846, to Julian Workman and Hugo Reid, of the mission of San Gabriel. A copy of the deed is contained in a letter now in my possession, from Mr. Reid to Commodore Stockton. The words of Gov. Pico are:

> "Authorized beforehand by the most excellent assembly of the department to dispose of the missions, for the payment of their debts, and avoiding of the total ruin of them, as well as to proportion resources that may serve for the general defense in case of a foreign invasion, which according to recent dates, is not far off," etc. etc.
>
> "The facts above narrated, with many attending circumstances, led me to believe that the authorities of California designed to create as large as possible a British interest in the country, or in other words, to convert, wherever it could be done, public or Mexican property

> in California into British property. These things were mostly done hurriedly, and mostly at the same fixed period of time, and taken in connection with my collision with the authorities in March, '46, and the declaration of the same authorities that I had come into the country to excite a revolt, and the disposition shown by the American settlers in offering to aid me, and the consequent proceedings against them, further led me to believe that the action of the authorities was influenced by apprehension of danger from the Americans. I believe that the action of the authorities in the grant to Macnamara was precipitated by the revolution in the north."

Immediately following this testimony of Fremont's, is a letter addressed to General Kearney, too long to be inserted here, strongly recommending his attention to the pecuniary affairs of the natives of California, and our own countrymen.

Fremont asks the committee to "consider the California claims under two divisions, those accruing under the first movement for independence, before the war with Mexico was known in California, and those arising after the flag of the United States was raised. It is very proper so to consider them; for although the United States, as receiving all the fruits of the movement for independence is as justly bound to pay the expenses of that movement as of the operations afterwards carried on under her own flag." Upon the ground then of the United States receiving the fruits of the revolutionary movement, he asks that government to consider and relieve him of the liabilities accruing under it.

In addition to the grants made of the missions named by Fremont, I would add, according to my belief, parts of Santa Clara, St. Johns, San Jose, and the Presidio lands; of the last however, I am not so certain. The papers respecting the Macnamara grant, etc., I propose to furnish next week, together with some testimony connected with the occupation of this territory which may prove interesting to many of your readers.

Respectfully, G.H.

READING 9

"The Bear Flag Revolt"

***The Californian*, 1847**

OUR READERS WILL REMEMBER THAT WE PROMISED TO make our paper a history of the country, a promise which we shall try to redeem.

At this time, it is a matter of great doubt in the United States, where the first flag of the American Revolution was hoisted, and what kind of thing it was, evidently from the fact that no person thought it a matter of sufficient importance to make a record of it in such way as to transmit the facts to posterity.

Our object in penning this article is to make permanent record of all the particulars of the hoisting of the "Bear Flag," under the impression, that, as that was the first move in revolutionizing this country, it will some time be interesting to know where, when, by whom, and what kind of Flag it was.

On the 14th June, 1846, a party of Americans without a leader, gathered and took possession of the fortified town of Sonoma, on the North side of the Bay of San Francisco, and made prisoners of three Mexican Officers, a General, a Lieut. Colonel and Captain. On the same day there was a partial organization under the name of the "Republic of California," and agreed to hoist a flag made of a piece of white cotton cloth with one red stripe on the bottom, and on the white a grisly Bear with a single star in front of him, it was painted or rather stained with lamp-black and poke-berries. Along the top was the words "REPUBLIC OF CALIFORNIA."

WAR WITH MEXICO

FIGURE 2.5. The Battle of San Pasqual (1846)

READING 10

The Treaty of Guadalupe Hidalgo

1848

Article VIII

Mexicans now established in territories previously belonging to Mexico, and which remain for the future within the limits of the United States, as defined by the present treaty, shall be free to continue where they now reside, or to remove at any time to the Mexican Republic, retaining the property which they possess in the said territories, or disposing thereof, and removing the proceeds wherever they please, without their being subjected, on this account, to any contribution, tax, or charge whatever.

Those who shall prefer to remain in the said territories may either retain the title and rights of Mexican citizens, or acquire those of citizens of the United States. But they shall be under the obligation to make their election within one year from the date of the exchange of ratification's of this treaty; and those who shall remain in the said territories after the expiration of that year, without having declared their intention to retain the character of Mexicans, shall be considered to have elected to become citizens of the United States.

In the said territories, property of every kind, now belonging to Mexicans not established there, shall be inviolably respected. The present owners, the heirs of these, and all Mexicans who may hereafter acquire said property by contract, shall enjoy with respect to it guarantees equally ample as if the same belonged to citizens of the United States.

Article IX

The Mexicans who, in the territories aforesaid, shall not preserve the character of citizens of the Mexican Republic, conformably with what is stipulated in the preceding article, shall be incorporated into the Union of the United States. and be admitted at the proper time (to be judged of by the Congress of the United States) to the enjoyment of all the rights of citizens of the United States, according to the principles of the Constitution; and in the mean time, shall be maintained and protected in the free enjoyment of their liberty and property, and secured in the free exercise of their religion without restriction.

Article X (Removed by Congress)

All grants of land made by the Mexican government or by the competent authorities, in territories previously appertaining to Mexico, and remaining for the future within the limits of the United States, shall be respected as valid, to the same extent that the same grants would be valid, to the said territories had remained within the limits of Mexico. But the grantees of lands in Texas, put in possession thereof, who, by reason of the circumstances of the country since the beginning of the troubles between Texas and the Mexican Government, may have been prevented from fulfilling all the conditions of their grants, shall be under the obligation to fulfill the said conditions within the periods limited in the same respectively; such periods to be now counted from the date of the exchange of ratification's of this Treaty: in default of which the said grants shall not be obligatory upon the State of Texas, in virtue of the stipulations contained in this Article.

The foregoing stipulation in regard to grantees of land in Texas, is extended to all grantees of land in the territories aforesaid, elsewhere than in Texas, put in possession under such grants; and, in default of the fulfillment of the conditions of any such grant, within the new period, which, as is above stipulated, begins with the day of the exchange of ratification's of this treaty, the same shall be null and void.

CONFLICT OVER LAND

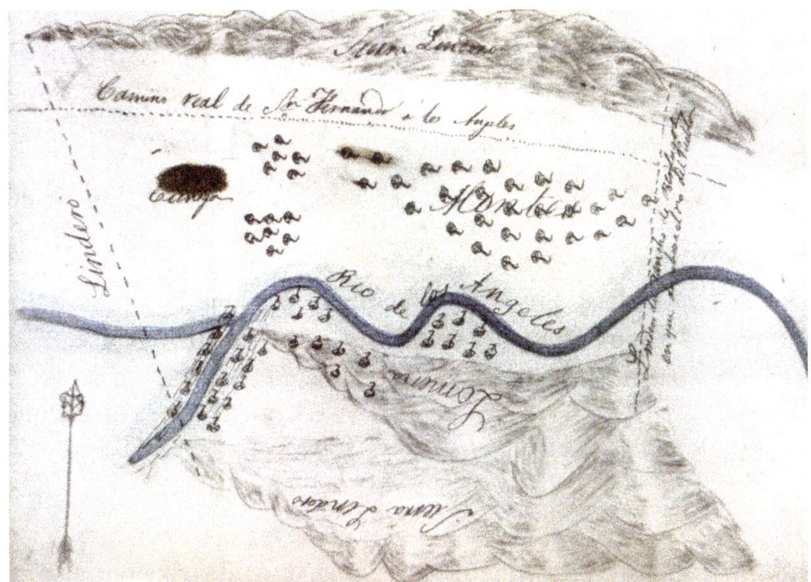

FIGURE 2.6. Sketch Map, or Diseño, of the Scott Tract of Rancho San Rafael (1857-1871)

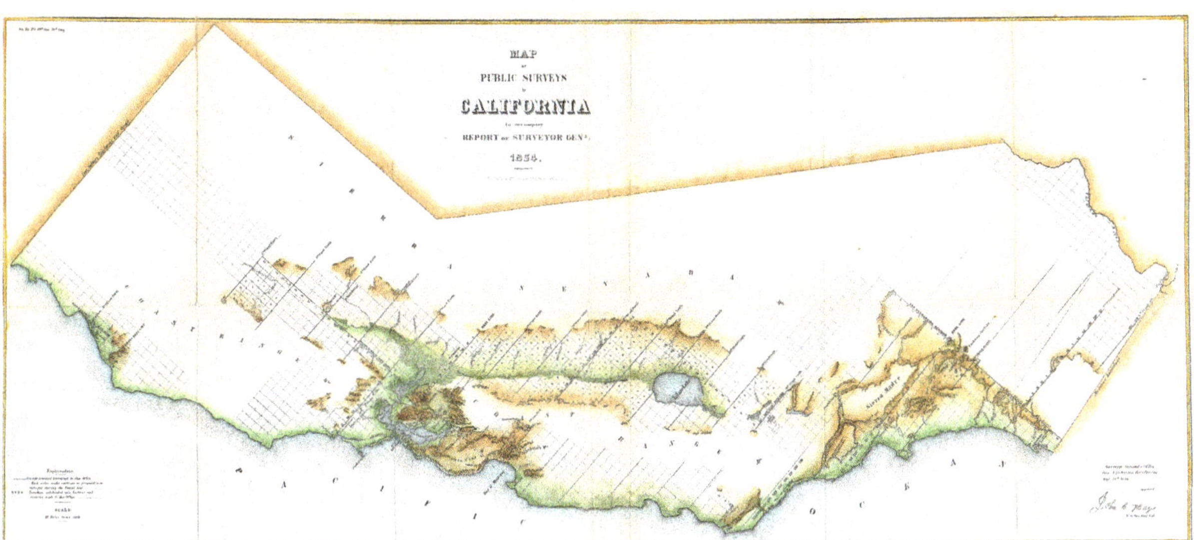

FIGURE 2.7. Land Survey Map of California (1854)

READING 11

The Land Act of 1851, Sections 2–7

Sacramento Transcript, February 17, 1851

"THE LAND BILL OF MR. GWIN."

The following is the copy of a bill offered by Senator Gwin in the United States Senate. It is offered as an amendment or substitute to Senator Fremont's bill, to ascertain and settle the private land claims in the State of California.

Mr. Gwin moves to amend as follows:

"Amend the title to read as follows: A bill to provide for the examination and settlement of titles and claims to land in California. And strike out all after the enacting clause, and insert the following: That for the purpose of ascertaining and settling the private land claims in the State of California, three commissioners shall be appointed by the President, by and with the advice and consent of the Senate, who shall hold their sessions at such times and at such places as the President shall direct.

Sec. 2.

And be it further enacted, That all persons claiming lands in California by virtue of any right or title derived from the Spanish or Mexican Government previous to the seventh day of July, eighteen hundred and forty-six, shall present the same to the said commissioners when sitting as a board, who shall proceed to examine the same when ready for hearing, and shall decide whether the same is valid or invalid. And the district attorney for the proper district shall appear before the commissioners, and attend to the several claims in behalf of the United States, for which he shall be allowed a reasonable compensation. And the marshal of the district, when the board is in session, shall appoint a deputy marshal to attend upon the same, for which he shall receive the same compensation as is allowed to the marshal for his attendance upon the district court of his district.

Sec. 3.

And be it further enacted, That in deciding the question of validity or invalidity of said claims, the board of commissioners shall be governed by the treaty of Guadalupe Hidalgo, the law of nations, the laws, usages, and customs of the government from which the claim is derived, the decisions of the Supreme Court of the United States so far as they apply, and the law of prescription in favor of possessory rights as applicable to individuals.

Sec. 4.

And be it further enacted, That all testimony in relation to such claims shall be taken in writing, and preserved recorded in bound books; and for the purpose of taking such testimony, the board itself when in session, or either commissioner at his chambers, or the secretary of the board hereinafter provided for, shall be authorized to administer oaths, to examine and cross-examine witnesses, to file the evidence with the secretary of the board to be used when the case comes on for a hearing, the claimant always having due notice of taking such testimony when not done at his own instance.

Sec. 5.

And be it further enacted, That the said commissioners shall be allowed each, six thousand dollars per annum, and twenty cents a mile for their necessary travelling in the discharge of their duties.

Sec. 6.

And be it further enacted, That the said commissioners shall appoint a secretary skilled in the Spanish and English languages, and such clerks as may be necessary, not to exceed five in number, and said secretary shall make up the proceedings of the board and act as interpreter, and be allowed three thousand dollars a year, and twenty cents a mile for necessary travelling, and the fees of office hereinafter established; and the said clerks shall be allowed each, fifteen hundred dollars a year.

Sec. 7.

And be it further enacted, That in all cases of rejection or confirmation of any claim by the board of commissioners, it shall and may be lawful for the claimant or the United States to present a petition to the district court of the proper district, setting forth fully the nature of the claim, names of original and present claimants, with the deraignment of title, accompanied by a transcript of the report of the board of commissioners, and of the papers on which it was founded; and it shall thereupon, and at the next ensuing term of the district court aforesaid, be the duty of the said court to render a judgment, and upon the application of the party, against whom the judgment is rendered, grant an appeal to the Supreme Court of the United States; and the said Supreme Court of the United States shall thereupon proceed finally to adjudicate such claims, according to the principles, so far as they are applicable, which are recognized in the act of Congress, approved twenty-sixth May, eighteen hundred and twenty-four, entitled "An act enabling the claimants to lands within the limits of the State of Missouri, and Territory of Arkansas, to institute proceedings to try the validity of their claims:" *Provided, however*, That notice of the intention to file such petition shall be entered on the journal of said commissioners within twenty days after such decision, and such petition shall be filed in the district court within six months from the date of the decision of the tribunal aforesaid. And all lands covered by the claims which may be finally rejected by said court, or not brought before the said court, or prosecuted within the period of three years, shall, *ipso facto*, revert to the public domain, saving for a time not exceeding three years, after their disabilities shall have been removed, the rights of infants, femes coverts, and insane persons; and for all claims finally confirmed, either by the tribunal or court aforesaid, patents shall issue upon the rendition to the General Land Office of a plot of survey, duly approved and certified by the Surveyor General....

QUESTIONS FOR STUDY

1. What conclusions can you draw about Californio society by examining the portraits? What do these images communicate about race, gender, and family relationships?
2. During the 1820s and 1830s there was a lot of speculation about what should happen to California. Should it remain a part of Mexico? Should it be transferred to the United States? To England? If you had been a

resident of California at that time, what argument might you have made for and against each of those options? Why?

3. The Bear Flag Revolt today has been largely forgotten, subsumed into the larger events of the Mexican American War. Would it be fair to consider the revolt as a precursor or prequel to the War? Why or why not?
4. The Land Act of 1851 (also known as the Gwin Act) created a three-member Board of Land Commissioners to try and settle the validity of Spanish and Mexican land grants in California. Compare and contrast the legal traditions of Mexico and the United States when it came to land. How might those traditions help explain why United States in 1848 refused to simply recognize the land grants as valid? Were the actions of the United States fair and just?

CREDITS

1. Fig. 2.1: "Pio Pico Family (1850)," http://aztlan.sdsu.edu/chicanohistory/picture_gallery/c03pg.html. Copyright in the Public Domain.
2. Fig. 2.2: "Arcadia Bandini Sterns de baker," Copyright in the Public Domain.
3. Fig. 2.3: "Abel Stearns," Copyright in the Public Domain.
4. William Robert Garner, "William Robert Garner Promotes the American Annexation of California," ed. Donald Monroe Craig, pp. 95-96. Copyright in the Public Domain.
5. Fig. 2.4: "Bear flag of the Republic of California (c. 1846)," http://en.wikipedia.org/wiki/File:Firstbearflag.jpg. Copyright in the Public Domain.
6. *Californian*, vol. 3, no. 13, pp. 2. Copyright in the Public Domain.
7. "The Bear Flag," *Californian*, vol. 1, no. 26, pp. 3. Copyright in the Public Domain.
8. Fig. 2.5: Colonel Charles Woodhouse, USMCR, "Battle of San Pasqual," http://en.wikipedia.org/wiki/File:SanPasqual.jpg. Copyright in the Public Domain.
9. "The Treaty of Guadalupe Hidalgo," http://www.southwestbooks.org/treaty.htm#articlex. Copyright in the Public Domain.
10. Fig. 2.6: "Sketch map, or diseño, of the Scott Tract of Rancho San Rafael (1857-71)," http://en.wikipedia.org/wiki/File:Scott_Tract_Burbank.png. Copyright in the Public Domain.
11. Fig. 2.7: "Map of Public Surveys in California to accompany Report of the Surveyor General, 1854," http://commons.wikimedia.org/wiki/File:1854_Land_Survey_Map_of_California_%28wall_map_size%29_-_Geographicus_-_California-landsurvey-1854.jpg. Copyright in the Public Domain.
12. "Land Act of 1851." Copyright in the Public Domain.

03

California Gold Rush and the New Economy

INTRODUCTION

In 1848, the year of the discovery of gold near the American River, there were only fourteen thousand non-Native residents in California. By 1852, their numbers had swelled to 223,856. This rapid population growth and the prosperity generated by the gold rush ushered California into statehood in 1850. They also allowed California to leap ahead of the rest of the United States, politically, economically, and socially. John Sutter (1803–1880) exemplifies the transitional nature of this era in California's history. Born to Swiss parents in Germany, he traveled to the United States in 1834 and arrived in California by 1839. The following year he became a Mexican citizen and received a land grant in the Sacramento Valley. He named it "New Helvetia," or "New Switzerland." His residence came to be known as Sutter's Fort. Sutter also founded a lumber mill in the Sierra Nevadas called Sutter's Mill. In 1848 one of his employees, James Marshall, found gold at Sutter's Mill, a discovery that turned into a mixed blessing for Sutter (see "Captain Sutter's Account of the First Discovery of Gold"). But there is no question that the gold rush irrevocably changed California and set in motion conflicts that continued to shape the state for decades to come.

The stereotype of the California gold rush is one of a grizzled, bearded American miner panning for gold (Figure 3.1). Yet, the gold rush was a global phenomenon (Figure 3.2). The lure of gold brought people not just from the United States but from Great Britain, France, Germany, Mexico, Peru, Chile, China, Hawaii, and other regions of the world. They came by ship and by wagon, on horseback and on foot. Although these migrants were overwhelmingly male, small numbers of women and children also came to the region. Fifty-two years later, the *San Francisco Chronicle* interviewed three of those women to capture their memories of life during the Rush. Mrs. Frances Anne Van Winkle had arrived in Napa in 1846, one of the first Anglo American women to get married in California. Her sister, Mrs. Susan Cooper Wolfskill, also shared her reminiscences with the newspaper. Mrs. Noble Martin had arrived at Sutter's Fort in 1849, when she was fifteen. All three women describe a world very different from the one they had left behind in the United States (see reading 17 "The Foremothers Tell of Olden Times").

A few men and women who came to California got rich mining (see reading 13 "The Gold Mine"). Many others did not, but found that the gold rush presented them with other opportunities. Alvin Coffey (1822–1902) was born a slave in Kentucky and later moved to Missouri with his owner's family. Coffey was then included in a party journeying to California, where he was able to make enough money in the mines to purchase his freedom and that of his wife and children. The reunited family eventually settled in Red Bluff, where they prospered as homesteaders (see reading 14 "Pioneers of Negro Origin"). Individuals with entrepreneurial spirits found many ways to make money. They opened businesses like dry goods stores, boarding houses, and banks. They provided entertainment, dealing cards and serving liquor. Some women turned to prostitution. Everyone had to find a way to make his or her way in the rapidly changing gold rush economy.

As California struggled to establish the basic institutions of a functioning society, miners created their own social and judicial conventions. Without a operational legal system in California, miners frequently developed their own laws to govern a particular mining camp (see reading 15 "The Miner's Ten Commandments"). The pursuit of "easy wealth" generated conflict and, unfortunately, violence and discrimination became elements of life in gold rush society. Louise Amelia Knapp Smith Clappe (1819–1906) moved to California from Massachusetts with her physician husband. She took the pen name Dame Shirley and published The Shirley Letters from the California Mines, a collection of twenty-three amusing, insightful, and sometimes appalling letters about life in California, letters she had originally written to her sister Molly. In "Louise Clappe writes about Vigilantism," she shares observations about men taking justice in their own hands from a rare woman's perspective.

Women and non-American miners were especially vulnerable to this type of vigilante justice. Hubert Howe Bancroft, probably the greatest of the nineteenth-century California historians, offers some perspective on the intersection of race, gender, and violence in the events in a small mining camp during the summer of 1851 (see reading 18 "The Downieville Tragedy"). In San Francisco, a Committee of Vigilance formed, also in 1851, in an attempt to address lawlessness in that community. That July the Committee lynched accused Australian murderer James Stuart. His associates Samuel Whittaker and Robert McKenzie were accused of "various heinous crimes" and lynched in August 1851 (Figure 3.3).

Within just a few years, mineral wealth became even more elusive as large mining companies came to control the industry. Hydraulic and quartz mining replaced panning and digging for gold. These newer, more efficient mining technologies also required large capital investments, ultimately transforming most individual miners into paid laborers who worked for big corporations. Hydraulic mining in particular permanently scarred the California landscape (Figure 3.4). It also helped produce one of the state's first legal cases involving the potentially negative environmental impact of a human activity (see *Woodruff v. North Bloomfield Gravel Mining Co.*). Finally, the discovery of mineral wealth not just in California but elsewhere in the West necessitated the building of the first transcontinental railroad, completed in 1869 (Figure 3.5). A physical manifestation of the notion of Manifest Destiny, the railroad connected the eastern commercial and growing industrial centers with the resources in the West—and California.

DISCOVERY OF GOLD

READING 12

Captain Sutter's Account of the First Discovery of Gold

1854

"I WAS SITTING ONE AFTERNOON," SAID THE CAPTAIN, "just after my siesta, engaged, by the bye, in writing a letter to a relation of mine at Lucern, when I was interrupted by Mr. [James] Marshall, a gentleman with whom I had frequent business transactions – bursting hurriedly into the room. From the unusual agitation in his manner I imagined that something serious had occurred, and, as we involuntarily do in this part of the world, I at once glanced to see if my rifle was in its proper place. You should know that the mere appearance of Mr. Marshall at that moment at the Fort, was quite enough to surprise me, as he had but two days before left the place to make some alterations in a mill for sawing pine planks, which he had just run up for me, some miles higher up the Americanos [American River]. When he had recovered himself a little, he told me that, however great my surprise might be at his unexpected reappearance, it would be much greater when I heard the intelligence he had come to bring me. 'Intelligence,' he added, 'which if properly profited by, would put both of us in possession of unheard-of-wealth – millions and millions of dollars, in fact.' I frankly own, [words missing in typescript] when I heard this that I thought something had touched Marshall's brain, when suddenly all my misgivings were put at an end to by his flinging on the table a handful of scales of pure virgin gold. I was fairly thunderstruck and asked him to explain what all this meant, when he went on to say, that according to my instructions, he had thrown the mill-wheel out of gear, to let the whole body of water in the dam find a passage through the tail race, which was previously to narrow to allow the water to run of in sufficient quantity, whereby the wheel was prevented from efficiently performing its work. By this alteration the narrow channel was considerably enlarged, and a mass of sand and gravel carried of[f] by the force of the torrent. Early in the morning after this took place, Mr. Marshall was walking along the left Bank of the stream when he perceived

something which he at first took for a piece of opal, a dark transparent stone, very common here – glittering on one of the spots laid bare by the suddenly crumbling away of the bank. He paid not attention to this, but while he was giving directions to the workmen, having observed several similar glittering fragments, his curiosity was so far excited, that he stooped down and picked one of them up. 'Do you know,' said Mr. Marshall to me, 'I positively debated within myself two or three times whether I should take the trouble to bend my back to pick up one of the pieces and had decided on not doing so when farther on, another glittering morsel caught my eye – the largest of the pieces now before you. I condescended to pick it up, and to my astonishment found that it was a thin scale of what appears to be pure gold.' He then gathered some twenty or thirty pieces which on examination convinced him that his suppositions were correct. His first impression was, that this gold had been lost or buried there, by some early Indian tribe – perhaps some of those mysterious inhabitations of the west, of whom we have no account, but who dwelt on this continent centuries ago, and built those cities and temples, the ruins of which are scattered about these solidary wilds. On proceeding, however, to examine the neighboring soil, he discovered that it was more or less auriferous. This at once decided him. He mounted his horse, and rode down to me as fast as it could carry him with the news.

"At the conclusion of Mr. Marshall's account, and when I had convinced myself, from the specimens he had bought with him, that it was not exaggerated, I felt as much excited as himself. I eagerly inquired if he had shown the gold to the workpeople at the mill and was glad to hear that he had not spoken to a single person about it. We agreed not to mention the circumstances to any one, and arranged to set off early the next day for the mill. On our arrival, just before sundown, we poked the sand about in various places, and before long succeeded in collecting between us more than an ounce of gold, mixed up with a good deal of sand. I stayed at Mr. Marshall's that night, and the next day we proceeded some little distance up the south Fork and found that gold existed along the whole course, not only in the bed of the main stream, where the [water] had subsided but in every little dried-up creek and ravine. Indeed, I think it is more plentiful in these latter places, for I myself, with nothing more than a small knife, picked out from [a] dry gorge, a little way up the mountain, a solid lump of gold which weighted nearly an ounce and a half.

"Notwithstanding our precaution not to be observed, as soon as we came back to the mill we noticed by the excitement of the working people that we had been dogged about, and to complete our disappointment, one of the Indians who had worked at the gold mine in the neighborhood of La Paz cried out in showing us some specimens picked up by himself, – Oro! – Oro – Oro!!! –"

READING 13

"The Gold Mine"

Californian, August 14, 1848

A FEW MONTHS AGO WE WERE IN THE HABIT OF SPEAKing of the agricultural resources and the commercial qualities of California, as being the source of her greatest wealth, and although now they are not inferior to any portions of the world, the soil constitutes but a small part of her wealth, all interests having been absorbed in the working of the mines.

The present number of the "Californian" is intended for circulation abroad as well as at home, and will, by giving a minute and general view of the all absorbing topic, the gold mine, be found useful to persons to send to their distant friends. The information which we shall give has been gathered from actual observation, and from persons who have been engaged at the mines, and from the most authentic sources, as it is desirable that the facts be correctly known through other counties, and especially through the United States.

Some time in the spring, Messrs. Marshall and Bennet, in opening a ditch for a tail race for a saw-mill, which had been built on the American Fork of the Sacramento, found some gold, which the current had collected in the bottom of the race, which, after being examined, was found to be very pure. It soon began to attract attention, and some persons discovered the gold in the river below and for some distance above, in large quantities, so much so that persons who only gave credit to one third of what was said about it left their homes and went to work in the mines. It was the work of but a few weeks, to bring almost the entire population of the territory together to pick up the precious metal. The result has been, that in less than four months, a total revolution has been effected in the prospects and the fate of Alta California. Then, the capital was in the hands of a few individuals engaged in trade and speculation, now labor has got the upper hands of capital, and the laboring men hold the great mass of the wealth of the country—the gold.

There are now about four thousand white persons, besides a number of Indians engaged at the mines, and from the fact that no capital is required, they are working in companies on equal shares or alone with their basket. In one part of the mine called the "dry diggins," no other implements are necessary thay an ordinary sheath knife, to pick the gold from the rocks. In other parts, where the gold is washed out, the machinery is very simple, being an ordinary trough made of plank, round on the bottom, about ten feet long and two feet wide at the top, with a riddle or sieve at one end to catch the larger gravel, and three or four small bars across the bottom, about half an inch high to keep the gold from going out with the dirt and water at the lower end. This machine is set upon rockers, which gives a half rotary motion to the water and dirt inside. But far the largest number use nothing but a large tin pan or an Indian basket, into which they place the dirt and shake it until the gold gets to the bottom and the dirt is carried over the side in the shape of muddy water. It is necessary in some cases, to have a crowbar, pick and shovel, but a great deal is taken up with large horns, shapen spoon fashion at the large end.

From the fact that no capital is necessary, a fair competition in labor without the influence of capital, men who were only able to procure one month's provisions, have now thousands of dollars of the precious metal. The laboring class have now become the capitalists of the country.

As to the richness of the mine, were we to set down half the truth, it would be looked upon in other countries as a "Sinbad" story, or the history of "Alladin's Lamp," which required that its possessor should but wish, and his wishes should be accomplished. Many persons have collected in one day, of the finest grade gold, from three to eight hundred dollars, and for many days together averaged from 75 to $150. Although this is not universal, yet the general average is so well settled, that when a man with his pan or basket does not easily gather 30 to 40 dollars in a day, he moves to another place, so that taking the general average, including the time spent in moving from place to place and in looking for better "diggings," we are of the opinion that we may safely set down an ounce of pure gold or $16 per day to the man. Suppose there are 4000 persons at work, they will add to the aggregate wealth of the territory about 4000 ounces, or about 60,000 dollars a day.

The value of the gold, like all things else, is regulated by the demand. Four months ago, flour was sold in the market for four dollars per hundred, now sixteen; beef cattle six, now thirty; ready made clothing, grocer's and other good have not risen in the same proportion, but are at least double their original cost. If we make bread and meat the standard by which to determine the value of gold, then it is only worth one fourth of what it is elsewhere. But if gold and silver be the standard, then the bread and meat is worth four times what it was. But the relative value of the grain gold, compared with gold and silver coin, can only be changed by the action of government for, however abundant the gold may be, it must produce its relative value in coin, and while a five dollar gold piece will be received in the treasury as five dollars, so long must an ounce of gold be worth *sixteen dollars.*

As to the future hopes of California, her course is onward, with a rapidity which will astonish the world. Her unparalleled gold mines, silver mines, iron ore and lead, with the best climate in the world, and the richest soil, will make it the garden spot of creation.

FORTY-NINERS

FIGURE 3.1. An Anglo Forty-Niner at the American River (1850)

FIGURE 3.2. Engraving of Chinese Gold Miners

READING 14, ALVIN A. COFFEY

"Pioneers of Negro Origin"

I STARTED FROM ST. LOUIS, MO., ON THE 2ND DAY OF April in 1849. There was quite a crowd of the neighbors who drove through the mud and rain to St. Joe to see us off. About the first of May we organized the train. There were twenty wagons in number and from three to five men to each wagon.

We crossed the Missouri River at Savanna Landing on about the sixth of May. There were several trains ahead of us. At twelve o'clock three more men took our place and we went to camp. At six in the morning, there were three more who went to relieve those on guard. One of the three that came in had cholera so bad that he was in lots of misery. Dr. Bassett, the captain of the train, did all he could for him, but he died at ten o'clock and we buried him. We got ready and started at eleven the same day and the moon was new just then.

We got news every day that people were dying by the hundreds in St. Joe and St. Louis. It was alarming. When we hitched up and got ready to move, Dr. said, "Boys, we will have to drive day and night."

There were only three saddle horses in the train, Dr. Bassett, Mr. Hale, Sr., and John Triplet owning them. They rode with the Dr. to hunt camping places. We drove night and day and got out of reach of the cholera. There was none ahead of us that we knew of.

Dave and Ben Headspeth's train was ahead of us. They had fourteen or fifteen wagons in the train and three to five men to a wagon. Captain Camel had another such train. When we caught up with them, we never heard of one case of cholera on their trains.

We got across the plains to Fort Laramie, the sixteenth of June, and the ignorant driver broke down a good many oxen on the trains. There were a good many ahead of us, who had doubled up their trains and left tons upon tons of bacon and other provisions.

When we got well down Humboldt to a place called Lawson's Meadow, which was quite a way from the sink of the Humboldt, the emigrants agreed to drive there. There was good grass at Lawson's Meadow. We camped there a day and two nights, resting the oxen, for we had a desert to cross to get to Black Rock where there was grass and water.

Starting to cross the desert to Black Rock at four o'clock in the evening, we traveled all night. The next day it was hot and sandy. When within twenty miles of Black Rock, we saw it very plainly.

A great number of cattle perished before we got to Black Rock. When about fifteen miles from Black Rock, a team of four oxen was left on the road just where the oxen had died. Everything was left in the wagon.

I drove one oxen all the time and I knew about how much an ox could stand. Between nine and ten o'clock a breeze came up and the oxen threw up their heads and seemed to have new life. At noon, we drove into Black Rock.

Before we reached Sacramento Valley, we had poor feed a number of nights. The route by the way of Humboldt was the oldest and best known to Hangtown. We crossed the South Pass on the Fourth of July. The ice next morning was as thick as a dinner plate. About two days before we got to Honey Lake we were in a timbered country. We camped at a place well known as Rabbit Hole Springs. An ox had given out and was down, and not able to get up, about one hundred yards from the spring. A while after it got dark as it was going to be, the ox commenced bawling pitifully. Some of the boys had gone to bed. I said, "Let us go out and kill the ox for it is too bad to hear him bawl." The wolves were eating him alive. None would go with me, so I got two double-barreled shot-guns which were loaded. I went out where he was. The wolves were not in sight, although I could hear them. I put one of the guns about five or six inches from the ox's head and killed him with the first shot. The wolves never tackled me. I had reserved three shots in case they should.

When we got in Deer Creek in Sacramento Valley, we divided up wagons. Some went to Sacramento Valley to get provisions for the winter and came up to Redding Springs later. We camped several days at Honey Lake but the grass on Madeline Plains was not very good. While Headspeth and a guide we had were hunting the best path to Sacramento road, the cattle recruited up nicely. We took several days to go from Honey Lake to Sacramento Valley.

Those that kept on from Deer Creek to Redding Springs camped at Redding Springs the thirteenth day of October, 1849. Eight to ten miles drive was a big one for us at the latter end. The last four miles the cattle had nothing to eat but poison-oak brush. We cut down black oaks for them to browse on, and got to Redding Springs the next day at four o'clock. We watered the oxen out of buckets that night and morning. The next day we gathered them up, drove them down to Clear Creek where they had plenty of poison oak to eat.

On the morning of the fifteenth we went to dry-digging mining. We dug and dug to the first of November. At night it commenced raining, and rained and snowed pretty much all the winter. We had a tent but it barely kept us all dry. There were from eight to twelve in one camp. We cut down pine trees for shakes to make a cabin. It was a whole week before we had a cabin to keep us dry.

The first week in January, 1850, we bought a hundred pounds of bear meat at one dollar per pound. I asked the man how many pounds he had sold, and he said, "I've sold thirteen hundred pounds and have four hundred to five hundred pounds left in camp yet. I gave the men considerable for helping me dress it."

READING 15

"The Miner's Ten Commandments"

***Placerville Herald*, 1853**

I.

Thou shalt have no other claim than one.

II.

Thou shalt not make unto thyself any false claim, nor any likeness to a mean man, by jumping one: for I, a miner, am a just one, and will visit the miners around about, and they will judge thee; and when they shall decide, thou shalt take thy pick, thy pan, thy shovel and thy blankets with all thou hast and shall depart seeking other good diggings, but thou shalt find none. Then when thou hast paid out all thy dust, worn out thy boots and garments so that there is nothing good about them but the pockets, and thy patience is like unto thy garments, then in sorrow shall thou return to find thy claim worked out, and yet thou hath no pile to hide in the ground, or in the old boot beneath thy bunk, or in buckskin or in bottle beneath thy cabin, and at last thou shalt hire thy body out to make thy board and save thy bacon.

III.

Thou shalt not go prospecting before thy claim gives out. Neither shalt thou take thy money, nor thy gold dust, nor thy good name, to the gaming table in vain; for monte, twenty-one, roulette, faro, lansquenet and poker, will prove to thee that the more thou puttest down the less thou shalt take up; and when thou thinkest of thy wife and children, thou shalt not hold thyself guiltless—but insane.

IV.

Thou shalt not remember what thy friends do at home on the Sabbath day, lest the remembrance may not compare favorably with what thou doest here. Six days thou mayst dig or pick; but the other day is Sunday; yet thou washest all thy dirty shirts, darnest all thy stockings, tap thy boots, mend thy clothing, chop the whole week's firewood, make up and bake thy bread, and boil thy pork and beans, that thou wait not when thou returnest from thy long-tom weary. For in six days' labor only though canst do it in six months; and though, and thy morals and thy conscience, be none the better for it; but reproach thee, shouldst thou ever return with thy worn-out body to thy mother's fireside.

V.

Though shalt not think more of all thy gold, and how thou canst make it fastest, than how thou will enjoy it after thou hast ridden rough-shod over thy good old parents' precepts and examples, that thou mayest have nothing to reproach thee, when left ALONE in the land where thy father's blessing and thy mother's love hath sent thee.

VI.

Thou shalt not kill; neither thy body by working in the rain, even though thou shalt make enough to buy physic and attendance with; nor thy neighbor's body in a duel, or in anger, for by "keeping cool," thou canst save his life and thy conscience. Neither shalt thou destroy thyself by getting "tight," nor "stewed," nor "high," nor "corned," nor "half- seas over," nor "three sheets in the wind," by drinking smoothing down—"brandy slings," "gin cocktails," "whiskey punches," "rum toddies," nor "egg-noggs." Neither shalt thou suck "mint juleps," nor "sherry- cobblers," through a straw, nor gurgle from a bottle the "raw material," nor take "it straight" from a decanter; for, while thou art swallowing down thy purse, and the coat from off thy back thou art burning the coat from off thy stomach; and if thou couldst see the houses and lands, and gold dust, and home comforts already lying there—"a huge pile"—thou shouldst feel a choking in thy throat; and when to that thou addest thy crooked walkings thou wilt feel disgusted with thyself, and inquire "Is thy servant a dog that he doeth these things!" Verily, thou shalt say, "Farewell, old bottle, I will kiss thy gurgling lips no more; slings, cocktails, punches, smashes, cobblers, nogs, toddies, sangarees and juleps, forever farewell. Thy remembrance shames one; henceforth, I cut thy acquaintance, and headaches, tremblings, heart-burnings, blue devils, and all the unholy catalogue of evils that follow in thy train. My wife's smiles and my children's merry-hearted laugh, shall charm and reward me for having the manly firmness and courage to say NO. I wish thee an eternal farewell."

VII.

Thou shalt not grow discouraged, nor think of going home before thou hast made thy "pile," because thou hast not "struck a lead," nor found a "rich crevice," nor sunk a hole upon a "pocket," lest in going home thou shalt leave four dollars a day, and going to work, ashamed, at fifty cents, and serve thee right; for thou knowest by staying here, thou mightst strike a lead and fifty dollars a day, and keep thy manly self respect, and then go home with enough to make thyself and others happy.

VIII.

Thou shalt not steal a pick, or a shovel, or a pan from thy fellow-miner; nor take away his tools without his leave; nor borrow those he cannot spare; nor return them broken, nor trouble him to fetch them back again, nor talk with him while his water rent is running on, nor remove his stake to enlarge thy claim, nor undermine his bank in following a lead, nor pan out gold from his "riffle box," nor wash the "tailings" from his sluice's mouth. Neither shalt thou pick out specimens from the company's pan to put them in thy mouth or pocket; nor cheat thy partner of his share; nor steal from thy cabin-mate his gold dust, to add to thine, for he will be sure to discover what thou hast done, and will straightaway call his fellow miners together, and if the law hinder them not, will hang thee, or give thy fifty lashes, or shave thy head and brand thee, like a horse thief, with "R" upon thy cheek, to be known and read of all men, Californians in particular.

IX.

Thou shalt not tell any false tales about "good diggings in the mountains," to thy neighbor that thou mayest benefit a friend who had mules, and provisions, and tools and blankets he cannot sell,—lest in deceiving thy neighbor, when he returneth through the snow, with naught save his rifle, he present thee with the contents thereof, and like a dog, thou shalt fall down and die.

X.

Thou shalt not commit unsuitable matrimony, nor covet "single blessedness;" nor forget absent maidens; nor neglect thy "first love;"—but thou shalt consider how faithfully and patiently she awaiteth thy return; yea and covereth each epistle that thou sendest with kisses of kindly welcome—until she hath thyself. Neither shalt thou cove thy neighbor's wife, nor trifle with the affections of his daughter; yet, if thy heart be free, and thou dost love and covet each other, thou shalt "pop the question" like a man.

A new Commandment give I unto thee—if thou has a wife and little ones, that thou lovest dearer than life,—that thou keep them continually before thee, to cheer and urge thee onward, until thou canst say, "I have enough—God bless them—I will return." Then from thy much-loved home, with open arms shall thy come forth to welcome thee, with weeping tears of unutterable joy that thou art come; then in the fullness of thy heart's gratitude, thou shalt kneel together before thy Heavenly Father, to thank him for thy safe return. AMEN—So mote it be.

FORTY-NINER.

WOMEN IN THE GOLD RUSH

READING 16

Louise Clappe Writes About Vigilantism

1851

IN A LETTER WRITTEN ON DECEMBER 14, 1851, LOUISE describes how the mining community established its own form of law and order:

The facts in this sad case are as follows. Last fall, two men were arrested by their partners on suspicion of having stolen from them eighteen hundred dollars in gold-dust. The evidence was not sufficient to convict them, and they were acquitted. They were tried before a meeting of the miners, as at that time the law did not even *pretend to wave its scepter over this place.*

The prosecutors still believed them guilty, and fancied that the gold was hidden in a coyote-hole near the camp from which it had been taken. They therefore watched the place narrowly while the suspected men remained on the Bar. They made no discoveries, however, and soon after the trial the acquitted persons left the mountains for Marysville.

A few weeks ago, one of these men returned, and has spent most of the time since his arrival in loafing about the different barrooms upon the river. He is said to have been constantly intoxicated. As soon as the losers of the gold heard of his return, they bethought themselves of the coyote-hole, and placed about its entrance some brushwood and stones in such a manner that no one could go into it without disturbing the arrangement of them. In the mean while the thief settled at Rich Bar, and pretended that he was in search of some gravel-ground for mining purposes.

A few mornings ago he returned to his boarding-place, which he had left some hour earlier, with a spade in his hand, and, as he laid it down, carelessly observed that he had been out prospecting. The losers of the gold went, immediately after breakfast, as they had been in the habit of doing, to see if all was right at the coyote-hole. On this fatal day they saw that the entrance had been disturbed, and going in, they found upon the ground a money-belt which had apparently just been cut open. Armed with this evidence of guilt, they confronted the suspected person and sternly accused him of having the gold in his possession. Singularly enough, he did not attempt a denial, but said that if they would not bring him to a trial (which of course they promised) he would give it up immediately. He then informed them that they would find it beneath the blankets of his bunk, as those queer shelves on which miners sleep, ranged one above another somewhat like the berths of a ship, are generally called. There, sure enough, were six hundred dollars of the missing money, and the unfortunate wretch declared that his partner had taken the remainder to the States.

By this time the exciting news had spread all over the Bar. A meeting of the miners was immediately convened, the unhappy man taken into custody, a jury chosen, and a judge, lawyer, etc., appointed. Whether the men who had just regained a portion of their missing property made any objections to the proceedings which followed, I know not. If they had done so, however, it would have made no difference, as the people had taken the matter entirely out of their hands.

At one o'clock, so rapidly was the trial conducted, the judge charged the jury, and gently insinuated that they could do no less than to bring in with their verdict of guilty a sentence of death! Perhaps you know that when a trial is conducted without the majesty of the law, the jury are [sic] compelled to decide not only upon the guilt of the prisoner, but the mode of his punishment also. After a few minutes' absence, the twelve men, who had consented to burden their souls with a responsibility so fearful, returned, and the foreman handed to the judge a paper, from which he read the will of the people, as follows: That William Brown, convicted of stealing, etc., should, in one hour from that time, be hung by the neck until he was dead.

By the persuasions of some men more mildly disposed, they granted him a respite of three hours to prepare for his sudden entrance into eternity. He employed the time in writing, in his native language (he is a Swede), to some friends in Stockholm. God help them when that fatal post shall arrive, for, no doubt, he also, although a criminal, was fondly garnered in many a loving heart.

He had exhibited, during the trial, the utmost recklessness and nonchalance, had drank many times in the course of the day, and when the rope was placed about his neck, was evidently much intoxicated. All at once, however, he seemed startled into a consciousness of the awful reality of his position, and requested a few moments for prayer.

The execution was conducted by the jury, and was performed by throwing the cord, one end of which was attached to the neck of the prisoner, across the limb of a tree standing outside of the Rich Bar graveyard, when all who felt disposed to engage in so revolting a task lifted the poor wretch from the ground in the most awkward manner possible. The whole affair, indeed, was a piece of cruel butchery, though that was not intentional, but arose from the ignorance of those who made the preparations. In truth, life was only crushed out of him by hauling the writhing body up and down, several times in succession, by the rope, which was wound round a large bough of his green-leaved gallows. Almost everybody was surprised at the severity of the sentence, and many, with their hands on the cord, did not believe even then that it would be carried into effect, but thought that at the last moment the jury would release the prisoner and substitute a milder punishment.

It is said that the crowd generally seemed to feel the solemnity of the occasion, but many of the drunkards, who form a large part of the community on these bars, laughed and shouted as if it were a spectacle got up for their particular amusement. A disgusting specimen of intoxicated humanity, struck with one of those luminous ideas peculiar to his class, staggered up to the victim, who was praying at the moment, and, crowding a dirty rag into his almost unconscious hand, in a voice broken by a drunken hiccough, tearfully implored him to take his "hankercher," and if he were innocent (the man had not denied his guilt since first accused), to drop it as soon as he was drawn up into the air, but if guilty, not to let it fall on any account.

The body of the criminal was allowed to hang for some hours after the execution. It had commenced storming in the earlier part of the evening, and when those whose business it was to inter the remains arrived at the spot, they found them enwrapped in a soft white shroud of feathery snow-flakes, as if pitying nature had tried to hide from the offended face of Heaven the cruel deed which her mountain-children had committed.

READING 17

"The Foremothers Tell of Olden Times"

San Francisco Chronicle, September 9, 1900

"WE CAME TO CALIFORNIA THE SAME YEAR AS THE ill-fated Donner party. It started about a month ahead of us, but it kept taking imaginary short cuts and hurrying until it met with frightful disaster. My father, who was captain of our train, led his party of about eighty people across trackless plains and mountains for five months, simply with the sun and the stars as guides, and came west almost as straight as the crow flies. He believed in moving every day, if only three miles and the result was that all our oxen were in better condition when they arrived in California than when they started. Several of the survivors of the Donner party, young George Donner and Mrs. Reed, came to our house in Napa after they were rescued. I heard the other day that Mrs. Reed's daughter, 'Patty' Reed, who was then a very little girl, is living on Franklin street in Oakland. She is Mrs. Martha Lewis now.

"Both father and mother were born in Kentucky, but like a good many other Kentuckians of those days, they moved out to Missouri, where we children were born.

"One day I read a pamphlet written by a man who had been in California. His name was Hastings, and he was a cousin to Judge Hastings. His description of the beautiful flowers blooming in winter, of the great herds of Spanish cattle in lovely fields, of glorious scenery, and of the ideal climate and blue skies, made me just crazy to move out there, for I thought such a country must be a paradise. Mother though so too, but father told us it was a dangerous trip and that Indians might kill all of us on the way. He had been a good ways west, hunting buffalo, and he knew something of the great stretches of plains. But we kept talking about California until father decided to put it to a family vote whether we should go or stay.

"Father went out with Fremont in 1845 to explore the Far Western country. The parties separated and returned. Father came home in time to lead our party, although we had already decided to go anyway."

"Altogether our trip was exceptionally fortunate. We made good time, came by the most direct route, had no sickness and lost but one person, a little baby that died after its mother had tried to doctor it herself.

"We were received at Napa by Mr. Yount, who had lived originally in Howard county, Missouri. He was just as glad to see us as if we had been his own family. He owned seven leagues of land there in the Napa valley, had 600 mares and thousands of horses and cattle. The whole valley was covered with grazing cattle. In those days the only Americans there were the Gregories, the Stewards, the Derbons and a few other families.

"All the Spanish families had Indian slaves. They never permitted them to walk, but made them go about on the trot all the time. Those Indians made good slaves, excellent. The Spanish vaqueros used to go up to what is now Ukiah and ride in among the Indian rancherias and drive out the boys and girls, leaving the mothers behind and killing the bucks if they offered any resistance. Then they would herd the captives down like so many cattle and sell them to the ranchers. About $100 was the standard price. A good girl would bring that, but some sold for as little as $50.

"I bought one Indian girl from a Spaniard for $100, but soon after that another Indian girl and two boys came to my house of their own accord and explained that they had no home and wanted to work. The four of them did all my work, washing, ironing, cooking and housecleaning. One of the girls was a splendid nurse. The shameful treatment of the Indians by the Spanish was never equaled by the whites. As Americans settled up the country the enslaving of young Indians naturally stopped.

"We had a Fourth of July celebration near Napa in 1847. It was given by us at the Yount place. It must have been the first affair of the kind in California. We had about forty guests, most of them Spanish people of some prominence in the country. I made an enormous pound cake for the center of the table. Nobody had brought an American flag to California, so my sister, now Mrs. Wolfskill of Winters, made a little one of some narrow red ribbon and cut some blue silk from her best dress, and sewed on but one star, for material was very scarce, and the whole thing was not bigger than a woman's handkerchief.

"Father had written across the little flag, 'California is ours as long as the stars remain.' The Spaniards took it all right, but Dr. Bailey became very much excited and snatched at the flag. All through the dinner he insisted upon removing it, declaring that the American flag should never wave over California.

"My husband, Dr. Semple, owned the only ferry-boat at Benicia. It was often said that he made money enough with it to sink that boat a half dozen times over, but he was one of the most remarkable speculators I ever knew, and went right through his money.

"At first we thought California would be a great stock country, a fine place for farming, an elegant climate to live in, but no one had any idea then that there was gold here. But in 1848 and 1849 Dr. Semple was the only man left in Benicia, and mother, my sister and I the only women. All the others had gone to the mines. We lived in Benicia just four years, then we moved to what is now Colusa.

"In Colusa, in the early days we raised vegetables to sell to the miners, and we grew grain and shipped it down to San Francisco on steamers. When I first saw Sacramento it was an apparently endless sweep of small tents, not a frame building anywhere in sight. That was in 1850. It was a terrifying place. I was frightened. Men were gambling on all sides. They were shooting and cursing and yelling. The noise and uproar were awful.

"I lived in Colusa for thirty-two years, never getting away much. It was along in the seventies before I saw San Francisco and I haven't visited Benicia for many years. Little by little, as more white people settled in Colusa, the Indians moved back farther from civilization. They disappeared somewhere. I still own a lovely home place of 670 acres at Colusa, and I've been offered $75 an acre for it and wouldn't take it. About ten miles from the house is an Indian rancheria, with a little colony of Indians. They sell chickens and pigs, and in the summer time they work in the harvest field and manage to get along pretty well.

Mrs. Susan Cooper Wolfskill of Winters, widow of the late John Wolfskill, who arrived in Los Angeles in 1834, is a sister of Mrs. Van Winkle. She is visiting her younger sister, Mrs. Martha Cooper Roberts, at 564 Fourteenth street, in Oakland. Mrs. Wolfskill supplements her older sister's reminiscences with some further interesting takes of the very earliest pioneering days.

"I saw the first gold ever discovered in California" said Mrs. Wolfskill. "Marshall came over to our house in Benicia and stayed all night.

He was on his way to San Francisco from Sutter's mill. He said he thought he had gold. He took out a little rag that looked like the bit of a bag that housewives keep aniseed in and opened it. We all looked at it in wonder. Three days after that Sam Brannan, a Mormon, came riding breathless into our place in Benicia and asked John Wolfskill, who was afterward my husband, for a fresh horse. He said that gold had been discovered, and that he was going up there to locate all the land he could and return to Monterey and file on it. Monterey was then the capital of California. But some time before that Brannan had been very unaccommodating to Mr. Wolfskill when he wanted horses to help bring his fruit trees from Los Angeles, so he would not let Brannan have a horse. Brannan rode on, urging his tired beast. He and [John] Bidwell were going to locate the whole gold-bearing country, but Mr. Wolfskill told them it was placer mining, and that they could not hold it all.

"Everybody was guarding the secret of gold in California in hope of monopolizing the product. My father was the first man to write of the discovery. He sent a long letter East to his old friend, Senator Thomas Benton, who had secured him the position of Indian Agent at Council Bluffs years before, and that letter of my father's was primarily the cause of the gold fever that swept through the Eastern States.

"In 1848 and 1849 we had a school in Benicia. Father started it and got seven pupils to come from a distance and board at our places.

"In 1849 and 1850 our only source of social amusement was dancing. And such dances! We used to ride horseback miles to attend them. I rode all the way from Benicia to Sonoma, about thirty miles, and then danced all night. And the only music for these balls was the fiddle. We left Benicia in 1852 and went to Green valley, and lived there three years. Then we moved to Colusa, and I stayed there until 1860, when I was married and went to Winters to live on the old Wolfskill place, where my husband died."

Mrs. Noble Martin of 2001 Haste street, Berkeley, widow of the late Senator Martin, was originally Miss Weare of Independence, Mo., and arrived at Sutter's Fort, near Sacramento, on November 20, 1849, when she was 15 years of age.

"We were just six months to the day crossing the plains," said Mrs. Martin. "Our destination was Sutter's Fort, and we did not consider that we were really in California until we had arrived there. Mike McClelland, who was also from Independence, kept the hotel at Sutter's Fort and was a family connection of ours.

"We came west by the old Santa Fe trail and passed through what is now the State of Kansas, but it was then Indian Territory. Of course, we received no mail and got no news on the way. It was not until 1860 that the Pony Express was started. As I remember it, our long journey was a continuous pleasure trip. When we arrived at Sutter's Fort the whole inclosure was a human beehive, just swarming with people, and there were people in the little rooms all about the court, and soldiers, perhaps twenty of them.

"After a few days' entertainment the women of our party moved over to Sacramento. I remember going down J street in a flat-bottom boat. We all camped out. I suppose there were 200 or 300 women in Sacramento at that time. From Sacramento we went up the river by boat to Marysville, and later to Bidwell's Bar, and to each of the other new mining camps as they were formed.

"I sluiced many and many a day. One member of our party picked up a $400 nugget on the Honecut.

"There were no bakeshops in those early days, and I made many an apple pie, just of common dried apples, and sold them for a dollar apiece. The women helped in that way to support he families, for mining was not always a certain means of livelihood.

"Christmas, 1852, I was at Point Reyes, at the cabin of Dr. Crandell, who owned the land there. I was all alone that day, not a human being within ten or twelve miles of me. It was raining. As I stood within the cabin and looked out the door across the ravine, a great mountain lion came out about 300 feet away. He looked toward the cabin and then let out a frightful yell. I shut the door and threw the crossbar into place.

"Later, father and mother lived at Alta Hill, near Grass Valley, but after my marriage to Dr. Martin I lived for many years at Dutch Flat, and then moved to Berkeley. Up there in Nevada county, father and mother lie at rest at the foot of a big thirty-foot rock that rises like a natural monument. They were married when father was 21 and mother 17, and they lived happily together all those years, father dying at the age of 89 and mother at the age of 85 within four months of each other. A remarkable thing was that father, after he was 80 years old, homesteaded the farm where he died."

VIGILANTE JUSTICE

READING 18, HUBERT HOWE BANCROFT

"The Downieville Tragedy"

1887

IT WAS A RARE THING IN California, extremely rare, for rough men to lay their hands upon a woman. About the only sentiment of youthful memories which with time and distance had not only remained but had become softly intensified, was that of home hallowed by the tender influence of mother, sister, or that nearer, sweet other self, wife. So woven among the fibres of the heart was it, so mingled with the sensuous blood, so wrapped within the folds of passionate imagination, that, like ash-covered coals, the drearier the aspect without, the warmer glowed the fire within.

Hanging of Whittaker and McKenzie, By the San Francisco Vigilance Committee.

FIGURE 3.3. Hanging of Whittaker and McKenzie by the San Francisco Vigilance Committee, on the west side of Battery Street between California and Pine Streets in San Francisco (1865)

Then wild indeed must be the fury that maddened them against a woman; and never was insensate wrath more manifest than among the miners of the Yuba for miles on either side of Downieville when, on the morning of July 5, 1851, it was known that a comrade had been slain, butchered with a long sharp knife, and by a woman. The matter of sex was suddenly lost sight of, swallowed in the gulp of passion which left nothing to the mind but the abominable bloody fact.

Joe Cannon killed! Cut to the heart, and by a woman! The words were confusing. The breath that uttered them came labored; thick it was, and murky in its significance. The blood, receding from the heart, clogged in the veins, and respiration was well nigh throttled by the messengers of the brain. Joe was the favorite of the camp, the finest fellow that ever swung a pick or dislodged a boulder. He was over six feet high, straight as a poplar, with limbs as clean as those of a newly barked madroño. In weight he fell not far short of two hundred and forty, and it was all muscle; his chest was like that of an ox, and the arms of Hercules hung from his shoulders. And yet he would not harm a fly; his heart was as tender as his sinews were tough. Joe gone! Stabbed to death, and by a woman!

Soon men began to speak in words. Fresh arrivals came pouring in. Strangers asked, Who is he? Who killed him?

It was a little woman; young, too—only twenty-four. Scarcely five feet in height, with a slender symmetrical figure, agile and extremely graceful in her movements, with soft skin of olive hue, long black hair, and dark, deep, lustrous eyes, opening like a window to the fagot-flames which, kindled with love or hate, shone brightly from within. Mexico was her country; her blood Spanish, diluted with the aboriginal American. Her name was Juanita. The man she killed, with one hand could have picked her up and tossed her into the Yuba River. He was an Englishman and an Australian colonist, but not a man of Sydney in the sense then current.

Though a stalwart Britisher, yet he could not let pass the immortal Fourth without assisting at its observances.

And this time they had made a glorious night of it. Joe Cannon, with the rest of them, was very drunk, and consequently very happy. From store to store, from house to house, up and down the streets and through all the streets they went, rapping up the inmates, compelling the master of the house to treat and then to join them. It was rare fun.

Passing the premises of a Mexican monte-dealer, Joe Cannon kicked at the door. As he was not in condition to stand steadily on one foot and carefully to weigh the force of the other as it went against the door, he may have given it a little harder blow than he intended or than was necessary. As the door was secured only by leathern hinges, it fell in. At least so the boys told him next morning—that he had kicked in the Mexican's door.

That was all right, said Joe. He knew the monte-dealer well, and had often bet an ounce or two in passing his table; the damage could not be great; he would go around after breakfast, pay it, and apologize. True, there was the wife, or she whom the man lived with as with wife: she might not perhaps appreciate the foreign patriotism which so disturbed rest—but she was a bashful, retiring little thing; no one thought of her. Besides, they were Mexicans, and their footing was not by any means too secure in the community as it was. A man, a miner, a big burly favorite, what were fifty Mexican gamblers and their mistresses to him? Nevertheless no man should be able truthfully to say that Joe Cannon ever did him wrong, drunk or sober.

Approaching the house, Joe found the door still down. The Mexican was within; and placing a hand on either door-post to steady himself withal, for his head seemed now as big as a barrel, and his legs were a little shaky, he began talking to the man in broken Spanish as best he could. Suddenly from a corner where she had lain concealed, quick as a flash the little woman sprang up, threw herself upon the strong man's breast, and buried her knife in his bosom. It was all done in an instant, and he who had come to make reparation for a trivial injury committed in a moment of frolic, he, the picture of physical perfection, the pride of the camp, lay as dead.

Why did she do it? Did this man visit her house to insult her? Had they ever met or had intercourse at any time; and was there ill-will existing on either side? No one knew. Who shall fathom a woman's heart? All those miners knew or cared to know was that for so slight a thing as she it was a monstrous blow. The bowie-knife was large and sharp, and to send it into his gigantic frame, through his shirt and through the breast-bone clear into the heart, that little arm must indeed have been tempered by most murderous passion.

And now, when the enraged miners with a blow of the fist burst her door and stood before her, Juanita manifested not the slightest fear; and yet she knew that she must die. It was not defiance, nor brazen impudence; she assumed no character—she acted only the primary sentiment of her nature, and that was stoical submission to inexorable fate, or more simply, cool courage.

Hastily putting in place some scattered articles, and glancing carefully at her dress—she was already attired in her best—she signified her readiness to go. The blaze of angry eyes, the forest of frowning faces through which blew deadly murmurings, were all lost on her; she was thinking of her own affairs, thinking should she send something to her friends, thinking about her household, and how her husband would do in her absence. Of course they would hang her; as for the paraphernalia of trial it might be some gratification to them, but it was nothing to her.

There yet stood near the centre of the town a large pavilion, which had been erected for the celebration ceremonies the day before; there was a raised platform, with chairs and table, just the place for the occasion, and there the dark-eyed bashful little murderess was conducted by her guard of two thousand.

Twelve men responded eagerly to the call for a jury; happy he who should have any part in this gentle strangulation. Glancing at each other and at the miners round them, they seemed to say, "All is safe and settled; woman or no woman, she hangs." Lawyers for the defence were backward in presenting themselves; there were plenty for the prosecution.

John B. Weller, then running for congress, was at the hotel overlooking the tribunal. He was besought to go out and speak to the mob, but he had no ambition that way. He was not of the stuff of which martyrs were made. There were times and places for all things: a time for advocating law and order, and a time for refraining from such advocation; and clearly this, in the eyes of John B. Weller, country-server, was one of the latter times.

So Juanita was tried; but the trial was a sad, one-sided affair, in which there was a total absence of that love of fair-play so characteristic of the American miner. No one dared to say a good word for her; no one was allowed to defend her. In so far as she was small and weak, and they were many, and great, and strong, in so far did their insensate fury intensify with the progress of affairs. For the moment the men of that region seemed baptized by Satan for the execution of a work of infernal grace.

When the verdict was formally declared, Juanita gave a quiet little laugh, as if to say, How droll! These great American men think in this aping of ancient forms they have given their prisoner a trial. Stroke conscience the right way and you can do anything with it.

In the four hours allowed her before her execution, Juanita made her will verbally, arranged her affairs, and gave her few effects away. During it all her heroism carried her far beyond the usual stolid fortitude of her race. At a time when men tremble and pray she was her natural self, neither gay nor sad. She was as far from looking lightly on the matter as giving way to senseless sorrow.

The builder of the bridge that spanned the Yuba had left at about the middle of it two uprights with a beam across, as if for the express purpose of hanging. It was just the place for the occasion, though from that point, with the flowing river underneath, and on either side with the rolling hills in front, and in the background the purple-misted mountains glowing in the light of the almighty sun, it was too beautiful a world for a young, free, light-hearted woman to wish to leave.

With a light elastic step, surrounded by her friends, chatting with them quietly on the way, Juanita walked down to the bridge. She shook hands with them all, but not a tear, not a tremor was visible. By means of a step-ladder she mounted to a scantling which had been tied for her to stand on between the uprights underneath the beam, took from her head a man's hat which had been kindly placed there by a friend, shied it with unerring accuracy to its owner, meanwhile smiling her thanks, then with quick dexterity she twisted up her long black tresses, smoothed her dress, placed the noose over her head and arranged the rope in a proper manner, and finally, lifting her hands, which she refused to have tied, exclaimed, *Adios, señores! and the fatal signal was given.*

Commenting on this tragedy, the Sacramento *Times and Transcript* says:

> "The act for which the victim suffered was one entirely justifiable under the provocation. She had stabbed a man who had persisted in making a disturbance in her house and had greatly outraged her rights. The violent proceedings of an indignant and excited mob, led on by the enemies of the unfortunate woman, were a blot upon the history of the state. Had she committed a crime of a really heinous character, a real American would have revolted at such a course as was pursued toward this friendless and unprotected foreigner. We had hoped the story was fabricated. As it is, the perpetrators of the deed have shown themselves and their race."

This editor goes far out of his way both to distort the facts and then to draw from them false conclusions. The woman was not a friendless foreigner, nor was her act justifiable. The man she murdered offered her no violence, and she had no right to kill him. The people were right to hang her, but they were wrong to do it madly and in the heat of passion.

FIGURE 3.4. Gold miners excavating an eroded bluff with jets of water at a placer mine in Dutch Flat, California, between 1857 and 1870.

MINING AND THE ENVIRONMENT

READING 19

Woodruff v. North Bloomfield Gravel Mining Co.

1884

HYDRAULIC MINING, AS USED IN THIS OPINION, IS THE process by which a bank of gold-bearing earth and rock is excavated by a jet of water, discharged through the converging nozzle of a pipe, under great pressure, the earth and debris being carried away by the same water, through sluices, and discharged on lower levels into the natural streams and water-courses below. Where the gravel or other material of the bank is cemented, or where the bank is composed of masses of pipe-clay, it is shattered by blasting with powder, sometimes from 15 to 20 tons of powder being used at one blast to break up a bank. . . . For example, an eight-inch nozzle, at the North Bloomfield mine, discharges 185,000 cubic feet of water in an hour, with a velocity of 150 feet per second. The excavating power of such a body of water, discharged with such velocity, is enormous; and unless the gravel is very heavy or firmly cemented, it is much in excess of its transporting power. At some of the mines, as at the North Bloomfield, several of these Monitors are worked, much of the time night and day, the several levels upon which they are at work being brilliantly illuminated by electric lights, the electricity being generated by water power. A night scene of the kind, at the North Bloomfield mine, is in the highest degree weird and startling, and cannot fail to strike the stranger with wonder and admiration.

• • •

The portion of the valley here referred to as covered with sand is that portion of the Yuba River extending across the Sacramento valley from the foot-hills to its junction with Feather River at Marysville—a distance of about 12 miles. Formerly, before hydraulic mining operations commenced, the Yuba River ran through this part of its course in a deep channel, with gravely bottom from 300 to 400 feet wide, on average, with steep banks from 15 to 20 feet high, at low water, on either side. From the top of the banks, on each side, extended a strip of bottom lands of rich, black, alluvial soil, on average a mile

FIGURE 3.5. Map showing the new transcontinental route of the Atlantic and Pacific Railroad and its connections.

and a half wide, upon which were situated some of the finest farms, orchards and vineyards in the state. Beyond this first bottom, was a second, constituting a basin between the higher lands on either side of from a mile and a half to three miles wide. Not only has the channel of the river through these bottoms been filled up to a depth of 25 feet and upwards, but this entire strip of bottom land has been buried with sand and debris many feet deep, from ridge to ridge of high land, and utterly ruined for farming and other purposes to which it was before devoted, and it has consequently been abandoned for such uses.

• • •

Woodruff's interests involved are by no means insignificant, no matter how much may have been said to belittle them. His block of stores, built on one of the most eligible business locations in Marysville, at a cost of at least somewhere between $40,000 and $60,000, his nearly 1,000 acres of farming land—among the best in the state—in Sutter county, called the Hock Farm, and his Eliza tract of over 700 acres on the opposite side of the river, in Yuba county and upon which a little settlement, embracing business houses and a public regular steamboat landing, once existed of which 125 acres in the aggregate on the two tracts are conceded to have already been destroyed certainly constitute an estate of no inconsiderable value.

• • •

The brief flood occasioned by the breaking of the English dam, in June last, afforded a striking illustration of what is liable hereafter to occur. This enormous deposit of debris in the Yuba, and near Marysville, and in the streams in the mountains above, is a continuing, ever-present, and, so long as hydraulic mining is carried on as now pursued it will ever continue to be, an alarming and ever-growing menace, a constantly augmenting nuisance, threatening further injuries to the property of complainant, as well as the lives and property of numerous other citizens similarly situated. Against the continuous and further augmentation of this nuisance the complainant must certainly be entitled to legal protection.

• • •

The supreme court of California has never recognized the validity of any custom to mine in such a manner as to destroy or injure the property of others, even in the district of diggings where the local customs and usages of miners are sanctioned by the statutes. But the California reports are full of cases where the principle has been enforced in the mines that every one must so use his own property as not to injure another.

• • •

After an examination of the great questions involved, as careful and thorough as we are capable of giving them, with a painfully anxious appreciation of the responsibilities resting upon us, and of the disastrous consequences to the defendants, we can come to no other conclusion than that complainant is entitled to a perpetual injunction. But as it is possible that some mode may be devised in the future for obviating the injuries, either one of those suggested or some other, and successfully carried out, so as to be both safe and effective, a clause will be inserted in the decree giving leave on any future occasion, when some such plan has been successfully executed, to apply to the court for modification or suspension of the injunction.

Let a decree be entered accordingly.

QUESTIONS FOR STUDY

1. Given that the odds of "striking it rich" overnight were always relatively low, why was the Gold Rush able to draw so many people from all over the world so quickly?
2. An estimated 95% of the people who came to California during the Gold Rush were men; only 5% were women. What brought women to California at this time? What were their experiences like? Do you think men and women experienced the Gold Rush differently? Why or why not?
3. What do the legal principles of the mining society tell us about what gold miners valued?
4. How did gender and race shape vigilante justice in California? If Juanita had been a man would the outcome have been different? What if she had been an Anglo woman?
5. What was the environmental impact of hydraulic mining in California? How did the Supreme Court of California in *Woodruff v. North Bloomfield Gravel Mining Co.*, decide to deal with the issue? Why? What might be the long-term consequences of this court decision?

CREDITS

1. "Capt. Sutter's Account of the First Discovery of the Gold." Copyright in the Public Domain.
2. "The Gold Mine," *Californian*, no. 4, pp. 2. Copyright in the Public Domain.
3. Fig. 3.1: L.C. McClure, "An Anglo Forty-Niner at the American River (1850)," http://commons.wikimedia.org/wiki/File:Gullgraver_1850_California.jpg. Copyright in the Public Domain.
4. Fig. 3.2: Roy Daniel Graves, "Engraving of Chinese Gold Miners," http://en.wikipedia.org/wiki/File:Chinese_Gold_Miners_b.jpg. Copyright in the Public Domain.
5. Sue Bailey Thurman, ed., "Alvin A. Coffey," *Pioneers of Negro Origin in California*. Copyright © 1952 by Acme Publishing Company.
6. James M. Hutchings, "The Miner's Ten Commandments," *Placerville Herald*. Copyright in the Public Domain.
7. Louise Amelia Knapp Smith Clappe, *The Shirley Letters from California Mines in 1851-52*. Copyright in the Public Domain.
8. "The Foremothers Tell of Olden Times," *The Chronicle*. Copyright in the Public Domain.
9. Fig. 3.3: Barber and Howe, "Hanging of Whittaker and McKenzie," http://en.wikipedia.org/wiki/File:Whittaker_andMcKenzie_hanging_Barber_1865p644.jpg. Copyright in the Public Domain.
10. Hubert Howe Bancroft, "The Downieville Tragedy," *The Works of Hubert Howe Bancroft*, vol. XXXVI: *Popular Tribunals*, vol. 1, pp. 577-588. Copyright in the Public Domain.
11. Fig. 3.4: "Gold Miners Excavating," http://en.wikipedia.org/wiki/File:X-60072.jpg. Copyright in the Public Domain.
12. Fig. 3.5: "Map Showing the New Transcontinental Route of the Atlantic & Pacific Railroad," http://www.loc.gov/resource/g3701p.rr003300/. Copyright in the Public Domain.
13. "Woodruff v. North Bloomfield Gravel Mining Co.," *The Federal Reporter*, vol. 18, pp. 756-757, 759-760, 763, 764, 765, 767, 770, 786, 792-793, 797, 802, 808-809. Copyright in the Public Domain.

04 Conflict and Identity in a New State

INTRODUCTION

The discovery of gold hastened the need for civil government as large numbers of gold seekers rushed to find their fortunes in California. In 1849, Californians sought statehood. After an animated debate in Congress over the slavery issue, California entered the Union as a free state on September 9, 1850. The gold rush also fundamentally changed the economic base and the ethnic makeup of California, with people arriving from all over the world. By the late 1850s, it was one of the most diverse regions in the world, a trend that continued throughout the following decades (Table 4.1; Figure 4.2). This growing diversity also created conflict, as Anglo Californians increasingly asserted the primacy of their right to the abundant wealth of the new state. These conflicts occurred within the context of the efforts to fashion an identity for the state and for themselves as Californians.

Race	1860		1870		1880	
White	323,177	85.0%	499,424	89.1%	767,181	88.7%
Colored	4,086	1.1%	4,272	0.8%	6,018	0.7%
Chinese	34,938	9.2%	49,277	8.8%	75,182	8.7%
Japanese	0	0.0%	33	<0.1%	86	<0.1%
Civilized Indians	17,798	4.7%	7,241	1.3%	16,277	1.9%
Total	**379,999**		**560,247**		**864,744**	

TABLE 4.1. California Population by Race (U.S. Censuses 1860-1890)

For the Native American population, the confrontation with Anglo settlers proved fatal. On the eve of American conquest in 1845, approximately one hundred fifty thousand Indians lived in California; by 1870, their numbers had dropped to only thirty thousand. By the turn of the century, fewer than eighteen thousand Indian people survived, leaving them astounded and demoralized, and their cultures devastated. Most deaths resulted from the ravages of disease epidemics, exacerbated by starvation and poverty. Displaced by settlers and gold seekers from their traditional lands, Indians resorted to stealing cattle to survive, resulting in violent retaliatory attacks on them (see reading 20 "Indian Troubles in El Dorado"). Other attacks were unprovoked massacres, leading many historians to use the term genocide to describe them. Vigilante groups, financed by local citizens, hunted down Indians and killed them; some were reimbursed for their costs from the state coffers. One of the most lethal of these attacks occurred on Indian Island in Humboldt Bay and nearby villages on February 26, 1860 (see reading 21"The Humboldt Butchery of Indian Infants and Women"). Asurvivor of this massacre, Jane Sam, left us with a detailed account of the events—the only indigenous perspective, as far as can be determined (see reading 22 "Jane Sam (Wiyot) Witnesses the Indian Island Massacre").

The Washoe Indian tribe exemplifies the impact of American arrival in the region. Native to the region around Lake Tahoe, the Washoe lifestyles revolved around their environment and seasonal migrations in search of food supplies. The California gold rush and the subsequent silver rush in Nevada a few years later disrupted this balance. Thousands of miners and immigrants flooded Washoe lands in a relatively short time period. These arrivals depleted the natural food sources, while the logging and mining industry denuded the forests. What happened to the land also happened to the people. Many settled near white towns and took jobs on ranches and as domestics to make some money. Others continued to hunt and fish, selling their catch to the newly arrived migrants. The Washoe material culture also began to change, but they continued to speak their language and hold on to some of their cultural practices. The forced assimilation policies placed further pressures on the Washoe. Children were forcibly taken from their homes and sent to the Stewart Boarding School to be "Americanized" while the communal nature of indigenous life was considered a threat to modern American living. Yet, the Washoe persisted (Figure 4.1). Today, approximately fifteen hundred enrolled members of the Washoe Tribe of Nevada and California live on tribal lands scattered in the Reno, Carson Valley, and Gardnerville areas of Nevada and in Woodfords, California.

The rising number of gold seekers, combined with the mounting costs and complexity of mining operations, also created growing tensions among miners. White "American" miners specifically expressed their resentment of the other national groups represented in the camps. While they usually accepted Europeans, they had less tolerance for Mexican miners and none for Chinese. In April 1850, the new California legislature responded by passing the Foreign Miners' License Law, requiring people not "native to or natural born citizens of the United States" to pay $20 per month for the right to mine in California. The tax drove many Latino miners back to their home countries; immigrant miners who stayed staged protests and the law was repealed. When gold rush immigration reached its peak in 1852, bringing another sixty-seven thousand people to the state, the legislature adopted a new foreign miners' tax of $4 per month. This tax was aimed specifically at the Chinese, who made up nearly a third of the 1852 arrivals (Figure 4.3).

Chinese miners found increasingly harsh treatment at the hands of their fellow miners. Many had already left the camps and moved to San Francisco, where they soon established themselves in the city's business community and created America's first Chinatown. While many immigrant groups chose to settle in their own ethnic communities where they could reproduce customs from the homeland, Chinatowns additionally grew out of necessity, as places of protection against the growing anti-Chinese violence. With their numbers growing, the Chinese encountered increasing prejudice and discrimination. In Los Angeles, for instance, a mob of over five hundred men entered Chinatown on October 24, 1871, to attack, rob, and murder Chinese residents in a racially motivated riot. The mob systematically killed eighteen Chinese immigrants, making this so-called Chinatown War the largest incident of mass lynching in American history (Figure 4.4).

The anti-Chinese sentiments were exacerbated by the fact that the transcontinental railroad had ended California's comparative isolation from economic cycles in the rest of the United States. By the mid-1870s, when a national economic depression reached California, the Chinese became the scapegoats for the state's economic woes. In 1877, labor leader Denis Kearney organized the Workingman's Party of California around the issue of the Chinese as the "indispensable enemy." Kearney and others tapped into deep anxieties about the Chinese and their fitness for assimilation (see reading 23 "Why the Chinese Do Not Go"). The Workingman's Party advocated for the exclusion of the Chinese, leading to a nationwide debate (Figures 4.5-4.6). In 1882, the US Congress responded with the passage of the Chinese Exclusion Act, barring further Chinese immigration for ten years (see reading 24 "The Chinese Exclusion Act"). Congress extended the act for another ten years in 1892 and also required that all Chinese obtain a certificate of residence, without which she or he faced immediate deportation (Figure 4.7). In 1902, Congress extended the act indefinitely until it was repealed in 1943.

INDIGENOUS CALIFORNIANS IN THE NEW STATE

READING 20

"Indian Troubles in El Dorado"

***Sacramento Transcript*, January 22, 1851**

WE LEARN FROM DR. MATTHEW CROFT, WHO ARRIVED IN the city yesterday, evening, that the Indians have again broken out on the miners and others, residing along the frontier of El Dorado county. It appears that, from the time of the disbanding of Col. Rodgers' volunteers to the present, the Indians have been committing depredations and killing miners whenever opportunity offered.

Dr. C. has in his possession the proceedings of a meeting of miners and others, held at Johnson's Rancho, which is located near the South Fork of the American river, which he designs forwarding immediately to Gov. McDougal. The frontier men call earnestly on Government to protect them, and represent that the Indians are not only daily driving off stock, and lying in wait to murder them if they venture any distance from their cabins, but that it is

FIGURE 4.1. Washoe Indians—The Chief's Family

a daily circumstance to hear of miners being killed whilst engaged in their labors. The Indians are in the habit of coming close to the rancho in daylight, and killing the horses and other stock around. On Sunday, last two persons, a short distance only from the house, were fired on, and a young man named Smith was seriously wounded. There are three rancherias within twelve miles of Johnson's, where there is gathered a large body of Indians, and the whites are compelled to guard the house both by night and day.

A petition has been drawn, up, asking the Legislature, 1; to authorize the raising of a small volunteer force, and we trust that those in authority will give the application that prompt attention- which the necessities of the case demand.

READING 21

"The Humboldt Butchery of Indian Infants and Women"

***New York Times*, April 12, 1860**

SAN FRANCISCO, FRIDAY, MARCH 16, 1860.

The particulars of the horrid massacre of peaceable Indians, one bright Sunday morning, (Feb. 25,) I detailed in my last steamer letter. Since then, many who were in the vicinity have been in town, and the coherence and agreement of their several stories show that we have arrived at the truth in the matter. It appears that the brutal murderers were not over-anxious to meet the male Indians; that a spy who had attended an annual dance on Indian Island (about a mile from Eureka, the County Seat of Humboldt) the evening previous, conveyed the intelligence that there was not a gun, bow or arrow on the island, that the savages were entirely defenceless. The whites then approached, about 6 o'clock in the morning, fired upon and killed three men, who were asleep in a cabin at some little distance from where the women lay, then, entering lodge after lodge, they dirked the sleeping, and with axes split open and crushed the skulls of the children and women. The total killed on the island were fifty-five, of whom only five were men. On South Beach, about a mile away from Eureka, in another direction, an hour or two before, the same party of whites had killed 58, most of them women and children. No defence was made. Many of the women were making an honest living in the families of the whites. The half-breeds pleaded for their lives in good English. On the following Wednesday 40 more were butchered on the South Fork of the Eel River. The Humboldt Times, which justifies this short method of getting rid of disagreeable neighbors, says that many of those killed on Eel River were bucks and bad fellows. Still later, by a few days, 35 were slaughtered on Eagle Prairie -- total of the butchered within one week, 188. The victims had lived on terms of peace with the whites, and relied on them for security. They were not even charged with thieving. Their great crime was that the whites suspected that some hostile mountain Indians had taken refuge among them when hard pressed. The names of the brave men who brained the children have not been published. One writer for the Bulletin says, however, that there is a fellow in Eureka who boasts that with his own hatchet he slew 30 women and children in one day, and that another man who professes to have been captain of the outlaws says that he alone killed 60 infants.

READING 22

Jane Sam (Wiyot) Witnesses the Indian Island Massacre

1860

THE DANCE WAS OVER [IN] ONE DAY. THE WIND BLEW and rough weather. On account of this nobody went home. That night after the dance all were asleep. There were four houses and one sweat house.... The door was blocked by white men as the people were asleep, not expecting anything to happen. They were not on the lookout. When they found out what was up they began to scatter and was struck down by clubs, knives, and axes, all met the same fate, children, women, and men. I got out and hid in a trash pile. That was how I was saved.

When I got away from the trash pile I sneaked away near the edge of the marsh by a blind slough [and] laid there. I did not hear any noise or scream from the people. Must of all been killed, sure enough. These white men took all things such as beads, baskets, fur, hide, bows, and arrows. All the property belonging to the dead that was not taken was destroyed by burning. Women and children were killed when they lay asleep or they did not make any effort to escape, as they thought the white men would not molest them. A few men got away, the exact number being forgotten. At break of day I saw two boat loads of white men going across to Eureka. These were the men that done the massacring.

It took all the forenoon to gather up all...[the] bodies [of] men, women, children, and babies [that] could be found. One living child was found in the arms of his dead mother and today he is [still] living....It took all day to bury the dead. The next morning they was through burying what bodies were buried on the Island. The rest of the bodies...were taken to Mad River for burial. Some were taken to the Peninsula and some to South Bay, some to Freshwater. That same night there was a massacre at the mouth of Eel River and at the South Jetty where men, women, and children were killed. What got away were taken to Bucksport [Fort Humboldt] by the soldiers. I do not know how long they were kept at Bucksport. From there we were taken to the Indian reservation.

FOREIGN-BORN MINERS

FIGURE 4.2. White and Chinese Miners Pose for a Photo at Auburn Ravine (1852)

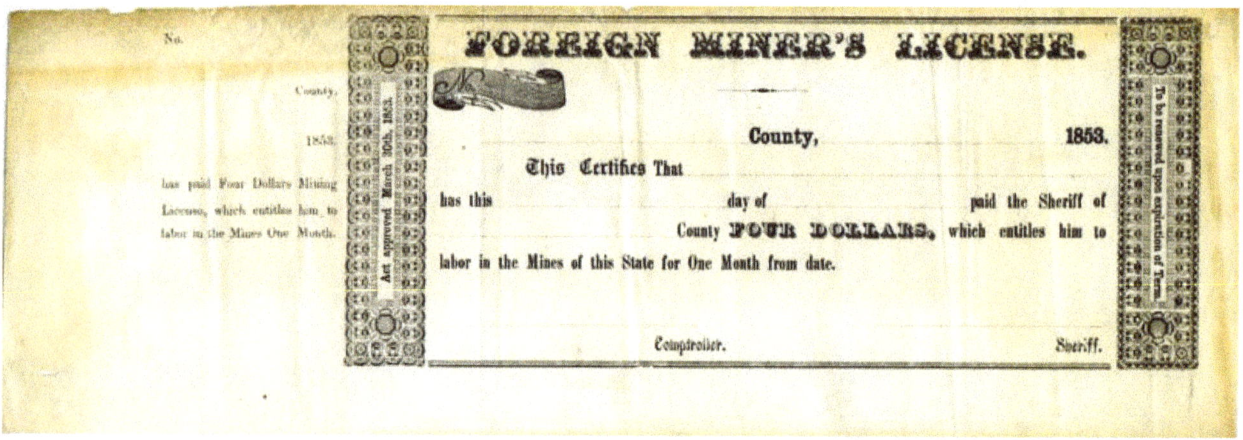

No.

County,

1853.

has paid Four Dollars Mining License, which entitles him to labor in the Mines One Month.

Act approved March 30th, 1853.

FOREIGN MINER'S LICENSE.

No.

County, 1853.

This Certifies That

has this day of paid the Sheriff of County **FOUR DOLLARS,** which entitles him to labor in the Mines of this State for One Month from date.

Comptroller. Sheriff.

To be renewed upon expiration of Term.

FIGURE 4.3. Blank Foreign Miners Tax License (1853)

INTERACTIONS WITH THE CHINESE

READING 23

"Why the Chinese Do Not Go"

***Sacramento Daily Union*, January 10, 1879**

IT HAS BEEN OFTEN ENOUGH OBSERVED THAT ALL THE agitation against the Chinese has bad no appreciable effect upon them in this State. The Sand Lot cry, "The Chinese must go!", has in fact long since become simply ridiculous, for everybody sees that the Chinese do not go. On the contrary, they find constant and profitable employment, and they have no inducement to leave a State where they are as a rule doing very much better than they ever did before in their lives. They do not go because the people of California, while protesting against their presence, continue to utilize their labor in a hundred ways.

In this matter private interest dominates public interest. The very men who go to the Sand Lots and applaud Kearney's speeches, are supporters of Chinese labor. Thousands of them have all their washing done by Chinese. The wives of scores or hundreds of them employ Chinese help. They smoke cigars made by Chinese. They contribute in many ways, directly and indirectly, to keep the Chinese in the State. White women buy their vegetables of Chinese hucksters, and not only vegetables, but fish, fruit and many other things. Nor is it probable that, however much

FIGURE 4.4. Calle de los Negros in Los Angeles Chinatown, the Site of the Chinese Massacre of 1871 (c. 1882)

talk there may be, any concerted effort to put a stop to this traffic would prove successful. A San Francisco journal the other day printed some comments on these facts, implying that California had no right to ask Congressional interference in the premises while such strong evidence was attainable that the Chinese are really not regarded as objectionable. At the first glance this kind of criticism appears sound; but it will not bear analysis. Cheap labor and its productions will always command a market, without regard to any moral or political considerations that may be involved. The instinct of thrift is too strong in the units of society for us to expect any other results. Whatever A or B may hold in a general and abstract way upon the Chinese question, where concrete matters are concerned the strong probability is that they will endeavor to get the most service or goods possible for their money.

So long as Chinese cheap labor is available it will be employed, either openly or secretly, and this would occur in any considerable community of human beings anywhere.

The expulsion of the Chinese is not demanded on the ground that they represent cheap labor; if such a plea was advanced it might be turned to the prejudice of other nationalities than the Chinese. They are regarded by the thoughtful as objectionable because they represent a substitution of unchangeably foreign and hopelessly unassimilative material for that which is malleable and assimilative. They do not come here with any view to permanent residence or naturalization. They bring their own peculiar and uncongenial civilization with them, and wherever they go they set up a small section of the Chinese Empire.

There is therefore no parallel between this kind of cheap labor and other kinds. We cannot look forward to the probability that some day all these Chinese will be American citizens, will speak English, will have adopted American habits and institutions. Chinese colonies never merge, as all experience proves. They have lived in Singapore and Java for generations, but they are still as completely Chinese as at the beginning. Cheap labor with them, therefore, is really a question between the peopling of this coast with Chinese or with white men and women. The fact that they are cheap assures the employment of as many as may come. It is idle to build remedial theories upon; the delusive supposition that self-interest can be subordinated to public policy in this connection.

This predominance of self-interest should rather be conceded as one of the inevitable conditions of human nature, and the fact of its existence should be advanced as demonstrating the necessity of governmental interference in the interest of American civilization. It is not a reproach to California that she cannot rid herself of this plague. Her helplessness is not the effect of a phenomenal inconsistency, nor is it any proof of insincerity in her complaints. All the circumstances which to the mere surface observer seem to indicate an indifference to, or even approval of, the presence of the Chinese, only emphasize the truth that the Chinese question is one demanding a statesmanlike solution, "since it is clearly beyond the reach of the Society that suffers from it."

VIEWS OF EXCLUSION

READING 24

The Chinese Exclusion Act

1882

AN ACT TO EXECUTE CERTAIN TREATY STIPULATIONS RELATING TO CHINESE.

Whereas in the opinion of the Government of the United States the coming of Chinese laborers to this country endangers the good order of certain localities within the territory thereof: Therefore,

Be it enacted by the Senate and House of Representatives of the United States of America in Congress assembled, That from and after the expiration of ninety days next after the passage of this act, and until the expiration of ten years next after the passage of this act, the coming of Chinese laborers to the United States be, and the same is hereby, suspended; and during such suspension it shall not be lawful for any Chinese laborer to come, or having so come after the expiration of said ninety days to remain within the United States.

SEC. 2. That the master of any vessel who shall knowingly bring within the United States on such vessel, and land or permit to be landed, any Chinese laborer, from any foreign port or place, shall be deemed guilty of a misdemeanor, and on conviction thereof shall be punished by a fine of not more than five hundred dollars for each and

THE ONLY ONE BARRED OUT.
ENLIGHTENED AMERICAN STATESMAN.—"We must draw the line *somewhere*, you know."

FIGURE 4.5. "The Only One Barred" (April 1882)

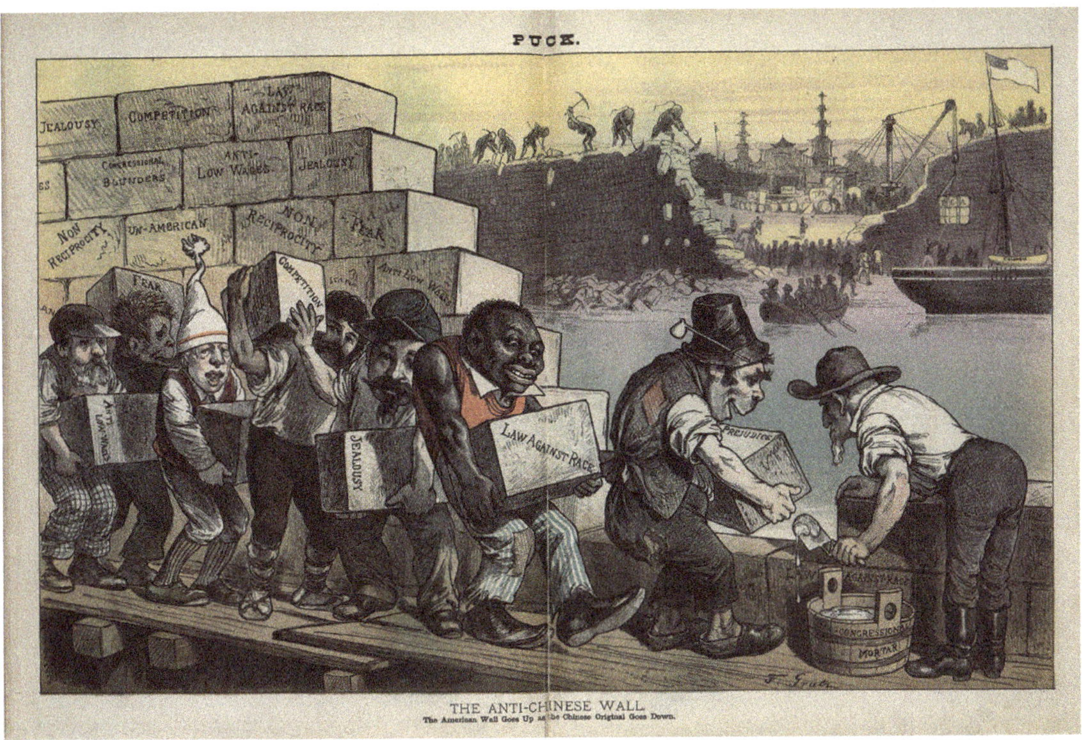

FIGURE 4.6. Friedrich Graetz, "The Anti-Chinese Wall" (March 1882)

every such Chinese laborer so brought, and maybe also imprisoned for a term not exceeding one year....

SEC. 4. That for the purpose of properly identifying Chinese laborers who were in the United States on the seventeenth day of November eighteen hundred and eighty, the collector of customs of the district from which any such Chinese laborer shall depart from the United States shall, in person or by deputy, go on board each vessel having on board any such Chinese laborers and cleared or about to sail from his district for a foreign port, and on such vessel make a list of all such Chinese laborers, which shall be entered in registry-books to be kept for that purpose, in which shall be stated the name, age, occupation, last place of residence, physical marks of peculiarities, and all facts necessary for the identification of each of such Chinese laborers, which books shall be safely kept in the custom-house.; and every such Chinese laborer so departing from the United States shall be entitled to, and shall receive, free of any charge or cost upon application certificate shall contain a statement of the name, age, occupation, last place of residence, persona description, and facts of identification of the Chinese laborer to whom the certificate is issued, corresponding with the said list and registry in all particulars. The certificate herein provided for shall entitle the Chinese laborer to whom the same is issued to return to and re-enter the United States.

SEC. 5. That any Chinese laborer desiring to depart from the United States by land, shall have the right to demand and receive, free of charge or cost, a certificate of identification similar to that provided for in section four of this act.

SEC. 6. Every Chinese person other than a laborer who may be entitled by said treaty and this act to come within the United States, and who shall be about to come to the United States, shall be identified as so entitled by the Chinese Government in each case, such identity to be evidenced by a certificate issued under the authority of said government, which certificate shall be in the English language or (if not in the English language) accompanied by a translation into English.

SEC. 7. That any person who shall knowingly and falsely alter or substitute any name for the name written in such certificate or forge any such certificate, or knowingly utter any forged or fraudulent certificate, or falsely personate any person named in any such certificate, shall be deemed guilty of a misdemeanor; and upon conviction thereof shall be fined in a sum not exceeding one thousand dollars, and imprisoned in a penitentiary for a term of not more than five years....

FIGURE 4.7. Chinese Certificate of Residence (1892)

SEC. 11. That any person who shall knowingly bring into or cause to be brought into the United States by land, or who shall knowingly aid or abet the same, or aid or abet the landing in the United States from any vessel of any Chinese person not lawfully entitled to enter the United States, shall be deemed guilty of a misdemeanor, and shall, on conviction thereof, be fined in a sum not exceeding one thousand dollars, and imprisoned for a term not exceeding one year.

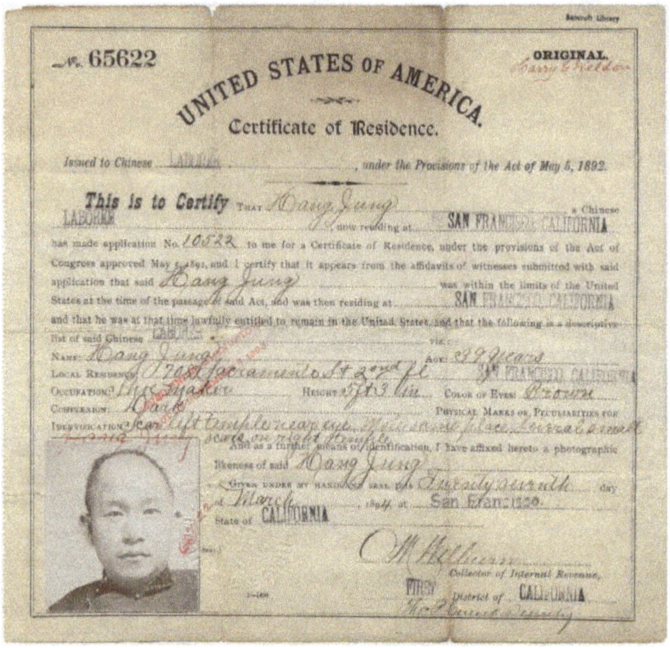

SEC. 12. That no Chinese person shall be permitted to enter the United States by land without producing to the proper officer of customs the certificate in this act required of Chinese persons seeking to land from a vessel. And any Chinese person found unlawfully within the United States shall be caused

to be removed therefrom to the country from whence he came, by direction of the President of the United States, and at the cost of the United States, after being brought before some justice, judge, or commissioner of a court of the United States and found to be one not lawfully entitled to be or remain in the United States.

SEC. 13. That this act shall not apply to diplomatic and other officers of the Chinese Government traveling upon the business of that government, whose credentials shall be taken as equivalent to the certificate in this act mentioned, and shall exempt them and their body and house- hold servants from the provisions of this act as to other Chinese persons.

SEC. 14. That hereafter no State court or court of the United States shall admit Chinese to citizenship; and all laws in conflict with this act are hereby repealed.

SEC. 15. That the words "Chinese laborers", wherever used in this act shall be construed to mean both skilled and unskilled laborers and Chinese employed in mining.

QUESTIONS FOR STUDY

1. What differences in tone and perspective appear in the sources that address the issue of California Indians? What explains these differences? How might have readers in different parts of the country have responded to the two newspaper articles? What are your reactions to these three accounts?
2. Why did the Chinese specifically become targets for exclusion? What arguments do the various documents offer for and against exclusion? What do they illuminate about America and Americans at the time? How do they reflect questions about who is an American?
3. Political cartoons are expressions of opinion. What opinions do the two cartoons in this chapter represent? What are the visual and verbal clues that hint at this opinion? What emotional appeals do they use? What groups might they have appealed to? What values do the cartoons express, overtly or implicitly?
4. What similarities do you perceive in the documents to more recent debates about immigration and immigrants in America? What are the differences?

CREDITS

1. Fig. 4.1: Thomas Housewort, "Washoe Indians - The Chief's Family," http://digitalcollections.nypl.org/items/510d47e0-b5e6-a3d9-e040-e00a18064a99. Copyright in the Public Domain.
2. "Indian Troubles in El Dorado," *Sacramento Transcript*, vol. 2, no. 75, pp. 2. Copyright in the Public Domain.
3. "The Humboldt Butchery of Indian Infants and Women," *The New York Times*. Copyright in the Public Domain.
4. Jane Sam, "Genocide and Extortion" *The North Coast Journal Weekly*. Copyright in the Public Domain.
5. Fig. 4.2: "California Gold Rush miners," http://www.learnnc.org/lp/multimedia/12286. Copyright in the Public Domain.
6. Fig. 4.3: "Blank Foreign Miner's License," http://friendsofcalarchives.org/2013/09/gold-fever-and-foreign-miners/790-blank-foreign-miners-license/. Copyright in the Public Domain.
7. Fig. 4.4: "View of Calle de Los Negros," http://waterandpower.org/museum/Early_Plaza_of_LA_%28Page_1%29.html. Copyright in the Public Domain.
8. "Why the Chinese Do Not Go," *Sacramento Daily Union*, vol. 7, no. 270, pp. 2. Copyright in the Public Domain.
9. Fig. 4.5: "The Only One Barred Out," http://en.wikipedia.org/wiki/File:The_only_one_barred_out_cph.3b48680.jpg. Copyright in the Public Domain.
10. Fig. 4.6: F. Graetz, "The Anti-Chinese Wall," http://www.loc.gov/pictures/item/2012645635/. Copyright in the Public Domain.
11. Fig. 4.7: "Chinese American Certificate of Residence 1892," http://en.wikipedia.org/wiki/File:Chinese_American_Certificate_of_Residence_1892.jpg. Copyright in the Public Domain.
12. "Chinese Exclusion Act." Copyright in the Public Domain.

05

The Paradox of Progressivism

INTRODUCTION

The Progressive Era in American history refers approximately to the years between 1890 and 1920. Progressives were a loose coalition of individuals interested in reform. California Progressives were male and female; Protestant, Catholic, and Jewish; Republican and Democrat; Anglo American, Mexican American, and African American. They were interested in a host of issues, ranging from political reform to women's rights; and from immigration reform to ensuring a safe food supply. What tied them together was a collective belief in the power of education and in the role of local, state, and national governments to create positive change in society. Progressives were in many ways rather conservative. They believed in reform, not revolution. They believed, above all, that government—and good government in particular—potentially held the solution to many of the state's problems (see reading 28 "Good Government").

Railroads were one of the inspirations for Progressive reform efforts. In California, the most economically and politically powerful railroad corporation, and thus the one that most worried reformers, was the Southern Pacific Railroad (SP). The Southern Pacific had been created in 1884 when the Central Pacific Railroad, the Southern Pacific Railroad, and several coastal passenger and freight steamship lines were merged into a single corporation. By the 1880s the Southern Pacific thus held a monopoly over much of the transportation system in the state. It was also the single largest landowner. The SP had deep ties to the state's political system. One of the SP's presidents, Leland Stanford (who had also been president of the Central Pacific), served as both the governor of California in the 1860s and as one of its state senators in the mid-1880s. The corporation itself became notorious for pressuring and, in some cases, paying politicians in Sacramento to support its interests. While Progressives were not anticorporation or anticapitalist, they focused on finding, exposing, and preventing what they regarded as abuses of power. Political cartoons were one way to bring attention to such abuses. In 1910, for example, a young, East Coast–based artist named Beaumont Fairbank drew a cartoon called "The Right of Way" that criticized the impact of monopolies like the SP (Figure 5.1.). Rather than dismantling the railroads outright, Progressives worked to rein in the power of such large corporations through regulation and ending monopolies (see reading 27 "'Bully Fight' Says Hiram Johnson").

Progressives also felt that reforming the political system was key to improving California. At a time when wealthy special interests could control the outcome of elections, they wanted to return power to the individual voters. Hiram Johnson (1866–1945) began his political career crusading against corruption in San Francisco. His ambitious reform agenda earned him the notice of the political cartoonists of the day (Figure 5.2). In 1910 the reform-minded Lincoln-Roosevelt League urged Johnson to run for governor. That year he was elected to the first of two terms and began his ascent to become one of the state's most influential Progressive Republicans. Johnson went on to help found the national Progressive Party in 1912. That year he ran as its vice-presidential candidate on a ticket with Theodore Roosevelt. They lost the election, but in 1916 Johnson was elected to the first of several terms as a US senator representing California.

During Johnson's first year as governor, California also adopted three tools of political reform that would do more to shape the state in the twentieth century than perhaps any others: the initiative (often referred to as propositions); the referendum; and the recall. California is not the only state with these tools. Indeed, Progressives both in the United States and around the world viewed them as vital to combating the political corruption common in the late nineteenth and early twentieth centuries. However, modern Californians use these three political tools far more frequently than any other state, often in ways the Progressives likely never would have anticipated (see Chapters 11 and 12).

Progressives in California also championed women's suffrage. Pro-suffrage activists had first tried, and failed, to win women the right to vote in 1896. Both the press and the public debated the question of whether women should have the right to vote, and what sort of voters women might be (see section "The Long Struggle for Woman Suffrage"). The second vote on women's suffrage in California happened in the fall of 1911. The election was a close one; indeed, suffrage lost both in San Francisco and in Oakland. However, it carried in Los Angeles by more than five thousand votes, which was enough to secure victory. The women's suffrage victory made California the sixth state in the United States where women could vote in statewide elections. When Henry Mayer created his cartoon "The Awakening" in 1915, all the states that had granted women the right to vote were located in the American West (Figure 5.3). In January of that year, the US Congress defeated a suffrage amendment. American women, including those living in California, fought on. They ultimately had to wait until the ratification of the Nineteenth Amendment in 1920 before they could vote in federal elections.

Moral reform was yet another concern for some Progressives in the state. They argued that alcohol consumption, gambling, and prostitution all needed to be addressed politically due to their negative impacts on health and on the family. To try and combat prostitution, for example, Progressives in 1913 pushed the Red Light Abatement Act through the California State Legislature. This law took the novel approach of making landlords liable if their properties were used for prostitution. Some Californians viewed it as an innovative way to combat a social problem through legislation. Others remained skeptical about the benefits of the new law (see section "Progressive Reform and Morality").

Californians also used the power of government to address the environmental limitations they confronted in the early twentieth century. Faced with continued population growth, the state's two largest cities, San Francisco and Los Angeles, realized that rainfall alone would not and could not provide enough water to sustain them. Each turned to creating large-scale municipal projects that imported water from elsewhere in the state. Both also turned to taking water from other parts of the state, often over the opposition of residents in those locations. San Francisco decided on a dam and an aqueduct to secure a steady water supply for the city. Over the staunch opposition of conservationists, including John Muir, San Francisco dammed the Hetch Hetchy Valley in Yosemite (Figure 5.4). Through a series of machinations, the legality of which are debated to this day, Los Angeles built a massive aqueduct to siphon water from the Owens Valley to Southern California. This water was critical to the development of Los Angeles' suburbs, particularly in the San Fernando Valley. But siphoning it southward devastated the farmers of the Owens Valley, who had depended on that water for their crops and livestock (Figure 5.5). Perhaps understandably, many held a grudge against Los Angeles for generations. The debates and reforms of the Progressive Era thus had a lasting impact on the politics of the state. But they also touched nearly every other aspect of life in the state, in ways that continue to shape and influence the California of the twenty-first century.

RAILROAD REGULATION

READING 25, BEAUMONT FAIRBANK

Illustration: "The Right of Way"

1910

FIGURE 5.1. The Railroad Monopoly. Illustration shows a locomotive labeled 'Private Monopoly Special' racing down tracks labeled 'Opportunity' while two trains labeled 'Plain People Local' and 'Legitimate Business' have been side-tracked, giving the monopoly the 'right of way.'

HIRAM JOHNSON: DIRECT DEMOCRACY

READING 26, JOHN HARMON CASSELL

Illustration: "All Done in 20 Minutes"

1910

FIGURE 5.2. Political cartoon of Governor of California and United States Senator Hiram W. Johnson. He stands in a library amidst shelves of books and papers pertaining to contracts, laws, and legislative acts. Captioned, 'all done in 20 minutes!'

READING 27

"'Bully Fight,' Says Hiram Johnson: Lincoln-Roosevelt League Candidate Talks to Big Crowd in Berkeley"

***San Francisco Call*, July 30, 1910**

HIRAM JOHNSON, LINCOLN-ROOSEVELT LEAGUE CANDIdate for governor, told residents of North Oakland and South Berkeley, who filled Lincoln hall in Alcatraz avenue to overflowing tonight, that he was going to be the next governor of the state. He declared that he would come up from the Tehachapi with 18,000 plurality over all other candidates for the highest office in the state.

"It is a bully fight," he declared, "that we are making to free the state and it is no sham battle this year. In the words of the former president of the United States, I repeat, it is a bully fight."

Johnson said that while one of his opponents was declaring for the declaration of independence and another for good roads, he believed that the release of the people from the political domination of the Southern Pacific political bureau, with William F. Herrin at its head, the only issue of the battle. He said: "Shall the people of this state take back the reins of power which they have relinquished for the last 25 years, or shall they submit to the rule of the Southern Pacific machine and be guided by the tooting of a locomotive whistle?

"The freedom of the people is the only issue, and I have coaxed and pleaded on highways and byways with my opponents to come out for the freedom of California, to no purpose.

"You couldn't shoot enough spines in them with a gatling gun to make them mention the names of the Southern Pacific railroad and William F. Herrin.

"This campaign has no time for the improvement of the roads or discussing whether the duty on prunes should be lowered, while the freedom of the people of the state is trampled on. When the grip of the Southern Pacific bureau is released, then will be time enough for the people to improve their roads and make all other betterments.

"Ours is a campaign of equality. It is a campaign for the election of the United States senator by popular vote, for an impartial judiciary. Every man, rich or poor, in power or not, shall stand before the law as equal in every particular.

"This is the first opportunity under the new primary law to accomplish something in the way of political reform," he declared. "Every man who is familiar with conditions has said that a successful fight must be made at this time to ensure the freedom of the people. We have got to win, and we will win, no matter how hard the fight or how great the effort.

"You must understand that it is not the intention of our campaign to drive the Southern Pacific company out of business nor do we intend to fight all corporations. This campaign is directed against the lawless interests, the corporations which have been successful in evading the law and gaining by their dishonesty.

"The honest corporations will be conserved and protected. The Southern Pacific machine will be on an equal footing if it conducts its business in a legitimate manner and keeps its dirty fingers out of politics. If it doesn't, then it will be kicked out of the state."

Johnson also urged that the voters of Berkeley stand behind C. C. Young for assemblyman from the fifty-second district.

PROGRESSIVE POLITICAL REFORM

READING 28

Good Government

***Los Angeles Herald*, February 6, 1910**

IN OTHER CITIES THE NAME OF LOS ANGELES IN GOOD government campaigns is one to conjure with. Applause follows the statement: "They did it in Los Angeles. It is the Los Angeles way. We can do it here, and make it our way." Our friends in every part of the United States with eager expectation are waiting to see the Good Government forces complete their work and clean up the county and state governments. Then, and not till then, will they seriously consider uniting nationally in a movement for good government. The success of a national Good Government party depends on the success with which the citizens of Los Angeles complete the work of eliminating from the politics of the state the railroad machine which is synonymous with graft, corruption, boodle, plot and dishonor. The complete elimination of this machine moans for Los Angeles and for Southern California an era of unprecedented progress and prosperity. The advancement of the best interests of the city, county and state has been attended by Influences which interfered with those interests.

Even now, in spite of all the lessons that have been learned by the arch-conspirator, a system of rates loot in Greater Los Angeles is being practiced upon the business men. If they would send goods to their own seaport of San Pedro, they must needs stand and deliver to the railroad a rate which is higher than the rate for the long haul across the continent.

The regulation of rates is one of the absolute necessities attendant on the development and good government of Los Angeles. Unfair rates, like crooked government, militate against the interests of a city or community; and good government should be extended to railroad rates as well as to every other branch of the public service.

THE LONG STRUGGLE FOR WOMEN'S SUFFRAGE

FIGURE 5.3. Henry Mayer, "The Awakening" (1915)

READING 29

"The Argument Against Suffrage"

***San Francisco Call*, May 23, 1894**

WE HAVE RECEIVED A CIRCULAR FROM THE ANTI WOMAN suffragists—who are ladies—setting forth reasons why in the opinion of the signers the suffrage should not be granted to women. The circular states that women have no grievances which cannot be redressed through existing agencies; that the possession of the suffrage would not tend to enhance either the interests of woman or of society, but that on the contrary it would tend to degrade her by imposing a privilege which she could not exercise without confessing her inability to perform the corresponding duties which adhere to the responsibility of civil government.

This last is the most substantial argument that has been adduced against female suffrage. Women cannot be soldiers or policemen; they are out of place as lawyers or judges; therefore they ought not to be voters. Plausible as the argument seems, it is a fallacy, as a moment's reflection will show. A large proportion of men are unfit to be soldiers or policemen or lawyers, yet no one thinks of challenging their right to vote on that account. Men who are deaf, or blind, or lame, or afflicted with chronic infirmities are unfit for military service or for service as policemen, yet they enjoy the full rights of citizens.

The circular makes the point that all controversies resolve themselves at last into an appeal to the strongest, and that women could not make such an appeal. That proposition merely applies to societies in a natural state. In civilized societies the jus fortioris is no longer in force. In our time public opinion and the dictates of conscience are more powerful than physical force. Nations are more frequently restrained by the impolicy of injustice and by fears of the ultimate danger of pursuing a selfish course than by the dread of defeat in battle. If it were not so, weak nations would hold their existence at the mercy of strong nations, and powers like Germany and Russia and China, which can put millions of men into the field, would dominate the world.

That the circular emanates from a professor of obsolete theories may be inferred from the following paragraph:

> 8. It is assumed that the possession of the right of suffrage would be an elevating and refining influence for women. Has it been so with men? Certainly at no period of the history of the country have there been so many complaints as to the indifference of the educated classes and of the venality of ignorant citizens as at this time. Judging by the effect, therefore, of universal suffrage upon man, and considering the more emotional nature of woman, it is a fair inference that the conferring of the suffrage upon them would be a degrading rather than an elevating and refining influence.

A reasoner who argues that men have deteriorated under universal suffrage does not really deserve to be considered seriously. Such a person should be invited to compare the measure of intelligence possessed by the masses of the American people with that of the rural laborers of the last generation in Great Britain and to get his information from truthful sources. He might then be trusted to answer himself. The true doctrine in the subject is that the heavier the responsibilities which are laid upon an individual the larger his capacity becomes to fulfill them. We cannot form an opinion as to women's fitness to deal with political questions until we have made it an object for them to become acquainted with them.

Opponents of female suffrage should at least make an effort to show the mischiefs it would entail. Assertions that it would "unsex men and women by destroying the sanctity and privacy of the family circle and home life" are mere propositions, which rest neither on fact nor reasoning. As reasonably might it be said—as it used to be said—that the study of history and science by girls would unfit them for matrimony. If there is any danger lurking in the admission of women to the suffrage let it be shown. But to influence the drift of public opinion it must be a real danger which can be described in words that can be understood. It must not be vague platitudes about the home circle and the sacred duty of maternity. All that part of the business has been duly considered, and honorable women, who would rather be dead than fail in their duty to their homes and their families, are quite content to take the risk of becoming citizens as well as wives and mothers.

READING 30, CLARA M. SCHLINGHEYDE

"Ballot for Women Will Compel None to Mix in Politics"

***San Francisco Call*, September 14, 1911**

*IT ALWAYS HAS BEEN A MYSTERY TO ME WHY ANTI-*suffragists should become so exercised because other women want to vote. If they feel so keenly the possible disgrace of voting, their remedy lies so close at hand it is astonishing they have not seen it themselves. All they have to do is to stay away from the polls! Senate constitutional amendment No. 8 does not contemplate a posse comitatus (with apologies to John P. Irish) that shall drag the reluctant anti to the polls if she does not wish to go. What it does contemplate is that no woman shall be denied to express through the ballot her mother love, her home love and her country love if she chooses there to express it.

Right to Stay at Home

If the antis are not keen about going to the polls we concede them the right to remain away; but when an ever decreasing number of antis interferes with the liberties of an ever increasing number of suffragists, and attempts to shackle upon them the dead weight of bygone, outworn and edge frayed relics of traditions and prejudices, we protest against the unjust handicap. It is as though an airship were denied dominion because some persons prefer the prairie schooner.

But the worst of it is that when California does thunder "Yes," October 10, the antis will be the first to take transfers and hop blithely aboard the airship as though they had "never done nothin." Oh, yes, that is what always happens. They forget all about the contaminating influence of the polls. They rush into the awful mire of politics with an alacrity that persuades us they were only joking with themselves about these bugaboos; that they scorned their own hysterical fears of the awful evils that would follow in the train of woman suffrage; that they knew all along the ballot for women was a thousand times more dignified expression of opinion than indirect influence.

Sympathy for Opponents

But these are grim jokes and costly to a nation that needs its women in government. We have genuine sympathy for those women who find it difficult to adjust their step to the stride of progress, but it is not fair to expect that the vast number of quick step women should be asked to accommodate themselves to the straggling step of those who lag behind. Some of them may never catch up.

Said John D. Long, former secretary of the navy: "If a man or woman wants to exercise the right to vote, what healthy reason is there for denying it because other men and women do not wish to exercise it? If I desire to breathe the fresh air of heaven, shall I not cross my threshold because the rest of the family group prefers the stale atmosphere inside?"

PROGRESSIVE REFORM AND MORALITY

READING 31

California Civic League, Red Light and Injunction Bill

***Sausalito News*, March 8, 1913**

THE RED LIGHT AND INJUNCTION BILL (S.B. 320) NOW pending in the legislature is unquestionably the most important moral issue of the session. It is backed by many prominent men and by all the civic organizations of women throughout the State. The California Civic League urges you to place before the people of your community the facts as given in the enclosed letter and leaflet.

The revelations concerning the White Slave Traffic, the profits of commercialized vice and the spread of disease, have aroused general discussion throughout the United States, concerning our methods of dealing with the social evil. On the continent of Europe, where segregation in a district and regulation of vicious women, has been thoroughly tried out for more than fifty years, there is now widespread dissatisfaction with the results. At the recent Conference of Nations, held in Brussels, there was the greatest opposition to the system; while all the Vice Commissions in America—Chicago, Atlanta, Minneapolis, Saint Louis and Grand Rapids—have declared against segregation. During the last two years fourteen American cities have closed their Red Light districts while no cities have adopted the policy of segregation during the same period.

The Red Light Injunction Bill now pending in the California Legislature is directly opposed to segregation. It makes houses of ill-fame nuisances under the law, as they are in fact, and places the responsibility for their maintenance upon the owner and the landlord. It is made relatively easy to enforce because the case is to be tried in a Court of Equity and therefore without a jury; and because any citizen who has the evidence, as well as the district attorney, may bring suit.

California has admirable sections in its Penal Code for the protection of the persons of women; but illegal and informal segregation generally prevails in all cities and towns and it is all but impossible to close disorderly houses under the present system of procedure. At the same time this kind of segregation does not by any means thoroughly segregate the vicious element. The pending bill will not entirely suppress the social evil but will if passed, as is proven by the experience of Des Moines and Omaha, do away with the most conspicuous, the most alluring and the most offensive aspects of vice; it will prevent the exploitation of women for profit and give decent citizens a means of protection against a public nuisance.

READING 32

"Red Light Abatement Declared Impossible: Manager of Granada Hotel Says to Scatter Women Will Bring Disastrous Results"

San Francisco Call, April 24, 1913

"IMPOSSIBLE LEGISLATION" WAS THE TERM APPLIED TO the redlight abatement bill yesterday at the luncheon of the Downtown association of the Chamber of Commerce. Manager Metzger of the Granada hotel discussed many of the features of the measure.

"If you scatter these women all over the city, and no provision is made for them beyond ejecting them from the houses where they are found, they will be living in proximity to your sisters and daughters.

"These women really are a necessity, especially as this is a seaport town."

Chairman Frank Turner said he had heard Doctor Aked and others discuss the bill favorably, and that while personally he was in favor of it, the more arguments he heard on the subject the less sure he was of the correct position to take.

"Well, as for Doctor Aked," said Mr. Metzger, "he is one sided always, and he couldn't convince me of anything."

Thomas Dillon spoke briefly along the same lines as Mr. Metzger.

URBAN GROWTH AND WATER

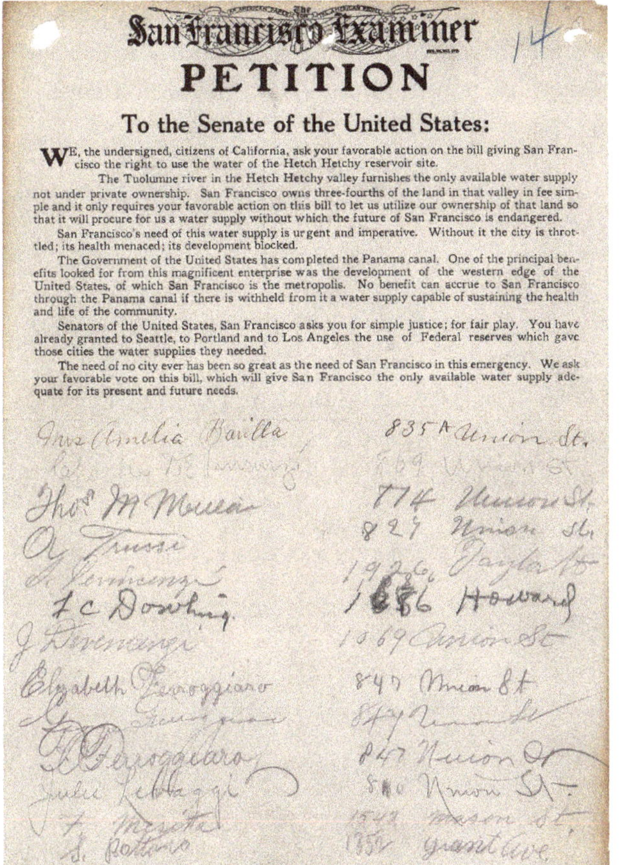

San Francisco Examiner

PETITION

To the Senate of the United States:

WE, the undersigned, citizens of California, ask your favorable action on the bill giving San Francisco the right to use the water of the Hetch Hetchy reservoir site.

The Tuolumne river in the Hetch Hetchy valley furnishes the only available water supply not under private ownership. San Francisco owns three-fourths of the land in that valley in fee simple and it only requires your favorable action on this bill to let us utilize our ownership of that land so that it will procure for us a water supply without which the future of San Francisco is endangered.

San Francisco's need of this water supply is urgent and imperative. Without it the city is throttled; its health menaced; its development blocked.

The Government of the United States has completed the Panama canal. One of the principal benefits looked for from this magnificent enterprise was the development of the western edge of the United States, of which San Francisco is the metropolis. No benefit can accrue to San Francisco through the Panama canal if there is withheld from it a water supply capable of sustaining the health and life of the community.

Senators of the United States, San Francisco asks you for simple justice; for fair play. You have already granted to Seattle, to Portland and to Los Angeles the use of Federal reserves which gave those cities the water supplies they needed.

The need of no city ever has been so great as the need of San Francisco in this emergency. We ask your favorable vote on this bill, which will give San Francisco the only available water supply adequate for its present and future needs.

FIGURE 5.4. *San Francisco Examiner* Petition Supporting Damming of Hetch Hetchy Valley

FIGURE 5.5. Los Angeles Aqueduct Map

QUESTIONS FOR STUDY

1. What did Progressives mean by "Good Government"? What types of issues did proponents of "Good Government" tackle? Why? How did their efforts help shape the future of California?
2. Compare and contrast the arguments for and against women's suffrage. What were they? Who do you think makes the stronger case, and why? Why do you think there was so much debate in the first place?

3. Why were Progressives so concerned about prostitution? What does this concern tell us about gender in the Progressive era? What impact might this law have had on prostitution?
4. Discuss the ethics of San Francisco and Los Angeles exporting water from other parts of the state to sustain their own growing populations. If these projects were taking place today, do you think the outcomes would have been different?

CREDITS

1. Fig. 5.1: Beaumont Fairbank, "The Right of Way," http://www.loc.gov/pictures/item/2011647591/. Copyright in the Public Domain.
2. Fig. 5.2: John Harmon Cassel, "John Harmon Cassell, All Done in 20 Minutes!," http://www.loc.gov/pictures/item/2009616501/. Copyright in the Public Domain.
3. "'Bully Fight,' Says Hiram Johnson," *San Francisco Call*, vol. 108, no. 60, pp. 1. Copyright in the Public Domain.
4. "Good Government," *Los Angeles Herald*, vol. 37, no. 128, pp. 8. Copyright in the Public Domain.
5. Fig. 5.3: Henry Mayer, "Henry Mayer, 'The Awakening' (1915)," http://www.loc.gov/pictures/item/98502844/. Copyright in the Public Domain.
6. "The Argument Against Suffrage," *San Francisco Call*, vol. 75, no. 174, pp. 6. Copyright in the Public Domain.
7. Mary Calkins Brooke, "Red Light Injunction and Abatement Law," *Sausalito News*, vol. XXVIX, no. 6, pp. 4. Copyright in the Public Domain.
8. "Red Light Abatement Declared Impossible," *San Francisco Call*, vol. 113, no. 145, pp. 10. Copyright in the Public Domain.
9. Fig. 5.4: "San Francisco Examiner petition supporting damming of Hetch Hetchy Valley (1913)," http://www.archives.gov/legislative/features/hetch-hetchy/examiner.html. Copyright in the Public Domain.
10. Fig. 5.5: The City of Los Angeles, "L.A. Aqueduct," http://en.wikipedia.org/wiki/File:Los_Angeles_Aqueduct_Map.png. Copyright in the Public Domain.

06

Myth and Modernity

INTRODUCTION

As California entered the twentieth century, Progressive reformers focused attention on the demands of the modern era in the state's economic and political life. At the same time, a distinct California identity was taking shape. San Francisco had developed a clear sense of itself around the mythology and story of the gold rush. Los Angeles, on the other hand, was still probing for a sense of itself as the city was growing rapidly. In their search for symbols and myths to establish an identity as a great city, Angeleno developers and promoters turned to an imaginary Mexican past, with the missions as its physical representation. Journalist Charles Fletcher Lummis especially recognized the potential capital worth of the old missions and their significance to a distinctly Southern California identity. The Mission Revival style became the physical representation of this connection to the mythic past, and a tool to lure tourists and to sell land to newcomers. This style became popular especially when the Santa Fe and Southern Pacific railroads embraced it with their stations and resort hotels. While representative of the past in form, these designs were also compatible with modern construction methods that used reinforced concrete (Figures 6.1 and 6.2).

Underlying this promotion of Southern California lay a racial myth that endorsed the region as the destined place for the Anglo Saxon race. While celebrating the missions and ranchos, this past was presented as "Spanish," distinct from "Mexican." The Mexican immigrants who worked on the railroads, in agriculture, and in other menial labor became increasingly marginalized in the barrios. Of special concern to Californians, however, were the Japanese migrants who started arriving on the mainland in the 1890s. Labeled an "undesirable race" and, as Asians, ineligible for citizenship, they became targets of growing discrimination and demands for exclusion. Like the Chinese before them, the Japanese were considered a serious economic and cultural threat to the Caucasian citizens of California. The debate reached international proportions when delegates from Tokyo, Japan, visited California to lobby against proposed anti-Japanese legislation (Figure 6.3). Regardless, California passed the Alien Land Law in 1913, implicitly targeting the Japanese (see reading 33 "Webb-Haney Alien Land Law").

Following the end of World War I, fears of radicalism fueled even further anti-foreign sentiment. The nativist demands led the US Congress to pass the Immigration Act of 1924, establishing a strict quota system and specifically targeting the Japanese, whose entry had been regulated solely through non-legislative measures (see reading 34 "Immigration Act of 1924"). In California, the exclusionists now organized the California Joint Immigration Committee, a successor to the Japanese Exclusion League, which had led the charge for the passage of the Immigration Act. Valentine Stuart McClatchy (1857–1938), a prominent California newspaper publisher, played a dominant role in both of these organizations. Many of the arguments McClatchy marshaled against Japanese Americans in the 1920s provided the framework for their internment during World War II (see reading 35 "Guarding the Immigration Gates"). Meanwhile, immigrants already in California were targeted with a variety of Americanization programs (see section "Americanization"; Figure 6.4.).

By the 1920s, Los Angeles had surpassed San Francisco in population and become the tenth largest city in the nation. This growth occurred as the automobile industry was maturing, and life in the city was increasingly organized around this most modern form of transportation. The automobile provided individual freedom of movement and eventually replaced the streetcars and other forms of transportation. It also introduced to California its trademark traffic congestion (Figure 6.5). As the population continued to grow, Angelenos spread out from the inner city in their automobiles. Los Angeles thus set the pattern for future urban development nationwide with its suburbs, automobiles, and strip malls.

Los Angeles also acquired a reputation as a place for bizarre behavior, religious cults, and unusual political groups. The evangelist Aimee Semple McPherson arrived in the city in 1921, after traveling the country staging tent revivals. In Los Angeles, she founded the Church of the Foursquare Gospel and built the Angelus Temple in Echo Park, playing an instrumental role in bringing conservative Protestantism to the American mainstream. Her message of old-time religion, accompanied by elaborate musical productions and showmanship, appealed to crowds numbering in the thousands every Sunday. Sister Aimee—as she was known—used modern technologies to advance that message. She created her own radio station, one of the first Christian stations in the country, to broadcast daily sermons. And she employed a publicist, becoming a darling of the journalists and newsreel crews (Figure 6.6).

By the 1920s, Los Angeles was also the center of the most visible form of cultural expression of the era: the movies. Hollywood production reached and affected most Americans as the popularity of the movies increased. In the process, the film industry effectively redefined and homogenized American culture. The movie industry continued the image of California as a place where opportunity abounded, a place where one could reach the dream of living it large. But movies were also linked to the perceived decline in the nation's moral standards, reflecting deeper concerns about the changing American landscape as the nation became increasingly "modern" in its outlook (see section "Hollywood").

Women also rose to prominence in this modern America of the movies. Called America's Sweetheart, Mary Pickford (1892–1979) reached legendary status as a silent film actress (Figure 6.7). By 1919, Pickford, along with Charlie Chaplin, Douglas Fairbanks, and D.W. Griffith, was among the heavyweights in the rapidly growing motion picture industry. All four, however, wanted to gain more financial and artistic control over the production and distribution of their films. On February 5, 1919, they joined forces to create their own film studio, which they called the United Artists Corporation. While Pickford's story provides insight into the opportunities that Hollywood afforded women, that of her contemporary Clara Bow (1905–1965) exemplifies the pitfalls of the celebrity culture that grew around movie stars (Figure 6.8). Bow became wildly popular after the 1927 film *It*, lending the actress her nickname, the "It" Girl. Her imagery and sexy performances specifically spoke to the 1920s flapper persona, making her a style icon. Fun loving and affable, Bow was also associated with a number of men off screen. These romantic forays made Bow the object of much hurtful speculation and gossip, eventually leading to an emotional breakdown and a sanitarium stay. Both women exemplify the emerging celebrity culture that continues to define Hollywood.

MISSION REVIVAL STYLE

FIGURE 6.1. Courtyard of Frank Miller's Glenwood Mission Inn, Riverside (1910)

FIGURE 6.2. Postcard Depicting San Diego's Union Depot (c. 1920)

IMMIGRATION RESTRICTION

FIGURE 6.3. Protesting Anti-Japanese Legislation, Photograph by Kamiya Soyeda (1913)

READING 33

Webb-Haney Alien Land Law

1913

§ 1. All aliens eligible to citizenship under the laws of the United States may acquire, possess, enjoy, use, cultivate, occupy, transfer, transmit and inherit real property, or any interest therein, in this state, and have in whole or in part the beneficial use thereof, in the same manner and to the same extent as citizens of the United States, except as otherwise provided by the laws of this state.

§ 2. All aliens other than those mentioned in section one of this act may acquire, possess, enjoy, use, cultivate, occupy and transfer real property, or any interest therein, in this state, and have in whole or in part the beneficial use thereof, in the manner and to the extent, and for the purposes prescribed by any treaty now existing between the government of the United States and the nation or country of which such alien is a citizen or subject, and not otherwise. ...

§ 7. Any real property hereafter acquired in fee in violation of the provisions of this act by any alien mentioned in Section 2 of this act, ... shall escheat as of the date of such acquiring, to, and become and remain the property of the state of California.

READING 34

Immigration Act of 1924

Definition of "Immigrant."

Sec. 3. When used in this Act the term "immigrant" means any alien departing from any place outside the United States destined for the United States, except (1) a government official, his family, attendants, servants, and employees, (2) an alien visiting the United States temporarily as a tourist or temporarily for business or pleasure, (3) an alien in continuous transit through the United States, (4) an alien lawfully admitted to the United States who later goes in transit from one part of the United States to another through foreign contiguous territory, (5) a bona fide alien seaman serving as such on a vessel arriving act a port of the United States and seeking to enter temporarily the United States solely in the pursuit of his calling as a seaman, and (6) an alien entitled to enter the United States solely to carry on trade under and in pursuance of the provisions of a present existing treaty of commerce and navigation.

Non-Quota Immigrants

Sec. 4. When used in this Act the term "non-quota immigrant" means—

(a) An immigrant who is the unmarried child under 18 years of age, or the wife, of a citizen of the United States who resides therein at the time of the filing of a petition under section 9;

(b) An immigrant previously lawfully admitted to the United States, who is returning from a temporary visit abroad;

(c) An immigrant who was born in the Dominion of Canada, Newfoundland, the Republic of Mexico, the Republic of Cuba, the Republic of Haiti, the Dominican Republic, the Canal Zone, or an independent country of Central or South America, and his wife, and his unmarried children under 18 years of age, if accompanying or following to join him;

(d) An immigrant who continuously for at least two years immediately preceding the time of his application for admission to the United States has been, and who seeks to enter the United States solely for the purpose of, carrying on the vocation of minister of any religious denomination, or professor of a college, academy, seminary, or university; and his wife, and his unmarried children under 18 years of age, if accompanying or following to join him; or

(e) An immigrant who is a bona fide student at least 15 years of age and who seeks to enter the United States solely for the purpose of study at an accredited school, college, academy, seminary, or university, particularly designated by him and approved by the Secretary of Labor, which shall have agreed to report to the Secretary of Labor the termination of attendance of each immigrant student, and if any such institution of learning fails to make such reports promptly the approval shall be withdrawn.

Quota Immigrants

Sec. 5. When used in this Act the term "quota immigrant" means any immigrant who is not a non-quota immigrant. An alien who is not particularly specified in this Act as a non-quota immigrant or a non-immigrant shall not be admitted as a non-quota immigrant or a non-immigrant by reason of relationship to any individual who is so specified or by reason of being excepted from the operation of any other law regulating or forbidding immigration.

Preferences within Quotas

Sec. 6. (a) In the issuance of immigration visas to quota immigrants preference shall be given

(1) To a quota immigrant who is the unmarried child under 21 years of age, the father, the mother, the husband, or the wife, of a citizen of the United States who is 21 years of age or over; and

(2) To a quota immigrant who is smiled in agriculture, and his wife, and his dependent children under the age of 16 years, if accompanying

or following to join him. The preference provided in this paragraph shall not apply to immigrants of any nationality the annual quota for which is less than 300.

(b) The preference provided in subdivision (a) shall not in the case of quota immigrants of any nationality exceed 50 per centum of the annual quota for such nationality. Nothing in this section shall be construed to grant to the class of immigrants specified in paragraph (1) of subdivision (a) a priority in preference over the class specified in paragraph (2).

(c) The preference provided in this section shall, in the case of quota immigrants of any nationality, be given in the calendar month in which the right to preference is established, if the number of immigration visas which may be issued in such month to quota immigrants of such nationality has not already been issued; otherwise in the next calendar month.

Numerical Limitations

Sec. 11. (a) The annual quota of any nationality shall be 2 per centum of the number of foreign-born individuals of such nationality resident in continental United States as determined by the United States census of 1890, but the minimum quota of any nationality shall be 100.

(b) The annual quota of any nationality for the fiscal year beginning July 1, 1927, and for each fiscal year thereafter, shall be a number which bears the same ratio to 150,000 as the number of inhabitants in continental United States in 1920 having that national origin (ascertained as hereinafter provided in this section) bears to the number of inhabitants in continental United States in 1920, but the minimum quota of any nationality shall be 100.

(c) For the purpose of subdivision (b) national origin shall be ascertained by determining as nearly as may be, in respect of each geographical area which under section 12 is to be treated as a separate country (except the geographical areas specified in subdivision (c) of section 4) the number of inhabitants in continental United States in 1920 whose origin by birth or ancestry is attributable to such geographical area. Such determination shall not be made by tracing the ancestors or descendants of particular individuals, but shall be based upon statistics of immigration and emigration, together with rates of increase of population as shown by successive decennial United States censuses, and such other data as may be found to be reliable.

(d) For the purpose of subdivisions (b) and (c) the term "inhabitants in continental United States in 1920" does not include (1) immigrants from the geographical areas specified in subdivision (c) of section 4 or their descendants,

(2) aliens ineligible to citizenship or their descendants, (3) the descendants of slave immigrants, or (4) the descendants of American aborigines.

(f) There shall be issued to quota immigrants of any nationality (1) no more immigration visas in any fiscal year than the quota for such nationality, and (2) in any calendar month of any fiscal year no more immigration visas than 10 per centum of the quota for such nationality, except that if such quota is less than 300 the number to be issued in any calendar month shall be prescribed by the Commissioner General, with the approval of the Secretary of Labor, but the total number to be issued during the fiscal year shall not be in excess of the quota for such nationality.

(g) Nothing in this Act shall prevent the issuance (without increasing the total number of immigration visas which may be issued) of an immigration visa to an immigrant as a quota immigrant even though he is a non-quota immigrant.

Exclusion from United States

Sec. 13. (a) No immigrant shall be admitted to the United States unless he (1) has an unexpired immigration visa or was born subsequent to the issuance of the immigration visa of the accompanying parent, (2) is of the nationality specified in the visa in the immigration visa, (8) is a non-quota immigrant if specified in the visa in the immigration visa as such, and (4) is otherwise admissible under the immigration laws.

(b) In such classes of cases and under such conditions as may be by regulations prescribed immigrants who have been legally admitted to the United States and who depart therefrom temporarily may be admitted to the United States without being required to obtain an immigration visa.

(c) No alien ineligible to citizenship shall be admitted to the United States unless such alien (1) is admissible as a non-quota immigrant under the provisions of subdivision (b), (d), or (e) of section 4, or (2) is the wife, or the unmarried child under 18 years of age, of an immigrant admissible under such subdivision (d), and is accompanying or following to join him, or (3) is not an immigrant as defined in section 3.

(d) The Secretary of Labor may admit to the United States any otherwise admissible immigrant not admissible under clause (2) or (3) of subdivision (a) of this section, if satisfied that such inadmissibility was not known to, and could not have been ascertained by the exercise of reasonable diligence by, such immigrant prior to the departure of the vessel from the last port outside the United States and outside foreign contiguous territory, or, in the case of an immigrant coming from foreign contiguous territory, prior to the application of the immigrant for admission.

(e) No quota immigrant shall be admitted under subdivision (d) if the entire number of immigration visas which may be issued to quota immigrants of the same nationality for the fiscal year has already been issued. If such entire number of immigration visas has not been issued, then the Secretary of State, upon the admission of a quota immigrant under subdivision (d), shall reduce by one the number of immigration visas which may be issued to quota immigrants of the same nationality during the fiscal year in which such immigrant is admitted; but if the Secretary of State finds that it will not be practicable to make such reduction before the end of such fiscal year, then such immigrant shall not be admitted.

(f) Nothing in this section shall authorize the remission or refunding of a fine, liability to which has accrued under section 16.

Deportation

Sec. 14. Any alien who at any time after entering the United States is found to have been at the time of entry not entitled under this Act to enter the United States, or to have remained therein for a longer time than permitted under this Act or regulations made thereunder, shall be taken into custody and deported in the same manner as provided for in sections 19 and 20 of the Immigration Act of 1917: Provided, That the Secretary of Labor may, under such conditions and restrictions as to support and care as he may deem necessary, permit permanently to remain in the United States, any alien child who, when under sixteen years of age was heretofore temporarily admitted to the United States and who is now within the United States and either of whose parents is a citizen of the United States.

READING 35, V.S. MCCLATCHY

"Guarding the Immigration Gates"

1925

A Menace to the Nation

FOR A QUARTER CENTURY AND MORE A DANGEROUS condition has been developing in the American nation, threatening its perpetuity. Before the war we were too busy making money to note the situation; during the war all our energies were concentrated on winning; but after the war, when we commenced to take stock, the realization of the facts dawned on us and urged us to apply a remedy.

Tests made in connection with the draft during the war period showed that the physical and mental standard of the average American citizen had very much lowered; that a not inconsiderable portion of the population was composed of individuals little better than morons; that an astonishingly high percentage had an average intelligence not superior to that of a child of 11 years of age. In looking about for the cause of this alarming situation, it was found that the type of immigrants admitted during the last quarter century was generally much less desirable for American citizenship than that which had come previously; that millions of these later immigrants had not only not been assimilated, but that great masses of them were apparently unassimilable, for some generations at least; that many who had been accepted as citizens were not only improperly equipped for citizenship, but had sought the privilege only for the advantages conferred, and with neither desire nor intent to fulfill the obligations thereof in time of stress.

The mere presence in the country of great numbers of those who are foreign, if not inimical, to American ideals and institutions constitutes a grave danger because of their possible influence on thought and action of growing Americans. Not only had the "melting pot" failed to function properly in that we had not digested much of the material accepted for residence and citizenship, but the future looked dark because the birth rate among these new immigrants of lower standards of living is high, while that among the old established assimilated stock steadily decreases to the vanishing point. In a democracy where the majority rules the steady proportional increase of mental and physical defectives must lead inevitably in time to the decline and death of the nation.

Through our open gates for some years before the war had come in each year as many as a million and a quarter immigrants, most of them of an undesirable character; and the reports from Consular representatives throughout Europe immediately following the war, indicated that if the gates were again opened we would be flooded each year by not less than 1,500,000 to 2,000,000 even less desirable immigrants, the culls and wastes of the great war.

The House Immigration Committee of Congress made exhaustive investigation of the subject; and, as public opinion was gradually educated, a preliminary restrictive immigration bill was passed in 1920, and renewed in 1922, and a comprehensive plan, based on "national origin," adopted in the Immigration Act of 1924, contemplating a quota immigration each year of 150,000.

In 1790, United States, by a Federal act, denied the privilege of naturalization to all except individuals of the white race. After our Civil War, that law was amended so as to admit blacks to that privilege, in the hope of solving the problem created by slavery; but in other respects the law has remained unchanged, and today, as 135 years ago, aliens of the yellow and brown races are debarred from citizenship.

In conformity with the spirit of that law the United States government has promptly adopted measures excluding as immigrants any element of the yellow or brown races when that element assumed dangerous proportions in immigration.

Why were the yellow and brown races of Asia, which include half the population of the globe, made ineligible for naturalization and excluded as immigrants? Not because we assume any racial superiority for the white race. China has a civilization which antedates that of Europe by centuries; and Japan has accomplished in 60 years by raising herself from a feudal condition to the modern plane of western political and industrial civilization what it took the white race four or five hundred years to do. The action as to the yellow and brown races was defensive purely: first in protection of our own people individually because of the lower standards of living of those races and our inability to meet them in economic competition. Second, because those races are so radically different from the white race in heredity, tradition, psychology, religion, ideals and everything that fixes racial identity that assimilation, in the sense of amalgamation or absorption, is not possible, or if possible, would be disastrous; and because to have either the yellow or brown race living side by side with whites in established communities, with equal rights, either here or in Asia, would be certain to breed racial trouble and international misunderstanding.

And of all the Asiatic races ineligible to citizenship under our law, the Japanese prove most dangerous when admitted, because, in addition to their advantages in economic competition, and our inability to assimilate them, characteristics which they share with other Asiatics, they are superior to the other Asiatic races in ambition, aggressiveness, co-operation, pride of race and determination to establish themselves as Japanese wherever they colonize, with a sensitive and powerful nation behind them.

Of all the English-speaking countries United States alone has permitted the Japanese, an alien, unassimilable race, with dangerous advantages in economic competition, to secure such a foothold in its territory.

In California before passage of the alien land law in 1913, the Japanese had acquired over 75,000 acres of rich land, and that quantity is being steadily increased by purchase on behalf of California-born Japanese. In 1920, according to the report of the State Board of Control, the Japanese had acquired control, through purchase or lease, of one-eighth of the irrigated lands of the state, in consequence of which the state alien land law was strengthened. In certain districts and communities they have secured control of various industries and occupations.

The nation's present established policy of closely restricting immigration is threatened at this time by danger from two sources:

> First, by possible amendments to the immigration act modifying the general restrictions, or removing them entirely so far as they apply to certain elements. In that category belongs the present movement to make exception for the Japanese from the provision excluding aliens ineligible to citizenship. And if the bars are let down anywhere, or to any degree, there will be insistent demand from many sources that they be let down still more. There should be a tightening and not a loosening of restrictions, regardless of the influences demanding concessions.
>
> Second, by surreptitious entry from Canada, Mexico and Cuba. According to Secretary of Labor Davis many thousands are entering in this way each month. They are generally of the most undesirable character, paying heavy fee or bribe for assistance in breaking the law and entering secretly a country which does not want them. It is not feasible to defend thousands of miles of sea coast and border adequately against such surreptitious entry, nor is detection of violators after entry easy in the absence of a system of registration, as urged by

> Secretary Davis, or some similar plan. It is conceivable that under the present conditions the immigration act, so far as concerns restriction of undesirable immigration, might soon become a dead letter.

The situation is one which must cause great concern to the American Legion and to the other organizations affiliated with it in immigration restriction. We fought during the war to save the nation from the onward march of an enemy eager for world conquest; we labored after the war to close the gates to insidious foes whose peaceful penetration would prove more disastrous to American citizenship than would an invading army; and now we must carefully guard gates and border against assault or surreptitious entry. In that sacred duty every citizen can and should perform effective service.

AMERICANIZATION

FIGURE 6.4. English Class for Korean Women at the YWCA International Institute, Los Angeles (1922)

READING 36

"A New Slant on Americanization"

***Pacific Rural Press*, December 11, 1920**

MRS. FRANK A. GIBSON, CHAIRMAN OF THE AMERICANIZATION Committee of the California Federation of Women's Clubs, has recently issued the outline of a program for this year's Americanization work. It is prefaced by the statement: "If each club will assume its share in the work as outlined, the C. F. W. C will be able to render a unique and valuable service to the State." The outline runs as follows:

Clubs will be asked to secure statistics as to number, nationality, location, occupation, recreation, etc., of at least their dominant local race groups. These statistics to be placed upon local maps and later transferred to county maps. The county maps to be finally assembled for the preparation of a State Nationality Map.

In gathering, statistics local Americanization problems in education, industry, housing, recreation, assimilation, etc., will present themselves for careful consideration. Brief papers on such subjects will make practical club programs of intense interest and, collected, may throw new light upon questions that are now perplexing the state.

In the line of original research, nothing will prove of more value than a study of the lives of foreign-born men and women, residents of California, who have rendered distinguished state or world service. Beginning with Junipero Serra, many counties will be able to collect data as to their own monuments and history and, incidentally, to learn something of the methods of the earliest vocational work on the Pacific Coast. Following Junipero, without regard to sequence, come such immigrants as Portola, Sutter, Muir, Modjeska, Sienkiewitz,: Sutro, Lubin, Murray, Morse, Stephens, Paderewski, Ricard, Furusuth, Tetrazzini, Mulholland of aqueduct fame, and McLeran, who built the Golden Gate Park. Each county, can add worthily to this group of wonderful men and women who, coming from other lands, have given of their genius to the land of their adoption.

Exhibits of Arts and Crafts

Each county is asked to secure an exhibit of the arts and crafts, the folksongs and dances peculiar to its foreign-born groups. These should be shown, perhaps, in the County Chambers of Commerce. Later, the more valuable part of each county collection should be assembled at the State Fair in 1921, where, with the State Nationality Map, it should be designated as The Foreign Arts and Crafts Exhibit of the. C. F. W. C.

We have given the program in full because it is worthy of careful consideration by every Californian. There has been a lot of loose talk about Americanization; a lot of energy has been wasted in desultory effort, and a lot of near crimes (to be conservative)have been committed in its name because we have been blazing away without knowing what we were shooting at.

What Is Americanization and Why and How!

Honest, now, when it comes right down to business, isn't our answer to the above query rather vague? During the spasm of hysteria that has now about spent its force, the answer seemed easy. To sentimentalize, and fumble, and bungle about in this slum and that shop and the other playground, teaching a bit of English here, taking an auto apart and putting it together again there, or giving a bum motion picture show in the other place—that was Americanization. To make everybody talk United States whether they had learned to speak it or not; to insist that everybody shout himself hoarse every time the picture of an American flag floated in Freedom's breeze across a movie screen; to smash phonograph records that had a foreign twang, and rip leaves from text books that made reference to obnoxious facts of history, and bar the doors of our temples of art to masters who happened to be born in a country whose name was anathema; to preach the gospel of unreason and hate, that was Americanization. Thank goodness, that is about past and gone. We are getting back to "Normaly," as the advertisements say. We are beginning to realize that before we shoot, we need to locate the target and decide what ammunition will achieve the best results. Funny somebody didn't think of that before, but then a person throwing fits doesn't do much thinking and neither does a nation. Somebody in the California Federation of Women's Clubs has been thinking and thinking straight. That program faithfully carried out will show us (something we do not now know) just what our job is. "Statistics and Maps"—Original research"—a year of that and we will have the target located. "Biography" (go back and read that list of names)—year of that ought to clarify our vision wonderfully. "The Foreign arts and crafts exhibit"—a view of that at the next State Fair may tempt some of us to hand the gun over to the other fellow. Anyway, a year of all this and we will go at our task in the spirit of the greatest apostle's masterpiece—"Now abideth faith, hope and love, but the greatest of these is love."

Rural Americanization

When they get down to making the maps for the counties, and conducting the researches, and digging out the local biographies, I wonder if they are not going to make a discovery. No claim to knowledge of city conditions is here made, so we cannot say that the problem in the country differs from that in the city. Maybe it doesn't though we are inclined to believe it does, and that different methods will be needed according as we deal with urban or rural conditions. Probably the proposed survey will settle that. What we started to say, however, was when the country is reached it will be found that most desirable form of Americanization is already well under way. We don't call it Americanization; we don't call it at all—but we are doing it!

We want a study made of the various boys' and girls' calf, pig, cow and other clubs being fostered by the Agricultural Extension force and the various breed associations. I know a "foreigner" who is now scurrying around for seven purebred calves for his seven boys. Call it what you will —that is building Rural American Citizenship!

We want a study made of the co-operative farmers' organizations that, on a supposedly cold-blooded business basis, are making brothers of us all. I know a "foreigner" (you have to listen carefully to understand him) who is the acting manager of a large co-operative plant that teems with the spirit of mutual helpfulness. Call it what you will—that is building safe and sane citizenship. We want a study made of the Home Demonstration work, a department of Agricultural Extension. I know a "foreigner," a woman who can't talk English, who is showing her sisters in a whole county how to cull poultry; another who has shown a county how to can mushrooms; another who has taught many of her neighbors the art of home cheese-making. And just recently these columns recorded the fact that, in the Livingston school lunch campaign, the foreign-born mothers were the most eager of all to carry out every last detail of the program. I mingled with the women of that community for several hours, drawing out the story of their fine work. Never once did I hear the word Americanization, but verily I say unto you, these women, with their scales and tape and hot soup, are developing genuine American Citizenship!

If we are not badly mistaken, what is quietly going on right now through the various branches of Agricultural Extension, Breed Associations and Cooperative Movements, is what Americanization should mean in the country and is the why and the how thereof. And no doubt the program of the California Federation of Woman's Clubs when carried out will find it and help it along.

IMAGES OF MODERNITY

FIGURE 6.5. Traffic Jam at Broadway and 7th Street, Los Angeles (c. 1920)

FIGURE 6.6. Sister Aimee Semple McPherson Preaching at the Newly-Built Angelus Temple (1923)

HOLLYWOOD

READING 37, CHARLES HANSON TOWNE

"The Monstrous Movies"

***Vanity Fair Magazine*, 1921**

The One Thing Missing

THEY TOLD ME A TALE IN HOLLYWOOD OF AN OLD TRAGEDIAN who, down and out, came to this cardboard city to eke out a living at the tail end of a rather brilliant career on the legitimate stage. He had supported Booth and Barrett, Mojeska and other renowned stars. At first he was thrilled by all the clamour and glamour of this new world. The novelty of the business appealed to his imagination, and he ranted and raved with fervor and gusto, as of old. But he missed the resounding lines of Shakespeare—I think he was mostly cast as the grandfather in tawdry pieces like *The Vengeance of Somebody*, or *The Perils of Somebody Else*; but bravely he did his duty. He was never late, he was always on hand when the scene was set. At the end of a month, however, he found there was something lacking. He could not quite tell what it was. Then, one day, it came to him. Of course—the clapping of hands, the whistle of the gallery-gods. What were a few electricians, a director, however sympathetic, and stray cameramen in shining puttees (heaven only knows why!) to those stormy audiences to which he had for so long been gloriously accustomed? He missed the repeated curtain calls, the instant response to his art across that golden semi-circle of footlights; and even when he saw himself projected upon the screen, he heard little or no applause in the big movie palaces. What though Keats had told him that "heard melodies are sweet, but those unheard are sweeter"? Bosh! it was not true. He craved, he demanded, the instant response that had always been his. He could not stand this silent drama; and, heartsick and homesick, he crawled back East, to talk over the times in the Actors' Home, with cronies who had flourished with him in those days of the Seventies when gaslight was the only illumination and the costume play was the joyous, youthful, inspiring thing.

Seriously, I marvel at the histrionic ability that can give a passionate performance just after breakfast. It is true that practically every screen actor and actress of note now demands accompanying music in order to work up to a trying scene. The honest Chaplin told me, however, that he seldom resorts to this artificial stimulus. "It's mostly bunk," he was frank enough to say, "pose of the most obvious kind. It is a detriment, rather than a help, for one is apt to get the wrong tempo, to keep his mind too insistently on the music, which soon becomes mechanical."

I quite agree with him, after observing various performers indulging in this dissipation. Still, musicians constantly travel from one studio to another to contribute their lyric strains to the vast enterprises at Hollywood. But the aristocrats of the films carry their own private orchestras, and are not dependent upon itinerant players. It is but a part of the enormous entourage of a successful star.

Money pours in like a cataract; it pours out in the same reckless fashion. The more prominent you are, the better you must live. The dear public likes to think of its idols resting, in their off moments, in palatial homes; and, once having seen these costly houses, it does not forget them. It is royal advertising.

And oh, how they work! It is not a life of ease and indolence. It consists of days and nights crowded with thrilling scenes; but many hours are spent in the difficult business of waiting about—the hardest task anyone can be given to do. They journey miles and miles in the course of taking of, perhaps, only a few scenes; arid they work themselves up to a high pitch of energy many times during an afternoon. The perspiration pours from their foreheads. The strenuous life, indeed, and no profession for anyone to follow, male or female, unless there is a natural endowment of health and strength.

If it is difficult for the stars, who are given every consideration, and whose pay-envelopes doubtless make amends for much physical effort, it is heart-breaking to see the supernumeraries who journey from lot to lot, seeking any kind of job. While youth is a great asset, there are just as many places where tired and wrinkled faces fit in; and the middle-aged "extra" has as good a chance as the vivacious and vapid looking flapper. The movies are a great democracy. They give employment to people of all kinds, since they are trying to photograph the world as it is. An old washerwoman who had been earning about ten dollars a week wandering from house to house doing up the beautiful linen of her customers, now earns ten dollars a day as one of the mob.

And many a mother rents out her baby, and knows just how to make it weep and smile at the proper moment, winning thereby the gratitude of a hard-pressed cameraman. Children, of course, are constantly in demand.

A certain Frenchman is supported by a remarkable dog that brings him in one hundred and twenty-live dollars a week; and there are those who allow parrots and monkeys to be their meal-tickets. "My cat is sick this week," I overheard a matron saying to a director. "Darn it all, I wish he'd pick up, for I need the dough!" It is hardly necessary to say that these animals are given every care, watched and coddled and daintily fed, lest some untoward accident or illness overtake them.

READING 38, HARMON STEPHENS

"The Relation of the Motion Picture to Changing Moral Standards"

1926

NO COMPETENT OBSERVER WILL DENY THAT CERTAIN changes in moral standards in the United States are to some extent linked up with moving picture exploitation. The relative importance of such influence in the complete picture of stimuli acting upon the public is a problem which is too complex for this discussion.

To make the subject more difficult, whether such changes are an aid or a deterrent to social progress is a question involving numerous interacting factors. As an example of a change in moral standards, we may cite the steadily mounting divorce rate. Whether such changes are a benefit or a calamity it is not the purpose of this article to attempt to determine. It is intended only to cite facts and opinions indicating the extent to which motion pictures have encouraged or intensified a number of changes in moral conduct.

Limited space makes it impossible adequately to treat both the hopeful and discouraging aspects of the problem. Since the pleasant and constructive features are being constantly presented to the public through well-organized propaganda, engineered by some of the most highly salaried men in the United States, the writer feels justified in dismissing this phase of the subject with general statements and devoting most of the space to disturbing elements which challenge our most serious attention.

It may be stated at once that most of the news reels, travel pictures and educational subjects are so presented as to provide cultural enrichment for the general public to an extent never before possible. Wholesome romance and adventure have been made available even to the illiterate, and have been a timely relief to the monotony of piece-working and machine-slaving. Wholesome pictures, particularly in recent years, have been in the majority, and progress in both artistry and technique has been marvelous. On the other hand, there have been recent releases more likely to undermine accepted moral standards than anything the writer has observed in fifteen years of special interest in motion pictures. Improved artistry and technique have often provided attractiveness for questionable things which crudeness formerly left uninviting. Furthermore, one's enthusiasm for a really fine picture is often jarred by incidental touches of vulgarity or sensual emphasis, which appear to have no importance to the picture except as a basis for sensational advertising.

Vital Need for Regulation

The fact that a majority of recent releases are wholesome provides no excuse for indulging in an orgy of blind optimism. Every few years since the infancy of the motion picture industry there have been periods of self-cleansing, abetted by threats of legal remedial measures, which have been helpful, but never sufficiently thorough to prevent relapses. Furthermore, while much of this cleansing has been due to high-minded motion picture men, who have visioned the relation between public welfare and the future of screen entertainment, no one can say to what extent the public has been misled by promises and propaganda devised to tide over a period of public arousement. It must also be stressed that conduct may be adversely affected by a relatively small number of anti-social exhibitions reaching the general public. Social safety demands constant control of imperious instincts, all too easily released under conditions resulting in tragic consequences. This is particularly true of young people and of the mentally immature.

The influence of a single pupil may prove a source of corruption to a class of fifty.

If as many as ten per cent of the pictures generally circulated were as extreme as some hereafter referred to, the situation would be very serious. The motion picture public reacts against an over-dose of anything, whether it be sex stuff, historical films, or spectacles. Within a few years, the exploitation can be repeated along altered lines, with an added technique that makes the effect of the individual films better or worse as the case may be. By 1916 most producers had seen the doom of the old style serpent-like vampire; her villainy was never in question, and in the audience one might hear whispered exclamations of "Isn't she terrible?"

Rousing Dormant Emotions of Youth

Before the optimists, however, had reached their peak of rejoicing over the passing of vampire stuff, a new type had appeared, the "baby vampire," who made "vamping" so attractive that to be called the "school vamp" lost whatever sting it had. The writer heard a little girl about ten years old proclaiming that she would like to become a vampire.

Later came the flapper heroines, some of whom broke most of the Ten Commandments with such vivacity and cleverness that they were rescued in the nick of time from paying any just penalty by an attractive hero of sturdy character, with the result of a "happy ever after" romantic ending. At one such exhibition, three young girls, aged about fourteen to sixteen years, were giving vent to such exclamations as "Isn't she darling?" and "Oh, I love her!" The object of their worship was a flapper heroine type who swore, smoked, imbibed cocktails freely, danced with sensual abandon and finally won the love of the hero as an aftermath of descending unchaperoned upon his bachelor apartment after midnight. A girl teacher, a recent university graduate, was heard to express similar admiration. Will anyone deny that making questionable conduct attractive adds to its danger?

Many people imagine that tacking on a moral or a penalty at the end of a film depicting adventurous anti-social conduct provides sufficient warning to the young. Dr. A. T. Poffenberger, of Columbia University, has made some study of this point. To quote:

> Motion pictures containing scenes vividly portraying defiance of law and crimes of all degrees may, by an ending which shows the criminal brought to justice and the victory of the right, carry a moral to the intelligent adult; but that which impresses the mind of the mentally young and colors their imagination is the excitement and bravado accompanying the criminal act, while the moral goes unheeded. Their minds cannot logically reach the conclusion to which the chain of circumstances will drive the normal adult. A survey of any group of posters advertising motion pictures will show a surprisingly large portion suggesting murder, burglary, violence, or crime of some sort. Considering the almost unlimited audiences which the advertising posters command, their careful control would seem a greater necessity even than that of the play itself.[1]

In one of the "white-slave" films which held sway a few years before the World War, the heroine is backed up against a bed behind locked doors struggling to avoid the brutal embraces of the villain. In the nick of time the hero batters down the door and rescues her, with the result of a romantic ending. A mother took her sixteen-year-old daughter to see this as a "lesson." She asked her girl what she thought about the picture and was astonished at this reply: "Oh, mother, wouldn't it be just wonderful to have a thrilling adventure like that?" This was in San Francisco. People lined up for over a block at the ticket window to see this exhibition, due to what the press agents call "hook-ups" with the press and clever appeals to morbid curiosity. A prominent preacher was given a whole Sunday feature page in which to praise such films for their wonderful "lesson." A few years later the National Board of Review issued a blanket ban against all "white slave" films featured as such. "White slavery" is now seldom referred to in photoplays. But there is no end of underworld life, eddying around brothels and "crook hangouts." The rape-like tactics of the lustful villain have been reincarnated and made "artistic "through the Apache "love" dance of the French underworld. The more brutal the waist, shoulder and throat grips, the harder the woman is thrown to the floor, the more fiery the passion, the greater the "love." The "kooch dance" wriggles, which the producers promised to eliminate several years ago, were vulgar, and will not come back again till they can be made in some fashion "artistic." But they were never the equal of the Apache dance in depicting intense, sexual abandon. In a recent photoplay, in which the plot is based upon Apache "love," a very decent sort of a wealthy American spends thousands of dollars upon an Apache queen of the underworld in an effort to win her away from her notorious male consort. In a luxurious apartment supported by the American, her maid attempts to teach the American some "cave-man" tactics to aid his quest, but his lessons are insufficient. In the final sequence of events, the Apache queen goes to her consort in their underworld dive, and by very sensual entreaty persuades him to dance. The resultant "love dance," partly deleted, is so brutal that she is nearly killed, but it reconciles them, and the American, sadder and wiser, goes his way, having learned the true nature of Apache love! The picture as a whole seems to be a sort of glorification of the rape-like tactics of what the dance artists and producers assume to be Apache love.

Is it inconceivable that such vivid picturizations of sadistic, lustful abandon should stimulate young people to act antisocially? There are of course other factors, but is that an excuse for minimizing this one? Statistics indicate an increase of thirty-three per cent in cases of criminal assault upon females. No doubt this percentage would be lowered if all factors entering into the reports were adjusted, but the guesses of certain optimists as to the relations of these factors are not likely to be as reliable as the cold figures. Furthermore, the rate at which reports of such cases are coming in where the offenders are boys or young men of normal or superior intelligence and good character should cause careful scrutiny of all possible inciting factors.

Before bringing in additional concrete illustrations of various statements, it is well to outline several points in attempting to estimate the effect of motion pictures upon conduct.

Movie Influence is Unique

First, we must bear in mind the psychology of mental shock. The term as here used refers to sensations of surprise, offense or horror which have no immediate tragic personal consequences, and to which one may become accustomed. It is not difficult to discover persons who are so hardened to vice and indecency that the most startling perversions make little impression upon them. No one will argue that such a lack of sensitiveness is desirable for the average citizen, and for the mentally immature it is a calamity. Much of the division of opinion as to the danger of certain pictures is due to the fact that some people are more accustomed to indecency than others. No one would argue that getting accustomed to a bad smell makes it desirable, or that getting used to seeing dirty milk bottles makes them safe. Many of the most dangerous influences never produce violent shock. Their effect is so gradually cumulative that the evil is not recognized till it is almost beyond repair.

The hope and yet the despair of humanity is that social groups never consciously encourage what is recognized as evil, yet they are constantly becoming so accustomed to one or more evils that they cannot be aroused in time to prevent great injury.

A second point relates to the relative influence upon conduct of the several mediums of expression. The writer received the following statement from a noted psychologist:

"On a scale measuring motivation of conduct, a given situation would probably rate lowest in print, next higher in still-pictures, next highest in motion pictures, and highest if reproduced in actual life." Sir Gilbert Parker once stated that photoplays might be expected to have more influence than spoken drama because they seemed more real.

It seems reasonable to assume that the motion picture comes nearer to reproducing real life situations than any other medium of expression. Dr. William

Healy, in his study of the individual delinquent, cites plenty of evidence of the effect upon minors of real life situations in the form of environment.

We find that educators, as far back as Quintillian and Plato and Aristotle, have insisted upon including in the reading of adolescents only such passages as would build ideals and character. If this is true of reading, how much more is it true of motion pictures? A third point of importance is that, according to the estimate of one producer, eighty per cent of the box office revenue is derived from what may be called family audiences. It has thus become almost impossible to separate adolescents from adults; they all receive the same fare. Comedies which the children cry for are put on the same bill with features suitable only for adults.

The situation has been admirably stated by Dr. Edward A. Ross:

> Never before have we had to confront the question whether the great tragedies of passion are fit for juveniles, because as literature they reached only those minds ripe for them. But filmed they attract the very young and we are obliged to ask ourselves: 'Are these treasures of literature the right thing for boys and girls to be occupied with?'
>
> Most emphatically I should say 'No.' No sensible parent wants his Billy or Molly to become familiar with the behavior of grown-ups under the power of the master passion until nature gives intimation that she is ready. He has already about all he can do to keep his young folks straight in the trying interval between their becoming physiologically men and women and their marriage. The last thing the thoughtful parent desires to see is this period prolonged and the strain increased. One reason for the hearty response to the juvenile recreation program is that it sets up a strong competitor with the sex interest. The founders of the outdoor corps-the Boy Scouts and the Camp Fire Girls-discovered another means of keeping down sex tension. But in comes the film and ravels out what has been knit up with such care. Week after week the children sit watching on the screen handsome heroes and lovely girls and lustful, leering villains. The man and the woman enamored and alone in a boat, in a studio, on a tropical island, in a forest glade, on a balcony, in a shipwreck. Youngsters of ten or twelve years watch scenes of fascination, pursuit, love-making, embracing, kissing, passionate abandon which the jaded, commonplace adult, somewhat disappointed with self or spouse or the drabness and adventurelessness of his daily existence, finds stirring and refreshing-but which are to children what fire is to tow.[2]

Is Youth Being Safeguarded?

A recent release which received unusual praise from the critics, and which indeed is unusual in its simple artistry, is peculiarly unfortunate as adolescent entertainment, if we are going to continue to ask young people to refrain from illicit adventures. This is Chaplin's first serious drama, *A Woman of Paris.* Agnes Smith has written an excellent review of this, appraising it, however, only from the adult standpoint. To quote:

> To get down to a consideration of the merits of *A Woman of Paris*: The story is ridiculously simple. A young French girl leaves a small town after a tragic love affair. She goes to Paris, captures the interest of a wealthy man and leads what the flappers jokingly call 'a life of sin.' Her 'life of sin ' is pictured as much more proper, congenial and serenely happy than most marriages. Chaplin has a gorgeous time indicating the relations of his erring couple without stepping on the toes of the censors.
>
> And he also has a gorgeous time indicating that 'living in sin' isn't half so terrible as it used to be in the productions of Ivan Abramson. The man and the girl are polite, considerate and genuinely fond of each other as two human beings. But, of course, the lover of the early tragedy has to show up and spoil a perfectly charming life of crime. The girl, true to her type, is sentimental and wants to marry him, even though she must share his poverty. His mother objects and the boy kills himself. Whereupon the girl reforms, as the saying goes, and breaks up one of the most pleasant illegal households in Paris.[3]

Before concluding this article, we may raise the question as to the progress being made by the producer's self-cleansing program before mentioned. The following comparison is thought provoking:

Previous to May, 1921, Emma Lindsay Squier described one or two scenes in a film which photoplay exchanges at first refused to handle because of its supposed indecency. To quote:

> There was another scene where the 'other woman' is using her seductive powers to entrap the man she wants. She undressed-behind a curtain-and donned a black chiffon negligee. It was handled delicately, but it was bold. The cutter's shears haven't left a remnant of that episode.[4]

> A little over five years later a feature film called *Up in Mabel's Room* was witnessed at Madison, Wis. This photoplay relates the complications brought about by what a theatre lobby advertisement described as a "cavorting chemise." At one point a certain Garry has been intruded upon in his bachelor apartment by Mabel, from whom he is supposed to have been divorced, and he is opposed to any reconciliation. Phyllis, Garry's fiancee, has decided to come and say good night (after a cabaret party) and Mabel wishes to break up the engagement.

Now comes a five minute sequence as follows: The butler announces that Garry's betrothed, Phyllis, wishes to come in to see him. Garry hustles Mabel behind a screen in his apartment. Phyllis enters as though in anticipation of a good night kiss. Mabel tosses her jacket over the screen. Garry tries to explain this to Phyllis. Then a close-up is shown of Mabel behind the screen removing her shoes, which she sets out in front of the screen. Garry explains to Phyllis that they belonged to his sister and were to be used as ash trays (e.g. of some of the comedy titles!). Then a close-up is shown of Mabel behind the screen stooping as though removing her stockings. Then the stockings are thrown over the screen, then a ladies under vest, then a pair of lacey little French panties. Garry now hustles the dismayed and astonished Phyllis out of the apartment and returns to face the screen at a distance of 15 feet or so. Mabel appears peeking from behind the screen, just her head, bare arm and shoulder, apparently naked, and calls "Ooo-ooh, Garry!" He is shocked and turns bashfully away. Again she calls, "Oh, Garry, come here!"

Garry refuses to even turn toward her, so she comes out from behind the screen, fully dressed save for her shoes. As she approaches he covers his eyes with his hands, supposing her to be naked. She turns him about so that he faces her, but he still keeps his hands tightly over his eyes, bashfully shocked. She pulls his hands away but he still keeps his eyes closed; then opens at her insistence, and sees he was fooled. He insists that she leave the apartment; she calmly goes over and starts replacing her underwear in a little vanity satchel, shaking out the French panties and holding them spread out in front of her bosom as she does so. This explains how she could throw such things over the screen and still be dressed. But the sequence was deliberately handled so as to make the audience believe she had actually disrobed.

The accuracy of this description was attested by a second observer who read it after witnessing the picture. This is but one of several questionable sequences in the same picture. At a Sunday matinee performance the shrill laughter of children completely drowned out the hilarity of adults. Young high school fellows were there with their girlfriends.

The picture was produced by a member organization of the Motion Picture Producers and Distributors of America, which association, through Mr. Hays, has for several years been assuring the public that member producing companies were no longer permitting questionable scenes.

The main title of the picture bore the legend, "Passed by the National Board of Review."

The writer has recently witnessed other photoplays produced by member companies of the Motion Picture Producers and Distributors of America which carried sequences equally questionable-sequences which some young college fellows referred to as "the hottest yet."

If we grant that the adolescent is less under parental control than ever before, and his conduct more influenced by whatever the community tolerates, then we should be very cautious lest we place too much confidence in dollar-guided standards.

The proper attitude to take would seem to be that expressed several years ago by H. Dora Stecker, at one time director of the Clifton Motion Picture Theatre of Cincinnati:

The machinery created by the industry through Mr. Hays is not a substitute for the efforts which the public is making, and has made, to protect itself; it is merely supplementary.

In Conclusion

In a short article it is possible to consider only a few aspects of the relation between changing moral standards and the motion picture. The highly important matter of sensational exploitation has barely been mentioned. It is a fine thing to have our attention called to wholesome entertainment. For that we should be grateful. It is another thing to have the most risque aspects of a picture, suitable only for adults, if for anyone, paraded before the eyes of the young on billboards, in leaflets distributed from door to door, in the family newspaper, and on the photoplay screen as an announcement of future entertainment, often in connection with a wholesome photoplay to which parents have been especially urged to take their children.

But enough has been presented to suggest that the motion picture has effected and will continue to vitally effect the moral conduct particularly of the young.

It is the writer's conviction that the recreation of the young can never be safely left to commercial exploitation. The commercial theatre was formerly regarded as adult entertainment.

Let us hope that the day will come when the needs of the young will be met through state or community supported circulating libraries of approved standard films-the coming classics of the screen-exhibited on a non-profit basis in school auditoriums or community theatres as a part of a balanced recreational program. Progress in this direction is well under way through the efforts of clubs, university extension divisions and forward looking civic organizations.

Notes

1. "Crime and the Movies," *Literary Digest*, May 7, 1921, p. 19. Quoted from an article in The Scientific Monthly by Dr. A. T. Poffenberger.
2. Excerpt from an address by Dr. Edward A. Ross, on February 11, 1926, before the National Motion Picture Conference at Chicago.
3. "The Screen in Review," by Agnes Smith, *Picture Play Magazine*, Jan., 1924, p.52.
4. "What Do Men Need," Emma-Lindsay Squier, *Picture Play Magazine*, May, 1921, p. 70.

WOMEN IN HOLLYWOOD

FIGURE 6.7. Mary Pickford (c. 1925)

FIGURE 6.8. Clara Bow (1905-1965)

QUESTIONS FOR STUDY

1. How does architecture help illuminate the past? What features do you notice the most in the structures pictured in the sources here? What do they tell us about the time in which they were created? What images of the past do they evoke?
2. What do the sources on immigration and immigrants tell us about the anxieties and concerns of Californians? What connections do you see with earlier concerns about immigration (see chapter 4)? Do you detect any differences? How do these sources help illuminate more recent discussions about who should and who should not be allowed in California?
3. What do the sources in this chapter tell us about the role of Southern California in shaping the image of the entire state? What impact did the region have in shaping the national culture?
4. This chapter contains several images of women. What do they communicate about the changing roles of women in American society? In what ways do they reflect 'traditional' female roles?

CREDITS

1. Fig. 6.1: "The courtyard of the Frank Miller's Glenwood Mission Inn, Riverside, ca.1910," http://commons.wikimedia.org/wiki/File:The_courtyard_of_the_Frank_Miller%27s_Glenwood_Mission_Inn,_Riverside,_ca.1910_(CHS-5261).jpg. Copyright in the Public Domain.
2. Fig. 6.2: C.C. Pierce, "San Diego-Union Depot post card ca 1920," http://commons.wikimedia.org/wiki/File:San_Diego-Union_Depot_post_card_ca_1920.jpg. Copyright in the Public Domain.
3. Fig. 6.3: "Kamiya Soyeda," http://www.loc.gov/pictures/item/ggb2005013616/. Copyright in the Public Domain.
4. Webb-Haney Alien Land Law. Copyright in the Public Domain.
5. The Immigration Act of 1924. Copyright in the Public Domain.
6. V. S. McClatchy, *Guarding the Immigration Gates*, pp. 3-10, 12-13. Copyright in the Public Domain.
7. Fig. 6.4: "Korean American women with their children in an English class at the International Institute of Los Angeles, 1922," Los Angeles Public Library, Order# 00002984. Copyright in the Public Domain.

8. "A New Slant on Americanization," *Pacific Rural Press*, vol. 100, no. 24, pp. 781. Copyright in the Public Domain.
9. Fig. 6.5: "Sister Aimee Semple McPherson preaching at the newly-built Angelus Temple in 1923," http://unitproj.library.ucla.edu/dlib/lat/display.cfm?ms=uclalat_1429_b3717_G3169&searchType=subject&subjectID=213433. Copyright in the Public Domain.
10. Fig. 6.6: Metro Transportation Library and Archive, "Traffic Jam at Broadway and 7th Street in Los Angeles (c. 1920)," http://www.kcet.org/updaily/socal_focus/history/la-as-subject/lost-tunnels-of-downtown-la.html. Copyright in the Public Domain.
11. Charles Hanson Towne, "The Monstrous Movies: Hollywood is Nothing So Much As Old Home-Week in Bedlam," *Vanity Fair Magazine*, pp. 51-52. Copyright in the Public Domain.
12. Harmon B. Stephens, "The Relation of the Motion Picture to Changing Moral Standards," *Annals of the American Academy of Political and Social Science*, vol. 128: The Motion Picture in Its Economic and Social Aspects, pp. 154-156. Copyright © 1926 by SAGE Publications. Reprinted with permission.
13. Fig. 6.7: "Mary Pickford (c. 1925)," http://commons.wikimedia.org/wiki/File:Mary_Pickford_portrait.jpg. Copyright in the Public Domain.
14. Fig. 6.8: "Clara Bow (1930)," http://commons.wikimedia.org/wiki/File:CBpic_Clara_Boop.png. Copyright in the Public Domain.

07 The Great Depression and the New Deal

INTRODUCTION

Many Californians confronted very real questions about where to turn and what to do as they lost their livelihoods and homes during the Great Depression of the 1930s. This economic calamity resulted from structural issues deep within the American economy, including overdependence on the manufacture of durable goods, growing income inequality, and too much stock market speculation, among other causes. California's distance from the financial centers of the East Coast initially helped insulate the state from the immediate impact of the stock market crash of 1929. But soon Californians, like Americans all over the country, faced collapsing banks and a shrinking job market. By 1932, California's unemployment rate hit 28 percent, a few points above the national rate of 23.6 percent. The landscape was now dotted with Hoovervilles—shanty towns named mockingly after President Herbert Hoover, who many blamed for plunging the country into the depths of the worst economic crisis in American history. One of the most dramatic examples of homelessness during the Depression years in California was Pipe City, also known as Miseryville, located at the foot of 19th Avenue in Oakland. Here, homeless men created makeshift dwellings out of surplus sewer pipes that belonged to the American Concrete and Steel Pipe Company, on company land (Figure 7.1).

While unemployment figures climbed, California agriculture drew additional tens of thousands to the state, looking for work picking crops. Many came from the southern Great Plains, an area ravaged by the ecological disaster known as the Dust Bowl. California native John Steinbeck immortalized these men, women, and children, often called Okies, in his 1939 novel The Grapes of Wrath. Before writing *The Grapes of Wrath*, Steinbeck had traveled up and down California reporting on the migrants from Oklahoma, Texas, and Arkansas who had moved to the state looking for work. During these travels, Steinbeck observed the complex relationships between the Okies and their employers (see reading 39 "The Harvest Gypsies"). The Okies came to California looking for their California Dream, only to find disappointment. Many became part of a migratory work force, living in government-constructed camps. While these camps afforded a sense of community, they also created resentment, both among the migrants themselves and their native California neighbors (see reading 40 "The 'Okies' Search for a Lost Frontier").

Mexicans had been excluded from the 1924 Immigration Act and had become a major part of California's agricultural workforce. But during the Depression, as employment opportunities declined, immigrant workers were now scapegoated for taking jobs away from native-born Americans. Even before the stock market crash, there was intense pressure from labor groups and municipal governments across the Southwest to reduce the number of Mexican immigrants. In 1930, the federal government launched intensive raids to identify aliens liable for deportation, in an effort to reduce relief expenditures and free jobs for native-born citizens. These federal efforts were accompanied by city and county pressure to repatriate destitute Mexican American families. In Los Angeles, for instance, the county welfare director asked federal immigration officials in early 1931 to send a team to supervise the deportation of Mexicans. The threat of unemployment, deportation, and loss of relief payments led many to leave voluntarily. Others were forcefully repatriated. Raids often swept up American-born individuals of Mexican descent as well as Mexican immigrants (see section "Repatriation").

Another sign of the uncertain times was growing labor unrest. California experienced numerous strikes in this decade, especially among the agricultural workers with dismally low wages. One gas station in Kern County expressed its support for strikers with a poster reminding them, "This is your country don't let the big men take it away from you" (Figure 7.2). The urban parts of California were not immune to labor unrest. The West Coast waterfront strike, also known as the Longshoremen's Strike, began on May 9, 1934. It started when Harry Bridges led his International Longshoremen's Association (ILA), which represented the dockworkers, in a vote to strike for control of hiring halls, better pay, and better hours. The strike effectively closed the port of San Francisco, quickly spreading to other ports up and down the West Coast. When the employers' organization, the Industrial Association, tried to reopen the port in San Francisco on July 5, the confrontation became violent (see reading 41 "2 Killed, 115 Injured in San Francisco Strike"). Known as Bloody Thursday, it helped Bridges rally the support of other unions in the city to join the strike. This general strike effectively shut down the city of San Francisco for four days, resulting in a victory for ILA. The following year, the federal Wagner Act created the National Labor Relations Board to protect the rights of workers to organize into unions. The general strike thus brought significant political power for labor unions that would last for decades.

The New Deal was President Franklin Delano Roosevelt's attempt to end the Depression through direct intervention in the economy. Following Keynesian economic principles, the Roosevelt administration argued that stimulating the economy through various works programs and other interventions would jump-start the recovery. Tens of thousands of men and women across the state joined New Deal programs. The federal spending that resulted had a permanent impact on the state's infrastructure. One example is the Golden Gate Bridge, which opened in 1937 (Figure 7.3). The bridge was built by union workers covered under the New Deal's Wagner Act. Two other New Deal programs, the Works Progress Administration (WPA) and the Public Works

Administration (PWA), funded the construction of roads to access the new bridge.

Bay Area photographer Dorothea Lange (1895–1965), one of the greatest documentary photographers in American art history, worked in the Resettlement Administration and the Farm Security Administration, federal agencies created as part of the New Deal. Her intimate images of those hardest hit by the Great Depression, many of them taken in California, helped create public support for further New Deal programs in support of the poor (Figures 7.4 and 7.5). Meanwhile, at the state level, Upton Sinclair and his End Poverty in California (EPIC) program promised a different kind of solution to the state's problems. Upton Sinclair (1878–1968) authored more than a hundred books, among them arguably his most famous work, the muckraking classic *The Jungle* (1906). In the 1920s he moved to California, where he turned to politics. Originally a Socialist, he changed to the Democratic Party in 1934 and ran for governor on a platform to End Poverty in California (see reading 42 "Upton Sinclair and EPIC").

Sinclair was not the only Californian offering a way to end the suffering caused by the Depression. Author and journalist Carey McWilliams (1905–1980) was a keen observer of social issues in California. In the 1930s he wrote one of the first nonfiction books focused on the plight of migrant agricultural workers and labor unrest in California, *Factories in the Field: The Story of Migratory Farm Labor in California* (1939). Readings 43 "The Good Doctor" and 44 "Ham and Eggs" are excerpts from one of his later books, the influential *Southern California: An Island on the Land* (1946). In these excerpts, McWilliams explores some of the private relief program ideas that developed in the state. All offered very different potential solutions to try and bring the Depression to an end.

THE DEPRESSION AND THE DUST BOWL

FIGURE 7.1. Pipe City, Oakland (1932)

READING 39, JOHN STEINBECK

"The Harvest Gypsies"

***San Francisco News*, October 7, 1936**

WHEN IN THE COURSE OF THE SEASON THE SMALL farmer has need of an influx of migrant workers he usually draws from the squatters' camps. By small farmer I mean the owner of the five to 100-acre farm, who operates and oversees his own farm.

Farms of this size are the greatest users of labor from the notorious squatters camps. A few of the small farms set aside little pieces of land where the workers may pitch their shelters. Water is furnished, and once in a while a toilet. Rarely is there any facility for bathing. A small farm cannot afford the outlay necessary to maintain a sanitary camp.

Furthermore, the small farmers are afraid to allow groups of migrants to camp on their land, and they do not like the litter that is left when the men move on. On the whole, the relations between the migrants and the small farmers are friendly and understanding.

In many of California's agricultural strikes the small farmer has sided with the migrant against the powerful speculative farm groups. The workers realize that the problem of the small farmer is not unlike their own.

On the other hand the large farms very often maintain their camps for the laborers. The large farms in California are organized as closely and are as centrally directed in their labor policy as are the industries and shipping, the banking and public utilities.

Indeed such organizations as Associated Farmers, Inc. have as members and board members officials of banks, publishers of newspapers and politicians; and through close association with the State Chamber of Commerce they have interlocking associations with shipowners' associations, public utilities corporations and transportation companies.

These farms are invariably run by superintendents whose policies with regard to labor are directed from above. But the power of these organizations extends far beyond the governing of their own lands.

It is rare in California for a small farmer to be able to plant and mature his crops without loans from banks and finance companies. And since these banks and finance companies are at once members of the powerful growers' associations, and at the same time the one source of crop loans, the force of their policies on the small farmer can readily be seen. To refuse to obey is to invite foreclosure or a future denial of the necessary crop loan.

These strong groups, then, do not necessarily represent the general feeling toward labor; but being able to procure space in newspapers and on the radio, they are able, not only to represent themselves as the whole body of California farmers, but are actually able to impose their policies on a great number of the small farms.

The ranches operated by these speculative farmers usually have houses for their migrant laborers, houses for which they charge a rent of from three to 15 dollars a month.

Let us see what this housing is like, not the $15 houses which can only be rented by field bosses (called pushers), but the three to five dollar houses forced on the laborers. The houses, one-room shacks usually about 10 by 12 feet, have no rug, no water, no bed. In one corner there is a little iron wood stove. Water must be carried from a faucet at the end of the street. Also at the head of the street there will be either a dug toilet or a toilet with a septic tank to serve 100 to 150 people. A fairly typical ranch in Kern County had one bath house with a single shower and no heated water for the use of the whole block of houses, which had a capacity of 400 people.

The arrival of the migrant on such a ranch is something like this—he is assigned a house for his family; lie may have from three to six children, but they must all live in the one room. He finds the ranch heavily policed by deputized employees.

The new arrival at the ranch will probably be without funds. His resources have been exhausted in getting here. But on many of the great ranches he will find a store run by the management at which he can get credit. Thus he must work a second day to pay for his first, and so on. He is continually in debt. He must work.

In the field he will be continually attended by the "pusher," the field boss, and in many cases a pacer. In picking, a pacer will be a tree ahead of him. If he does not keep up, he is fired. And it is often the case that the pacer's row is done over again afterwards.

Indeed any attempt to congregate is broken up by the deputies for it is feared that if they are allowed to congregate they will organize, and that is the one thing the large ranches will not permit at any cost.

The large ranch owners know that if organization is ever effected there will be the expense of toilets, showers, decent living conditions and a raise in wages.

The attitude of the workers on the large ranch is much that of the employer, hatred and suspicion. The worker sees himself surrounded by force. He knows that he can be murdered without fear on the part of the employer, and he has little recourse to law. He has taken refuge in a sullen, tense quiet. He cannot resist the credit that allows him to feed his family, hut he knows perfectly well the reason for the credit.

This repressive method results inevitably in flares of disorganized revolt which must be put down by force and by increased intimidation. The large growers' groups have found the law inadequate to their uses; and they have become so powerful that such charges as felonious assault, mayhem and inciting to riot, kidnapping and flogging cannot be brought against them in the controlled courts.

The attitude of the large growers' associations toward labor is best stated by Mr. Hugh T. Osburne, a member of the Board of Supervisors of Imperial County and active in the Imperial Valley Associated Farmers group. Before the judiciary committee of the California Assembly he said:

"In Imperial Valley we don't need this criminal syndicalism law. They have got to have it for the rest of the counties that don't know how to handle these matters. We don't need it because we have worked out our own way of handling these things. We won't have another of these trials. We have a better way of doing it. Trials cost too much."

"The better way," as accepted by the large growers of the Imperial Valley, includes a system of terrorism that would be unusual in the Fascist nations of the world. The stupid policy of the large grower and the absentee speculative farmer in California has accomplished nothing but unrest, tension and hatred. A continuation of this approach constitutes a criminal endangering of the peace of the state.

READING 40, CHARLES L. TODD

"The 'Okies' Search for a Lost Frontier"

***New York Times*, August 27, 1939**

"THEY TOLD ME THIS WAS THE LAND O' MILK AN' HONEY, but Ah guess the cow's gone dry, and the tumblebugs has got in the beehive."

That, in his own language, is the way the average Dust Bowl migrant feels toward California today. And how does California react to the migrant? As one West Coast grower puts it, "This isn't a migration—it's an invasion! They're worse than a plague of locusts!"

The situation might not be so tragic if there were an end in sight somewhere. But the "covered wagons" are still rumbling across the border—there were 20,000 new arrivals during the first five months of 1939, making a total of nearly 300,000 migrants now living in California. "What shall we do with them? How can we feed them? What about housing, medical care, relief?"

These are the questions California is asking today, and no one, not even the Federal Government, seems to know the ultimate answers.

Once California wanted, or thought she wanted, all the migratory labor the drought States could supply. A twenty-acre hop farm, for instance, adds as many as 500 pickers during the harvest, and "peak" labor was sometimes difficult to find. Today. however, there are thousands clamoring for jobs like that, and the "Okie," the migrant from the Dust Bowl, has all the advantage of desperation. Native pickers, pruners, grape-girdlers and cotton-choppers are hopelessly out-generaled. Mexicans, who formerly held a monopoly on "stoop" labor in the potato patches of Kern County and the lettuce fields of Imperial, have been routed by these work-hungry folk from the drought States: 20 per cent of them are from Oklahoma; hence the generic name, Okie.

An automobile, vintage 1926, drawing a home-made trailer loaded with tattered mattresses, a tent rig, cooking utensils, odds and ends of every description, rattles up to the gateway of a Federal Migratory Labor camp. There are two tow-headed, ragged children in the rear seat, a man and a woman in the front. The woman is hatless and is wearing a loose dress of uncertain age and color. Her neck and arms are almost as red as her husband's, and her face looks older than his. The man, wearing overalls but no shirt, climbs out of the car and walks over to the caretaker's office. If he is fortunate, there will be lodging for him and his family until he can organize his wits and get started again.

This particular newcomer was "tractored-off" a farm in a Southern State. The landowner bought two dozen tractors and let go nearly a hundred sharecropper families. He has been in California nearly two months—"mostly cotton-choppin' up near Bakersfield, me an' my wife, at 75 cents and acre...we manage about an acre an' a half a day between us."

There are former preachers, veterinaries, men with knowledge of the law, young people with credits from their State universities. Californians sometimes accuse them of being migrants "for the love of it"; others refer to them as "those modern pioneers." But whatever the answer may be, it is not so simple as that. Sensible men and women don't pick peas for 20 cents an hour just "for the love of it."

But the plight of the migratory worker is not quite so bad in 1939 as it was in 1936, thanks chiefly to the efforts of the Federal Government. Working through the Farm Security Administration set up under the Bankhead-Jones Farm Tenancy Act of 1937, the government has constructed thirteen camps, from Gridley in the North to Brawley in the South, capable of housing for a stated length of time some 2,500 families.

At best, these camps are a drop in the bucket, but the example they set has been far-reaching. Something like this had to be done. The old ditch-bank communities, where irrigating ditches provided drinking water, bathing and sewerage, took their toll not only among the migrants, but also in near-by towns. These Federal camps are models of good sanitation. In fact, for the first time in years the "Okie" is being recognized as a human being, although the government is making no long-term promises.

The significance of what is happening here is difficult to comprehend until one has partaken intimately of the life these more fortunate migrants know. Join the "Okies" in their Friday night boxing matches, their "smokers," or their weekly old-fashioned dances. Gossip with the women as they plumb the mysteries of an electric washing machine. Above all, watch them as they make their first entry into the camp, and notice their gradual relief and thawing out as the camp manager explains what is expected of camp residents. "Keep the place clean? Sure we'll keep it clean! Have ya got any extra blankets for the kids?"

From the camp "personals" one gets a sense of old-time gayety and neighborliness that is seldom felt in the outside world. New arrivals from the home state; the departure of old friends and the hope "that we will meet again on the migrant trail": plans for a barbecue; a meeting of the "Good Girls Club" in Unit 5; the "Mothers' Club"; Last night's Amateur Show...

As for humor, there is plenty of it—stemming straight from the era of Josh Billings, Artemus Ward and the "Yankee Book of Wit and Humor." There is poetry too—old ballads retouched for modern consumption, and new ballads celebrating the rigors of the great migration.

But there is bitterness here, as well as humor, both inside and outside the camps. Schools in Brawley, Indio, Gridley, and other towns are being taxed to capacity by the influx of the migrant children, many of whom are retarded through force of circumstance. Native Californians are fearful for their jobs in the face of this work-hungry horde from "foreign" States. And inside the camps there is a growing hopelessness, despite the clean showers and the washing machines. "We don't want to eat off the government—we want work!" they say.

More government camps? Perhaps, but that takes huge appropriations. and hinges heavily on political considerations. Bids have been let for four new camps in Texas, closer to the scene of the original disaster. But what then? Each camp has an average capacity of about 200 families, and residence is restricted to one year. They are but temporary answers to the problem.

The State of California has exhausted every known method of reducing the number of migrants. Border patrols were established and hundreds turned back. The roads into California are numerous, however, and there was desperation under the hoods of those old jalopies. The State has offered to pay transportation back to the place of origin, but many "Okies" went back and returned, bringing another member of the family with them. Whatever may be said for California's economic situation, it is a fine climate to be destitute in. Finally, California is now talking of "reducing peak-labor needs" through greater crop diversification. This might be a splendid thing for California agriculture, but it can be of little benefit to the migrants already there.

These local remedies are not being taken very seriously. The truth is, as President Roosevelt said in March, that the problem belongs to the nation at large. Despite the rebirth of Dust-Bowl farming, these refugees can never go back on their own again. Their very roots have disappeared.

Meanwhile, in the midst of all this confusion, one supreme necessity looms higher than all the rest. Something must be done and done soon. Somehow, somewhere, on this mighty continent, land must be found for these people to call their own. The camp at Arvin, with its tiny patch of land for every family head, makes that apparent. There is pride there, and a fulfillment. The "Okie" is land-hungry as well as work-hungry. His blood cries out for it. These are no hoboes or "blanket stiffs." They are ordinary American farmers in search of a lost frontier.

REPATRIATION

READING 41, CAREY MCWILLIAMS

"Repatriados"

***American Mercury*, 1933**

IN 1930 A FACT-FINDING COMMITTEE REPORTED TO THE Governor of California that, as a result of the passage of the Immigration Acts of 1921 and 1924, Mexicans were being used on a large scale in the Southwest to replace the supply of cheap labor that had been formerly recruited in Southeastern Europe. The report revealed a concentration of this new immigration in Texas, Arizona, and California, with an ever increasing number of Mexicans giving California as the State of their "intended future permanent residence." It was also discovered that, within the State, this new population was concentrated in ten southern counties.

For a long time Mexicans had regarded Southern California, more particularly Los Angeles, with favor, and during the decade from 1919 to 1929 the facts justified this view. At that time there was a scarcity of cheap labor in the region, and Mexicans were made welcome. When cautious observers pointed out some of the consequences that might reasonably be expected to follow from a rash encouragement of this immigration, they were shouted down by the wise men of the Chamber of Commerce. Mexican labor was eulogized as cheap, plentiful, and docile. Even so late as 1930 little effort had been made to unionize it. The Los Angeles shopkeepers joined with the industrialists in denouncing, as a union labor conspiracy, the agitation to place Mexican immigration on a quota basis....

During this period, academic circles in Southern California exuded a wondrous solicitude for the Mexican immigrant. Teachers of sociology, social service workers, and other subsidized sympathizers were deeply concerned about his welfare. Was he capable of assimilating American idealism? What anti-social traits did he possess? Wasn't he made morose by his native diet? What could be done to make him relish spinach and Brussels sprouts? What was the percentage of this and that disease, or this and that crime, in the Mexican population of Los Angeles? How many Mexican mothers fed their youngsters according to the diet schedules promulgated by manufacturers of American infant foods? In short, the do-gooders subjected the Mexican population to a relentless barrage of surveys, investigations, and clinical conferences.

But a marked change has occurred since 1930. When it became apparent last year that the programme for the relief of the unemployed would assume huge proportions in the Mexican quarter, the community swung to a determination to oust the Mexicans. Thanks to the rapacity of his overlords, he had not been able to accumulate any savings. He was in default in his rent. He was a burden to the taxpayer. At this juncture, an ingenious social worker suggested the desirability of a wholesale deportation. But when the Federal authorities were consulted they could promise but slight assistance, since many of the younger Mexicans in Southern California were American citizens, being the American-born children of immigrants. Moreover, the Federal officials insisted, in cases of illegal entry, upon a public hearing and a formal order of deportation. This procedure involved delay and expense, and, moreover, it could not be used to advantage in ousting any large number.

A better scheme was soon devised. Social workers reported that many of the Mexicans who were receiving charity had signified their "willingness" to return to Mexico. Negotiations were at once opened with the social-minded officials of the Southern Pacific Railroad. It was discovered that, in wholesale lots, the Mexicans could be shipped to Mexico City for $14.70 per capita. This sum represented less than the cost of a week's board and lodging. And so, about February, 1931, the first trainload was dispatched, and shipments at the rate of about one a month have continued ever since. A shipment, consisting of three special trains, left Los Angeles on December 8. The loading commenced at about six o'clock in the morning and continued for hours. More than twenty-five such special trains had left the Southern Pacific station before last April.

No one seems to know precisely how many Mexicans have been "repatriated" in this manner to date. The Los Angeles Times of November 18 gave an estimate of 11,000 for the year 1932. The monthly shipments of late have ranged from 1,300 to 6,000. The Times reported last April that altogether more than 200,000 repatriados had left the United States in the twelve months immediately preceding, of which it estimated that from 50,000 to 75,000 were from California, and over 35,000 from Los Angeles county. Of those from Los Angeles county, a large number were charity deportations.

The repatriation programme is regarded locally as a piece of consummate statecraft. The average per family cost of executing it is S71.14, including food and transportation. It cost Los Angeles county $77,249.29 to repatriate one shipment of 6,024. It would have cost $424,933.70 to provide this number with such charitable assistance as they would have been entitled to had they remained—a saving of $347,468.41.

One wonders what has happened to all the Americanization programmes of yesteryear. The Chamber of Commerce has been forced to issue a statement assuring the Mexican authorities that the community is in no sense unfriendly to Mexican labor and that repatriation is a policy designed solely for the relief of the destitute even, presumably, in cases where invalids are removed from the County Hospital in Los Angeles and carted across the line. But those who once agitated for Mexican exclusion are no longer regarded as the puppets of union labor.

What of the Mexican himself? The repatriation programme apparently, is a matter of indifference to this amiable ax-American. He never objected to exploitation while he was welcome, and now he acquiesces in repatriation. He doubtless enjoys the free train ride home. Probably he has had his fill of bootleg liquor and of the mirage created by pay-checks that never seemed to buy as much as they should. Considering the anti-social character commonly attributed to him by the sociological myth-makers, he has cooperated nicely with the authorities. Thousands have departed of their own volition. In battered Fords, carrying two and three families and all their worldly possessions, they are drifting back to el terenaso—the big land. They have been shunted back and forth across the border for so many years by war, revolution, and the law of supply and demand, that it would seem that neither expatriation or repatriation held any more terror for them.

The Los Angeles industrialists confidently predict that the Mexican can be lured back, "whenever we need him." But I am not so sure of this. He may be placed on a quota basis in the meantime, or possibly he will no longer look north to Los Angeles as the goal of his dreams. At present he is probably delighted to abandon an empty paradise. But it is difficult for his children. A friend of mine, who was recently in Mazatlan, found a young Mexican girl on one of the southbound trains crying because she had to leave Belmont High-School. Such an abrupt severance of the Americanization programme is a contingency that the professors of sociology did not anticipate.

READING 42, SECRETARIA DE RELACIONES EXTERIORES, MEXICO CITY

Letter Distributed to San Diego's Mexican and Mexican American Population

1932

THE GOVERNMENT OF MEXICO, WITH THE COOPERATION and aid of the Welfare Committee of this County, will effect the repatriation of all Mexicans who currently reside in this County and who might wish to return to their country.... Those persons who are repatriated will be able to choose among the States of Sonora, Sinaloa, Nayarit, Jalisco, Michoacán, and Guanajuato as the place of their final destination, with the understanding that the Government of Mexico will provide them with lands for agricultural cultivation...and will aid them in the best manner possible so that they might settle in the country.

Those persons who take part in this movement of repatriation may count on free transportation from San Diego to the place where they are going to settle, and they will be permitted to bring with them their furniture, household utensils, agricultural implements, and whatever other objects for personal use they might possess.

Since the organization and execution of a movement of repatriation of this nature implies great expenditures, this Consulate encourages you...to take advantage of this special opportunity being offered to you for returning to Mexico at no cost whatever and so that...you might dedicate all your energies to your personal improvement, that of your family, and that of our country.

If you wish to take advantage of this opportunity, please return this letter...with the understanding that, barring notice to the contrary from this Consulate, you should present yourself with your family and your luggage on the municipal dock of this port on the 23rd of this month before noon.

UNREST GROWS

FIGURE 7.2. Strike in Kern County (1938). A gas station in Kern County expresses its support for workers during an agricultural strike.

READING 43

"2 Killed, 115 Injured in San Francisco Strike"

***New York Times*, July 6, 1934**

NATIONAL GUARD TROOPS TOOK COMMAND OF THE SAN Francisco waterfront late today in the wake of fierce fighting which had exacted a toll early tonight of two dead, thirty wounded by gunfire and not less than eighty-five injured sufficiently to receive hospital treatment. Governor Merriam ordered Adjt. Gen. Seth Howard of the California National Guard to "take over the waterfront and protect life and property." Within a few minutes 1,750 war-equipped Guardsmen were on the march in this city and others around the bay.

Colonel R. E. Mittelstaedt, commander of the 250th Coast Artillery and commanding officer of waterfront troops, said as the mobilization began: "We have 4,000 additional men to back us up if necessary, and if that is not enough we will call the national army, the navy and the marine corps." But when the troops started moving a calmer attitude was reported among members of the strike committee of the International Longshoremen's Association.

Peace Order Reported

Barry Bridges, chairman of that committee, was reported to have ordered his rioting pickets to "cease hostilities" pending the formation at plans to appeal for a general strike. He was said to have told other committee members: "We cannot stand up to police machine guns and National Guard bayonets."

This climaxed a day never before duplicated in this city. The Embarcadero—San Francisco's name for its waterfront—ran blood. Strikers, non-strikers, policemen, newspaper reporters, photographers and onlookers fell victims to bricks, rocks, clubs, pistols and tear gas. Even the Ferry Building, central point for transmission of passengers and automobiles across San Francisco Bay, came into the line of disorder. Several commuters or visitors were caught in tear gas fumes and some were struck by bricks and stones.

Some Strangers Hurt

Among them were strangers to the city who were not even aware that there was danger at such a point. Those killed were Howard Sperry, 50 years old, felled with buckshot near local headquarters of the longshoremen's association, and an unidentified man who had described himself as an "intelligence officer" of the International Labor Defense.

The day began with clashes between police and rioting strikers as the industrial association resumed the movement of trucks carrying merchandise which had been stalled on piers and in warehouses here since May 9. At the same time the State Board of Harbor Commissioners prepared to restart trains moving on the State-owned and operated belt line railway. The movement was undertaken in light of a promise from Governor Merriam that he would send troops to the area if necessary.

As the day wore on two distinct clashes developed. Police won both encounters with shotguns and gas bombs after severe fighting. The principal fight was on Rincon Hill. Then Governor Merriam issued his call for troops. At 5 P. M. the first mobilized units began their movement to the waterfront—the first time since the great fire of 1906 that it has been necessary to call out the militia here.

Strikers estimated to number 500 were "picketing" the State armory as the mobilization was being completed. Amid the turmoil of pitched battle on the waterfront the port of San Francisco remained "open" today. The Industrial Association, which opened the port on Tuesday by moving trucks between Pier 38 and a warehouse several blocks away, had ten trucks in service all day. The Belt Line Railway also operated without interruption.

THE NEW DEAL

FIGURE 7.3. Golden Gate Bridge Under Construction (1934)

DOROTHEA LANGE PHOTOGRAPHS THE DEPRESSION

FIGURE 7.4. Mexican Mother and Child (1935). "Sometimes I tell my children that I would like to go to Mexico, but they tell me 'We don't want to go, we belong here.'"

FIGURE 7.5. Dispossessed Arkansas Farmers in Bakersfield (1935). Making do with gunny sacks and rags.

UPTON SINCLAIR AND THE CAMPAIGN TO END POVERTY IN CALIFORNIA (EPIC)

READING 44, S.J. WOOLF

"Upton Sinclair Describes His Evolution"

New York Times, September 16, 1934

SINCLAIR WAS EXTREMELY MODEST AS HE TOLD OF HIS literary successes. It was different when he spoke of his hardships. There was a smile of satisfaction on his face as he said: "I have been arrested four times—once for playing tennis on Sunday, once for walking up and down in front of John D. Rockefeller's office, once for selling a copy of the Bible to the police of Boston (I was released when some one told them it was the Bible) and once for reading a part of the Constitution while standing with the owner's permission upon private property."

I asked him how he happened to become a Democrat. His habitual smile broadened as he answered. His thin face calls up memories of Woodrow Wilson, and the strong lines about his mouth and cheeks, despite his smile, are reminiscent of the early Puritans. His voice is low and soft and his manner conciliatory even when he utters invectives against present conditions.

"I suppose I was born a Democrat, considering the fact that my father was an old-time Virginia gentleman. But you must not forget that I was brought up In New York, where the word Democrat was linked with Tammany Hall. My earliest political recollections are the things which the various legislative committees brought to light.

"It was impossible for me to align myself with the Democratic party in New York and so I became a Socialist. This did not prevent my being a Democrat in the best sense of the word. I am and always have been an advocate of the right of the people to manage their own affairs. God created the natural resources of wealth for the use of all mankind and not for the monopoly of a few. The means of producing and distributing the necessaries of life should be in the hands of the entire people, to be used for the people's benefit and not for any particular class.

"For years the Democratic party was in the bands of corruptionists and I continued my affiliation with the Socialist party despite the fact that I felt there was much in socialism which was filled with European ideology.

"The Democratic party has been turned over to the people. The money changers have been driven out and many of the ideas of socialism have been taken over by it.

"Today we are confronted with one of the gravest crises we have ever had to face. For the last seventy years this country has been governed by a business autocracy, and there has been a continuous struggle between that autocracy and our political democracy. Up to the present Big Business has always been the victor. But we have had only preliminary skirmishes. The final battle is on. If Big Business wins, we shall have fascism in this country and no real American wants that."

"Look at California," he went on. "It is a land ready to produce almost everything that human beings need. It has large factories filled with fine machines, it has good roads, and fertile farms. What is happening? The machines are idle, fruit is rotting on the ground and vegetables are being dumped in the bays because there is no one to buy them. There are thousands homeless and thousands of empty homes. More than a million are anxious for work and cannot secure It. Another million are being taxed out of homes and of farms to feed those starving ones who would be glad to labor for their food but are not allowed to.

"We are told that people are starving because we have produced too much food, that men and women have only rags because we have woven too much cloth, that they cannot work because we have too many factories, that they must sleep in the open because we have built too many homes.

"It is incomprehensible, yet it is a fact. It is so because corruption has been rampant in both business and politics and in the dealings between the two. At last there has come an awakening. Franklin Roosevelt has aroused a new spirit in the nation and with that behind him is making the Democratic party into a party of public welfare,"

"What about California?" I asked.

"I have worked out a plan that I propose to try there if I am elected. I say I have worked it out but I have had assistance from economists and experts. Our slogan is End Poverty in California and we call the plan EPIC from the first letter of each word.

"There is no excuse for poverty. All men and women who want work should have the opportunity to work and should be paid a decent wage. I propose that the State take over unworked farms and the factories that have been closed or are operating at a loss, and pay a fair rental to the owners.

"Upon the farms we shall put the unemployed farm workers and have them go to work. The factories, under the supervision of the State but with the owners as managers, maintaining their present organization, will start working at full production once more.

"The State will maintain a system of distribution whereby the food will be taken into the cities and the manufactured products taken out to the country. All the products will be made available at cost. Those who produce will receive the full social value of their product so that they will be able to buy what they have produced. Consumption will balance production. Production will be for use, not for profit.

"Our trouble is not overproduction, but underconsumption. What we have produced up to now does not belong to the people, but to a comparative few. That which the people do not own is of no use to them and might as well not exist. We propose that the unemployed shall produce food which they will eat and clothing which they will be able to wear without paying tribute to private owners.

"Of course, I can only outline our plan to you. The money to carry out this project will be raised by bonds. Our medium of exchange will be scrip. We shall revise the tax system and provide old-age pensions.

"If I am elected Governor," he continued, "the State of California will make an experiment which may determine the entire future of America. We are going to apply democracy to industry. If the people can provide food, clothing and shelter for themselves, then they will no longer have to work for masters and be ordered what to do and receive only a bare living in return. California will show the world that it believes that 'the laborer is worthy of his hire.'"

CAREY MCWILLIAMS DOCUMENTS THE DEPRESSION

READING 45

The Good Doctor

1946

*THE SENSATIONAL RISE OF THE UTOPIAN SOCIETY STIM*ulated dreams of abundance in many minds in Southern California and provoked a great outpouring of Utopian plans and panaceas. One of the most significant of these subsequent revelations was that conjured up by Dr. Francis Townsend. The "tall, lean, and gentle-voiced sexagenarian" had come to Long Beach from South Dakota in the great migration of the 'twenties. Failing to establish himself in the practice of medicine, he had organized a company to manufacture "dry ice" and, upon the failure of the company, had entered the real-estate office of R. Earl Clements. While loafing in the real-estate office one day, "the good doctor" came upon a paper written by Stewart McCord of Seattle which expounded the ideas, based upon technocratic economics, of "retiring oldsters upon a monthly annuity the spending of which was compulsory." Since real estate was not moving very rapidly at the time, the doctor proceeded to dress up McCord's idea a bit and to open a new office in 1954 with funds provided by R. Earl Clements, realtor. Thus was O.A.R.P., Ltd. (Old Age Revolving Pensions), born.

It is significant that this particular movement should have been launched in Long Beach, famous in local wisecracks as "a cemetery with lights." From its founding as a temperance colony, Long Beach has always attracted a disproportionate number of oldsters. Without the honkytonk atmosphere of most beach resorts, it has long been a paradise for the aged. With some 40,000 Iowans residing in the city, Bixby Park has for years been the favorite picnic ground for the various state societies. All one needs to do in order to understand the popularity of a Utopian pension scheme in Long Beach is to glance at the population statistics for the city. The age-level of Long Beach residents has always been somewhat higher than the average for other Southern California communities and definitely higher than the average for the state. The horseshoe pitching tournaments of California are invariably held in Long Beach with its

Water and land and sky and sand
And oil beneath the ground,
Where Iowans meet and sharpers cheat
And nary a native is found.

It is also significant that the founders of OARP should have been an elderly physician without a practice and a shrewd real-estate promoter. As part of the pension-plan promotion, "the good doctor" and his associate Clements established the *Townsend Weekly*, famous for its patent-medicine and gland-renovating advertisements, which soon had a weekly circulation of 100,000 copies. Governor Frank Merriam, a resident of Long Beach, a former Iowan, being sorely pressed by Mr. Sinclair in the gubernatorial campaign of 1934, endorsed the Townsend Plan as did Kathleen Norris, who, a short time previously, had announced that high taxes were driving her from California. By the end of 1934, the Townsend Plan had a state and national following that ran into the hundreds of thousands. Among those who joined up in the crusade "which only God could stop," was John Steven McGroarty, favorite columnist of the Los Angeles Times, poet laureate of California, who was elected to Congress on a Townsend Plan platform and who sponsored the plan in Congress.

Originating in Southern California, the Townsend Plan won thousands of followers in Oregon, Montana, Colorado, and began to spread throughout the Middle West and East. With thousands of oldsters across the nation chanting:

Two hundred dollars a month,
Youth for work, age for leisure,
Two hundred for the oldsters,
To be spent in ceaseless pleasure.

The movement gained steady momentum. As sole owners of the Townsend Weekly, with a circulation of 150,000 copies a week, Dr Townsend and Realtor Clements began to split a weekly net revenue estimated at $2,000. During 1935, OARP collected, largely in nickels and dimes, around $600,000 and in the peak year of 1936, collections totaled $950,000. In a congressional investigation in 1936, it was revealed that Townsend and Clements had each received $79,000 from the various subsidiary corporations which they had formed in connection with the pension-plan movement. One day in 1935 Dr. Townsend addressed a crowd of 35,000 in Northern California and, flying south, spoke to an audience of 50,000 pensionites assembled in Tujunga Canyon. In 1936 "the good doctor," in company with Gerald L. K. Smith and Father Charles Coughlin, formed the Union Party which nominated William Lemke for President. The same year marked the peak of the movement, for with the re-election of Franklin D. Roosevelt and the passage of the social-security program, the various pension-plan schemes lost much of their national significance, although still another chapter was to be written in California.

READING 46

Ham and Eggs

1946

DURING PERIODS OF GREAT SOCIAL STRESS IN INDUSTRIAL communities, the dispossessed are likely to smash factory windows, or to conduct hunger marches, or to dramatize their desperation in some concrete manner. But in an area without smokestacks where the sale of real estate has been the major industry, there are no visible symbols upon which the distressed masses can vent their fury. To the extent that their discontent can personalize a victim, it is likely to be the "money-lender," or the "big banker." Their hatred is inclined to be expressed in abstract form; their dreams to be dominated by abstract symbols, "money," "riches," "jewels," "wealth." Consequently, when they dream of Utopia, it is not of a well-planned, perfectly governed garden city, but of a perfect scheme or get-rich-quick system. Their archangel is not Sir Thomas More or Patrick Geddes, but the promoter who promises to deliver, the salesman with enticing phrases, the business magician.

The early mass political movements in Southern California, characterized by marked social inventiveness, were a healthy manifestation of a people's impulse to do something for themselves. Continued frustration of this impulse, however, soon began to produce rank and unhealthy social growths. Of all these latter-day growths, the Ham and Eggs movement is, by all odds, the most fantastic, incredible, and dangerous. The story of this movement which follows is largely based upon an interesting document by Winston and Marian Moore, entitled *Out of the Frying Pan*, published in Los Angeles in 1939. Incredible as they may sound, the facts set forth in this document, which I have summarized, have never been disputed or denied.

The story starts with the arrival in Los Angeles of Robert Noble, a neurotic but plausible rabble-rouser, young in years, attractive in appearance, dynamic in manner. He first appears as a platform and radio speaker in the Epic campaign of 1934. Shortly after the Epic campaign, he began to make a name for himself as a radio commentator on Station KMTR, attracting a large following by his attacks on an unpopular city administration. Observing the rapidity with which the Townsend Plan had spread throughout the region, he decided to conjure up a pension plan of his own based upon an article which he had read by Professor Irving Fisher on "stamp" money. Without bothering to prepare a plan, he simply began to speak on the air about a scheme that would pay the oldsters $25-Every-Monday. The slogan was excellent, the promise attractive, and soon the flow of nickels, dimes, and quarters began to increase in volume.

In the Hollywood building where Noble made his headquarters was also located the office of the Cinema Advertising Agency, operated by two brothers, Willis and Lawrence Allen, both talented promoters. Shortly before they had formed the Cinema Advertising Agency, Willis Allen had been involved in some promotional fancywork in connection with Grey Gone, a hair tonic. In need of assistance, Noble induced the Cinema Advertising Agency to manage his program and to negotiate, in the name of the agency, a contract for radio time on Station KMTR. As Noble's attacks on the city administration became increasingly violent and vitriolic, Capt. Earl Kynette was assigned the task of devising ways and means to take him off the air. After making a cursory inspection of the situation, Kynette decided to kill two birds with one stone: to get Noble off the air and to get in on the pension scheme himself. Suggesting that Noble was not the man to head the movement, Kynette made a cash loan to the Allen brothers which enabled them to carry off a clever *putsch.*

A "rump" meeting of the pensionites was accordingly held in September, 1937, in Clifton's Cafeteria, where many plots of the sort have been staged and where many movements have been born. The meeting adopted articles of incorporation prepared by the Aliens and then proceeded to elect an Allen-controlled board of directors. When Noble next appeared at Station KMTR, he found Willis Allen seated behind the microphone. And, when he called a meeting of the faithful to discuss this shrewdly executed maneuver, the meeting was disrupted by policemen making excellent use of stench bombs and tear gas. In desperation, Noble then attempted to throw a picket line around

Station KMTR, but Capt. Kynette was again on hand with the "boys," and the picket line melted away like snow in the sun. In a final effort to regain control of the movement, Noble filed papers with the Secretary of State in which he sought to protect the slogan $25-Every-Monday. Not the kind of operators to be thwarted by such a ruse, the Aliens immediately adopted the slogan $30-Every-Thursday which was more pleasing to the ear and more attractive to the purse. Noble was out. And soon the interesting Capt. Kynette was also "out" for, shortly after the Noble putsch was effected, he clumsily planted a time-bomb in the automobile of an investigator who was probing the city administration, was caught, tried, and sentenced to San Quentin Prison.

Left in undisputed control of $30-Every-Thursday, the Allen brothers did not know quite what to do with the movement. They needed, first of all, an effective spellbinder. The orator was soon discovered in the person of Sherman Bainbridge, whose voice has long echoed in the cafeteria meeting rooms of Los Angeles. It was Bainbridge who coined the invaluable slogan "Ham and Eggs" which the pensionites shout with the frenzy of storm-troopers yelling Sieg Heil! All meetings of the Payroll Guarantee Association are opened with the shouted salutation "Ham and Eggs" and each speaker who appears on the platform must preface his remarks with the salutation. If he neglects to do so, the crowd will shout "Ham and Eggs" until he does. The Aliens also needed a plan. Incredible as it may sound, they had been in control of the movement for eighteen months, conducting an intensive campaign by radio, newspaper, and open meetings, before so much as a line or a sentence had been placed on paper. They got the "plan" from Roy Owens, who for years had been an enthusiastic disciple of Father Divine. The plan contemplates the establishment of a state bank and the issuance of phony money to finance pension payments. They also needed "a situation," a springboard, from which they could really take off, and fate soon provided an occasion.

In San Diego—it would be San Diego—64-year-old Archie Price walked into a newspaper office one day and announced that, since he was too old to work and not old enough to qualify for a pension, he intended to commit suicide. The editor of the newspaper, a veteran in Southern California, scoffed at the suggestion. The next day Price committed suicide and was buried in a pauper's grave. Recognizing that Providence had provided them with the occasion for a spectacular mass demonstration, the Aliens organized a march on San Diego. "Less than a month after the death of Archie Price," write the Moores, "Sherman Bainbridge led a funeral cortege of thousands of cars from Los Angeles to San Diego, where Archie Price was exhumed and re-interred amid an avalanche of gorgeous bloom, to the sound of lovely music and surrounded by a multitude of mourners which would have done justice to a monarch. Sheridan Downey, later United States Senator from California, assisted Bainbridge in speaking at the ceremony and everything was very beautiful and impressive—and a little pitiful, because poor lonely Archie Price was so very dead." Poor lonely Archie Price became the Horst Wessel of the Ham and Eggs movement.

So rapidly did the Ham and Eggs movement grow after this incident that, in 1938, its sponsors presented the Secretary of State with a petition signed by more than 750,000 residents of California asking that the $30-Every-Thursday proposal be submitted to the voters as an initiative measure. If enacted, the proposal would have involved the issuance of $30,000,000 in warrants a week or an annual turnover of $1,560,000,000 in warrant money. As soon as the politicians were informed of the number of signatures on the petition (789,000 to be exact: 25% of the registered voters of the state), they all began to shout "Ham and Eggs" in a deafening chorus, one notable exception being Robert Walker Kenny. So effectively had the Allens tended to the organizational details that, by simply sending out a call for letters, they could inundate any state official with from 25,000 to 30,000 letters in forty-eight hours. Whatever they asked their followers to do was promptly done. If they were asked to give money, they gave money; if asked to write letters, they wrote letters; if asked to march, they marched; if asked to demonstrate, they demonstrated. From the beginning of the movement to the present time, it has been characterized by the conspicuous absence of rank-and-file democratic controls. On the eve of the 1938 election, the organization thus dictatorially controlled by the Allen brothers had a regular dues-paying membership of 200,000 and the organization itself was collecting an estimated $2,000 a day in contributions. All of the advertising and radio material of the Ham and Eggs movement has, of course, always been handled through the Cinema Advertising Agency which is owned by Willis and Lawrence Allen.

This fantastic proposal came within an ace of being adopted in November, 1938, being defeated by a vote of 1,398,000 opposed to 1,143,000 in favor of the proposal. Shortly after Culbert L. Olson took office in 1938, he was presented with a petition signed by 1,103,000 residents of California calling for a special election on the Ham and Eggs proposal. Once again the proposal received a staggering vote, but not enough to win. After the 1939 election, the movement began to decline, as the increasing prosperity of the defense program began to develop in California. When Governor Olson came up for re-election in 1942, he was defeated by his Republican opponent, Earl Warren, who was mysteriously in possession of the pension vote.

Today the movement languishes. In an effort to inject some new life into the movement, the Allen brothers have been collaborating with Gerald L. K. Smith, who was introduced at a meeting of the Payroll Guarantee Association by Willis Allen as "one of the greatest citizens of the United States." This venture is not surprising, for there has always been an undercurrent of anti-Semitism in the Ham and Eggs movement. It should be emphasized that $30-Every-Thursday, unlike the Utopian Society, the self-help co-operatives, and the Epic movement, is not a product of the depression. It really dates from 1938.

QUESTIONS FOR STUDY

1. Who were the Okies and what brought them to California? What kinds of conflicts emerged between the Okies and the ranch owners? What were the sources of some of those conflicts?
2. What messages do Dorothea Lange's photographs communicate about the Depression-era migrants and the Great Depression as an event? Why do you think she took these particular images? What specific clues can you point to in the images that support your conclusions?
3. What factors might explain the increased labor unrest of the Depression years? How were strikes perceived at the time? How would you assess the significance of the Depression years to the labor movement in general?
4. Compare and contrast various programs proposed and/or implemented to try and assist people during the Great Depression (EPIC, Ham and Eggs, Townsend Plans, etc.). Did they go too far? Not far enough? What about the New Deal? What, in your opinion, is the proper role of government during an economic crisis?

CREDITS

1. Fig. 7.1: M.L. Cohen, "Pipe City," http://collections.museumca.org/?q=collection-item/a6695326. Copyright © 1932 by Oakland Museum of California. Reprinted with permission.
2. John Steinbeck, "The Harvest Gypsies," *San Francisco News*. Copyright in the Public Domain.
3. Charles Todd, "The "Okies" Search for a Lost Frontier," *The New York Times*, pp. 10-11, 17. Copyright © 1939 by The New York Times Company. Reprinted with permission.

4. Fig. 7.2: Dorothea Lange, "Mexican Mother and Child (1935)," http://www.loc.gov/pictures/item/fsa1998017774/PP/. Copyright in the Public Domain.
5. Fig. 7.3: Dorothea Lange, "Dispossessed Arkansas farmers," http://www.loc.gov/pictures/item/fsa1998018423/PP/. Copyright in the Public Domain.
6. Fig. 7.4: Dorothea Lange, "Kern County, CA Strike," http://www.loc.gov/pictures/item/fsa2000001928/PP/. Copyright in the Public Domain.
7. "2 Killed, 115 Are Injured in San Francisco Strike," *The New York Times*, pp. 1, 8. Copyright © 1934 by The New York Times Company. Reprinted with permission.
8. Fig. 7.5: Charles M. Hiller, "Golden Gate Bridge Under Construction," http://www.loc.gov/pictures/item/90713569/. Copyright in the Public Domain.
9. S. J. Woolf, "Upton Sinclair Describes His Evolution: He Has Been Novelist and Socialist; Now as a Democrat He Still Crusades," *The New York Times*, pp. 9, 17. Copyright © 1934 by The New York Times Company. Reprinted with permission.
10. Carey McWilliams, "The Good Doctor," *Southern California: An Island on the Land*, pp. 299-301. Copyright © 1946 by Estate of Carey McWilliams. Reprinted with permission.
11. Carey McWilliams, "Ham and Eggs," *Southern California: An Island on the Land*, pp. 303-308. Copyright © 1946 by Estate of Carey McWilliams. Reprinted with permission.
12. Carey McWilliams, "Repatriados," *The American Mercury*. Copyright © 1933 by Estate of Carey McWilliams. Reprinted with permission.
13. "Repatriation During the Great Depression," Mexico City, Archivo de la Secretaría de Relaciones Exteriores, http://www.digitalhistory.uh.edu/disp_textbook.cfm?smtID=3&psid=3699. Copyright in the Public Domain.

World War II

INTRODUCTION

World War II proved a watershed moment for California. Because of its Pacific location and an existing industrial base, California benefited more than any other state from the mobilization for war and from federal contracts. Its military installations, shipyards, and airplane manufacturing plants were vital components in the nation's war effort. California's scientists also played an important role in war production. The California Institute of Technology developed new designs in rocketry, and research at the University of California at Berkeley led to the development of the first atomic bomb.

The defense industry boom created an acute demand for labor. This provided an opening for groups previously denied access to well-paying industrial employment (see reading 47 "Executive Order 8802: Prohibition of Discrimination in the Defense Industry"). Women specifically became targets of a recruitment campaign that used the imaginary Rosie the Riveter to attract women to work in shipyards and aircraft manufacturing (Figures 8.1 and 8.2). In places like the Kaiser Shipyards in Richmond, African American women worked side by side with white women. Approximately one thousand women were among the more than six thousand African Americans employed at the four shipyards operated by Henry J. Kaiser in Richmond. Here, Kaiser developed methods for prefabricating and mass producing Liberty Ships, a special type of cargo ship used in the war effort. Components built all across the country were transported to shipyards, where the vessels could be assembled in record time. During the war, Kaiser could build a Liberty Ship in about two weeks at a Kaiser yard. The SS *George Washington Carver* was the second American Liberty ship to be named for an African American (Figure 8.3).

Increasingly, women employees in the state's wartime industries were married with children, creating a host of new challenges for both the women and their employers. Childcare was among the most pressing of these issues. During the war years, the federal government provided funding for temporary childcare programs in "war impact areas." The bulk of this funding came to California because the greatest share of the nation's war industries was there. Yet, even at the height of the program, only about 13 percent of children benefited from it. Henry Kaiser again proved an innovator. With funding from the United States Maritime Commission, he opened twenty-four-hour childcare centers at his shipyards to boost productivity. Mothers working in the shipyard could drop off their children at these centers. They received day care, medical attention, and even hot meals. During the war, these Kaiser centers served about four thousand children. They were closed at the end of the conflict as mothers now were expected to return to their "traditional" roles as wives and mothers (Figure 8.4).

These employment opportunities attracted more than 1.5 million new migrants to the state between 1940 and 1944. Concentrated around the major urban areas, this population growth placed heavy burdens on the local communities, which struggled to meet the demand for housing and services. Local residents blamed the newcomers for "ruining" their cities, reflective of persistent images of migrants as "poor white trash" or "ignorant Southern Negroes." Other Californians worried about unsupervised youths and teenagers, particularly those who sported zoot suits. A classic "zoot suit" consists of a long coat and baggy trousers that fit tightly at the ankle. This rebellious form of fashion was popular with young men of African American, Euro American, and Mexican American descent throughout the United States in the 1940s (Figure 8.5). In Southern California the zoot suit became synonymous with the *pachucos*, a Mexican American youth subculture. The female counterpart was the *pachuca*. The pachucos' wild dress and often rowdy public behavior created tension with white authorities, who accused them of gang and even criminal activity. This conflict built on already-existing racial tensions between Mexican Americans and Euro Americans in wartime Los Angeles. In June 1943 those tensions exploded in an event now known as the Zoot Suit Riots.

People of Japanese ancestry took the brunt of public anger about the war (see reading 48 "The Question of Japanese Americans" and reading 51 "What You and I Can Do About It"). Under political pressure, especially from California, President Roosevelt signed Executive Order 9066 on February 19, 1942 (see reading 49 "Executive Order 9066"). This order set into motion the evacuation and mass incarceration of some 120,000 persons of Japanese ancestry on the West Coast. Most of the incarcerated were Nisei, or second-generation immigrants and American citizens; about half of them were children. They spent the war years in ten "relocation centers" in remote areas of mostly the American West (Figure 8.6). Justified as a military necessity, this incarceration had a profound impact in the community—socially, emotionally, and economically (see section "Images of Internment"; Figures 8.7 and 8.8).

In 1943, famed Bay Area photographer Ansel Adams (1902–1984) documented life in California's Manzanar internment camp. In granting him access to Manzanar, authorities had instructed Adams to not directly show its barbed-wire fences or guard towers in his photographs. However, he indirectly included them by taking photographs from the towers or by having them appear far in the background (Figure 8.9). Adams later wrote that his purpose for the Manzanar photographs was "to show how these people, suffering under a great injustice, and loss of property, businesses, and professions, had overcome the sense of defeat and dispair [sic] by building for themselves a vital community in an arid (but magnificent) environment" (Figure 8.10).

Through the efforts of leaders and advocates of the Japanese American community, Congress finally passed the Civil Liberties Act of 1988, popularly known as the Japanese American Redress Bill. The bill acknowledged that "a grave injustice was done" and mandated that Congress pay each surviving victim of internment $20,000 in reparations. These payments were sent with a signed apology from the President of the United States.

WARTIME LABOR

READING 47

Executive Order 8802: Prohibition of Discrimination in the Defense Industry

June 25, 1941

REAFFIRMING POLICY OF FULL PARTICIPATION IN THE Defense Program By All Persons, Regardless Of Race, Creed, Color, Or National Origin, And Directing Certain Action In Furtherance Of Said Policy

June 25, 1941

WHEREAS it is the policy of the United States to encourage full participation in the national defense program by all citizens of the United States, regardless of race, creed, color, or national origin, in the firm belief that the democratic way of life within the Nation can be defended successfully only with the help and support of all groups within its borders; and

WHEREAS there is evidence that available and needed workers have been barred from employment in industries engaged in defense production solely because of considerations of race, creed, color, or national origin, to the detriment of workers' morale and of national unity:

NOW, THEREFORE, by virtue of the authority vested in me by the Constitution and the statutes, and as a prerequisite to the successful conduct of our national defense production effort, I do hereby reaffirm the policy of the United States that there shall be no discrimination in the employment of workers in defense industries or government because of race, creed, color, or national origin, and I do hereby declare that it is the duty of employers and of labor organizations, in furtherance of said policy and of this order, to provide for the full and equitable participation of all workers in defense industries, without discrimination because of race, creed, color, or national origin;

And it is hereby ordered as follows:

1. All departments and agencies of the Government of the United States concerned with vocational and training programs for defense production shall take special measures appropriate to assure that such programs are administered without discrimination because of race, creed, color, or national origin;
2. All contracting agencies of the Government of the United States shall include in all defense contracts hereafter negotiated by them a provision obligating the contractor not to discriminate against any worker because of race, creed, color, or national origin;
3. There is established in the Office of Production Management a Committee on Fair Employment Practice, which shall consist of a chairman and four other members to be appointed by the President. The Chairman and members of the Committee shall serve as such without compensation but shall be entitled to actual and necessary transportation, subsistence and other expenses incidental to performance of their duties. The Committee shall receive and investigate complaints of discrimination in violation of the provisions of this order and shall take appropriate steps to redress grievances which it finds to be valid. The Committee shall also recommend to the several departments and agencies of the Government of the United States and to the President all measures which may be deemed by it necessary or proper to effectuate the provisions of this order.

Franklin D. Roosevelt
The White House,
June 25, 1941.

WOMEN AND WARTIME EMPLOYMENT

FIGURE 8.1. Women at Work on a Bomber, Douglas Aircraft Company, Long Beach, California (1942)

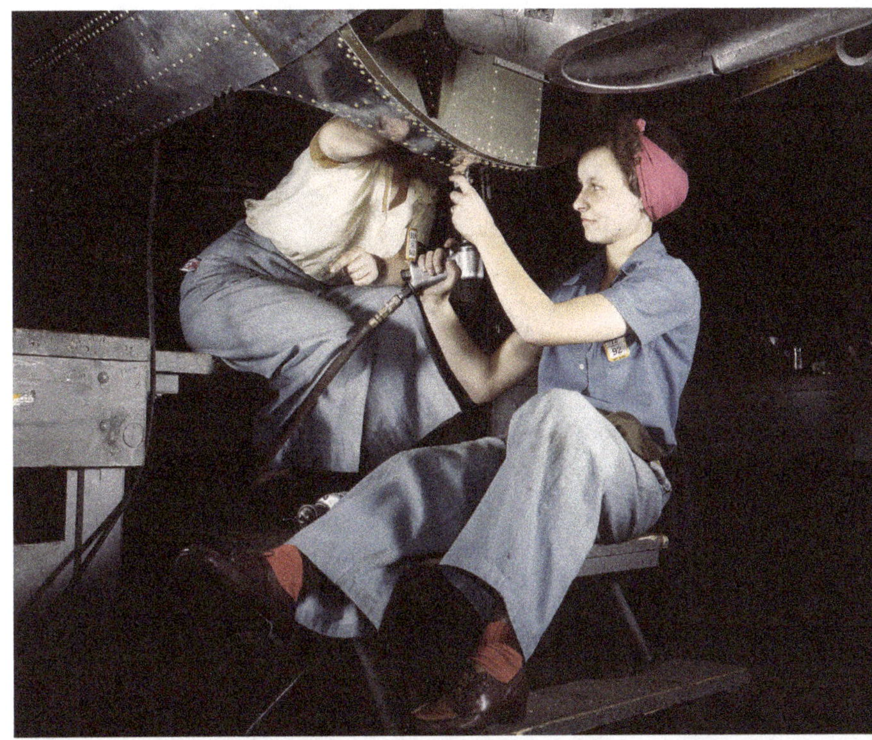

FIGURE 8.2. A "Wendy Welder" at Work at a California Shipyard (1943)

FIGURE 8.3. African-American Worker at Kaiser Shipyards (1943)

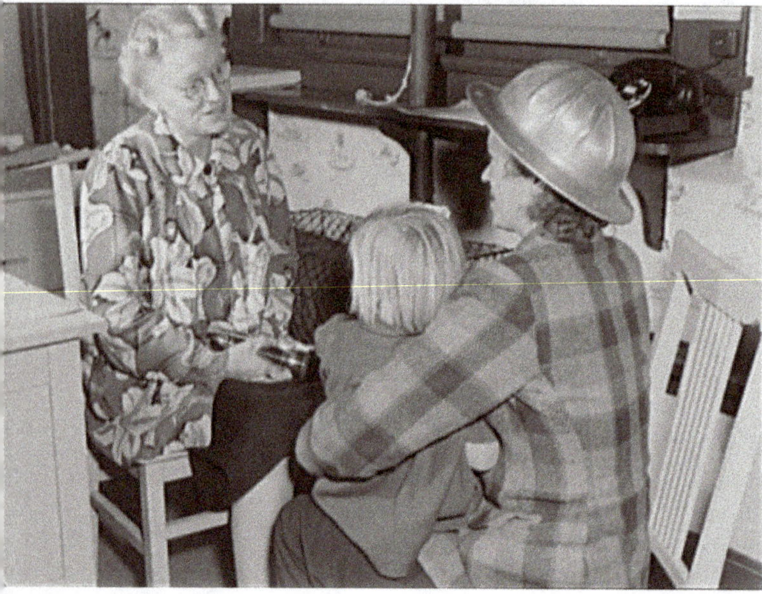

FIGURE 8.4. War Workers' Nursery. Mrs. Arlene Corbin, time checker at a Richmond shipyard, brings her daughter to a nursery school before going home to sleep after her shift that runs from midnight to 7:30 a.m. (1943)

ZOOT SUIT STYLE

FIGURE 8.5. Zoot Suits (1942)

JAPANESE AMERICANS AND INTERNMENT

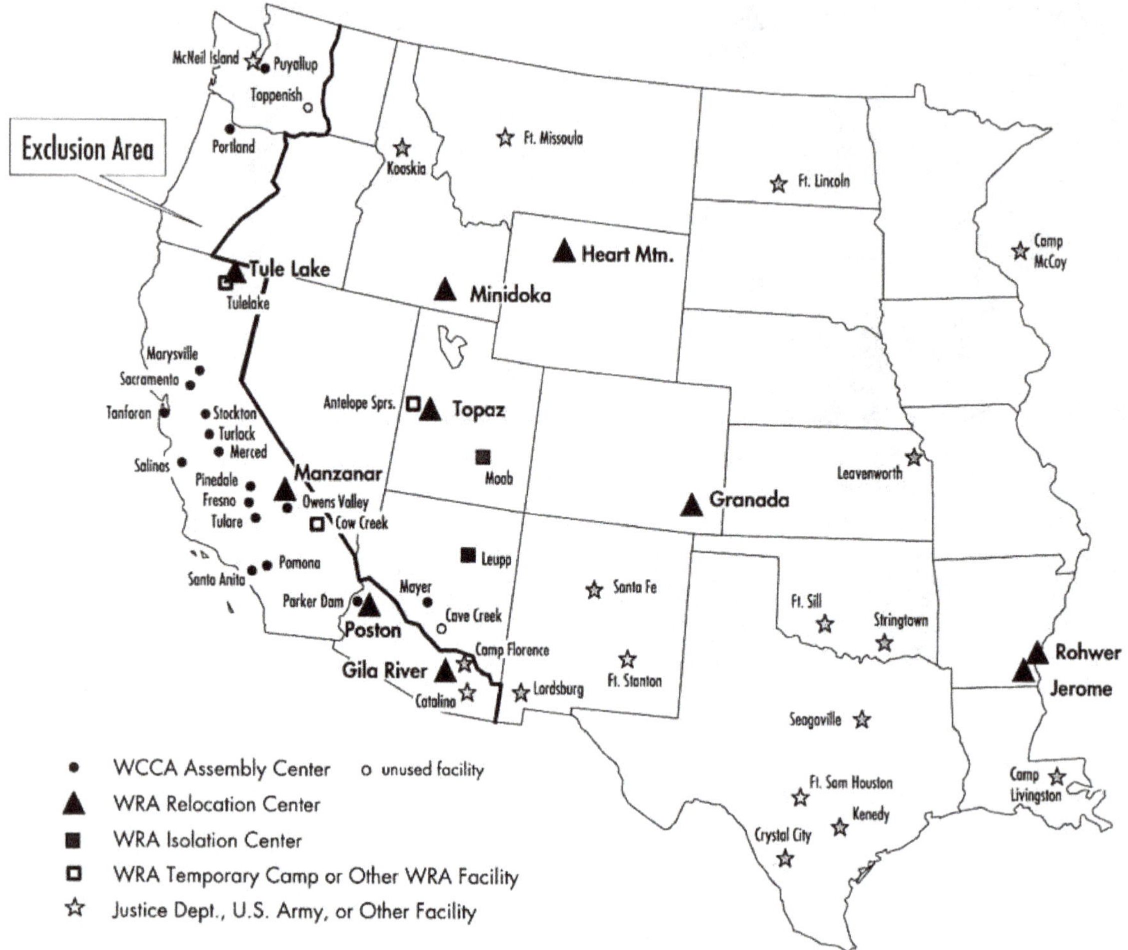

FIGURE 8.6. Map of World War II Japanese American Internment Camps

READING 48, W.H. ANDERSON

"The Question of Japanese-Americans"

***Los Angeles Times*, February 2, 1942**

PERHAPS THE MOST DIFFICULT AND DELICATE QUESTION that confronts our powers that be is the handling—the safe and proper treatment—of our American-born Japanese, our Japanese-Americans, citizens by the accident of birth, but who are Japanese nevertheless.

A viper is nonetheless a viper wherever the egg is hatched. A leopard's spots are the same and it's disposition is the same wherever it is whelped.

So a Japanese-American, born of Japanese parents, nurtured upon Japanese traditions, living in a transplanted Japanese atmosphere and thoroughly inoculated with Japanese thoughts, Japanese ideas and Japanese ideals, notwithstanding his nominal brand of accidental citizenship, almost inevitably and with the rarest of exceptions grows up to be a Japanese, not an American, in his thoughts, in his ideas and in his ideals, and himself is a potential and menacing, if not an actual, danger to our country unless properly supervised, controlled and, as it were, hamstrung.

Thus, while it might cause an injustice to a few to treat them all as potential enemies and to so limit and control their activities as to prevent the possibility of their becoming actually such, I cannot escape the conclusion—and I am by no means speaking idly or without a reasonable amount of knowledge on the subject—I cannot escape the conclusion that such treatment, as a matter of national and even personal defense, should be accorded to each and all of them while we are at war with their race.

READING 49

Executive Order 9066: Authorizing the Secretary of War to Prescribe Military Areas

February 19, 1942

WHEREAS THE SUCCESSFUL PROSECUTION OF THE WAR requires every possible protection against espionage and against sabotage to national-defense material, national-defense premises, and national-defense utilities as defined in Section 4, Act of April 20, 1918, 40 Stat. 533, as amended by the Act of November 30, 1940, 54 Stat. 1220, and the Act of August 21, 1941, 55 Stat. 655 (U.S.C., Title 50, Sec. 104);

Now, therefore, by virtue of the authority vested in me as President of the United States, and Commander in Chief of the Army and Navy, I hereby authorize and direct the Secretary of War, and the Military Commanders whom he may from time to time designate, whenever he or any designated Commander deems such action necessary or desirable, to prescribe military areas in such places and of such extent as he or the appropriate Military Commander may determine, from which any or all persons may be excluded, and with respect to which, the right of any person to enter, remain in, or leave shall be subject to whatever restrictions the Secretary of War or the appropriate Military Commander may impose in his discretion. The Secretary of War is hereby authorized to provide for residents of any such area who are excluded therefrom, such transportation, food, shelter, and other accommodations as may be necessary, in the judgment of the Secretary of War or the said Military Commander, and until other arrangements are made, to accomplish the purpose of this order. The designation of military areas in any region or locality shall supersede designations of prohibited and restricted areas by the Attorney General under the Proclamations of December 7 and 8, 1941, and shall supersede the responsibility and authority of the Attorney General under the said Proclamations in respect of such prohibited and restricted areas.

I hereby further authorize and direct the Secretary of War and the said Military Commanders to take such other steps as he or the appropriate Military Commander may deem advisable to enforce compliance with the restrictions applicable to each Military area hereinabove authorized to be designated, including the use of Federal troops and other Federal Agencies, with authority to accept assistance of state and local agencies.

I hereby further authorize and direct all Executive Departments, independent establishments and other Federal Agencies, to assist the Secretary of War or the said Military Commanders in carrying out this Executive Order, including the furnishing of medical aid, hospitalization, food, clothing, transportation, use of land, shelter, and other supplies, equipment, utilities, facilities, and services.

This order shall not be construed as modifying or limiting in any way the authority heretofore granted under Executive Order No. 8972, dated December 12, 1941, nor shall it be construed as limiting or modifying the duty and responsibility of the Federal Bureau of Investigation, with respect to the investigation of alleged acts of sabotage or the duty and responsibility of the Attorney General and the Department of Justice under the Proclamations of December 7 and 8, 1941, prescribing regulations for the conduct and control of alien enemies, except as such duty and responsibility is superseded by the designation of military areas hereunder.

Franklin D. Roosevelt
The White House, February 19, 1942.

READING 50

Instructions to All Persons of Japanese Ancestry

1942

WESTERN DEFENSE COMMAND AND FOURTH ARMY
WARTIME CIVIL CONTROL ADMINISTRATION
Presidio of San Francisco, California
April 1, 1942

INSTRUCTIONS TO ALL PERSONS OF JAPANESE ANCESTRY
Living in the Following Area:

All that portion of the City and County of San Francisco, lying generally west of the of the north-south line established by Junipero Serra Boulevard, Worchester Avenue, and Nineteenth Avenue, and lying generally north of the east-west line established by California Street, to the intersection of Market Street, and thence on Market Street to San Francisco Bay.

All Japanese persons, both alien and non-alien, will be evacuated from the above designated area by 12:00 o'clock noon Tuesday, April 7, 1942.

No Japanese person will be permitted to enter or leave the above described area after 8:00 a.m., Thursday, April 2, 1942, without obtaining special permission from the Provost Marshal at the Civil Control Station located at:

1701 Van Ness Avenue
San Francisco, California

The Following Instructions Must Be Observed:

1. A responsible member of each family, preferably the head of the family, or the person in whose name most of the property is held, and each individual living alone must report to the Civil Control Station to receive further instructions. This must be done between 8:00 a.m. and 5:00 p.m., Thursday, April 2, 1942, or between 8:00 a.m. and 5 p.m., Friday, April 3, 1942.

2. Evacuees must carry with them on departure for the Reception Center, the following property:
   a. Bedding and linens (no mattress) for each member of the family.
   b. Toilet articles for each member of the family.
   c. Extra clothing for each member of the family.
   d. Sufficient knives, forks, spoons, plates, bowls and cups for each member of the family.
   e. Essential personal effects for each member of the family.

   All items carried will be securely packaged, tied and plainly marked with the name of the owner and numbered in accordance with instructions received at the Civil Control Station.

   The size and number of packages is limited to that which can be carried by the individual or family group.

3. The United States Government through its agencies will provide for the storage at the sole risk of the owner of the more substantial household

items, such as iceboxes, washing machines, pianos and other heavy furniture. Cooking utensils and other small items will be accepted if crated, packed and plainly marked with the name and address of the owner. Only one name and address will be used by a given family.

4. Each family, and individual living alone, will be furnished transportation to the Reception Center. Private means of transportation will not be utilized. All instructions pertaining to the movement will be obtained at the Civil Control Station.

5. Go to the Civil Control Station at 1701 Van Ness Avenue, San Francisco, California, between 8:00 a.m. and 5:00 p.m., Thursday, April 2, 1942, or between 8:00 a.m. and 5:00 p.m., Friday, April 3, 1942, to receive further instructions.

J. L. DeWITT
Lieutenant General, U. S. Army
Commanding

READING 51

"What You and I Can Do About It"

***Los Angeles Times*, January 29, 1944**

IT IS WITH A FEELING OF HELPLESS RAGE THAT MOST OF us read of the barbaric practices visited by the Japanese upon Allied prisoners of war, Americans particularly. We search our souls for words adequately to denounce their callous atrocities, and fail to find them. Calling the authors of these inhuman tortures brutes and savages is merely to insult the real brutes and most, at least, of the primitives. To retort in kind upon the Jap prisoners and internees in our hands would merely be to lower ourselves to the same level of fiendish cruelty as that which horrifies and infuriates us. Comparatively few of us have weapons of war to use and fewer still have enemy Japs available on whom to use them.

As a matter of fact, there is plenty that we can do about it. Any of us.

Write your own ticket. The madder you are and the more Japs you want to kill in legitimate reprisal for the 7000 or more helpless heroes of Bataan who were starved, beaten and tortured to death in Jap prison camps, the larger should be your subscription to the Fourth War Loan.

Don't just take it out in talking. Very few Japs understand English anyway. But War Bonds are embryo machine guns and machine guns speak very fluent Japanese. Send a few—or several—of them over to deliver your personal opinion of what, in one of his lucid moments, Hitler referred to as the Japanese vermin. Enough of these will help speed up the slow-moving war in the Pacific.

If we are members of labor unions engaged in war Industries, the next time someone suggests that we stop production of Jap-killing weapons to agitate for higher wages or something, we can tell him to go to—well, call it Japan. It's almost the same thing, or will be after we get through sending Japs thither.

If we are not unionists, we can still help the loyal and patriotic majority of them to make it unhealthy to strike or to talk strike at the expense of servicemen who may thereby become prisoners of war and die miserable, lingering deaths at the hands of Jap murderers.

In an indirect but not too negative way, the Army-Navy revelations of enemy treatment of prisoners may help to straighten out or at least to shut up the sappy Jap-lovers who are emptying our internment camps and loosing potential spies and saboteurs on the country at large, against the earnest advice of our best-informed military authorities. In an apparent attempt to backfire the sworn McCoy-Mellnik-Dyess record, Tokyo is "protesting" against our treatment of Jap Internees. It is true that it has been scandalous—the scandal being that the Nips held under this soft restraint have been better fed, housed and otherwise privileged than a great many free Americans.

As Gen. DeWitt remarked: "A Jap is always a Jap."

IMAGES OF INTERNMENT

FIGURE 8.7. Air Raid Shelter Poster next to an Evacuation Order Poster, San Francisco (1942)

FIGURE 8.8. Temporary Assembly Center at Pomona Fairgrounds (1942)

FIGURE 8.9. Internment Camp at Manzanar, Photo by Ansel Adams (1943)

FIGURE 8.10. Group of Internees Reading Manzanar Newspaper, Photo by Ansel Adams (1943)

QUESTIONS FOR STUDY

1. In what significant ways did World War II set the stage for the future development of California?
2. What opportunities did wartime employment create for women? What kinds of challenges did this employment present?
3. If you were a Californian at the time, would you have defended internment? Would you have been likely to oppose it and with what arguments? What would have been the reaction to your opposition? How does the debate over internment reflect previous attitudes and prejudices against Asians? What safeguards do we have in place to prevent something like this from happening again?
4. If you were a person of Japanese ancestry at the time of evacuation orders and internment, how might you have felt about it? What options were there for opposing evacuation? What do the images in this chapter tell us about the experience and the ways in which the internees were trying to cope with it?

CREDITS

1. Franklin D. Roosevelt, "Executive Order 8802: Prohibition of Discrimination in the Defense Industry," http://www.ourdocuments.gov/doc.php?flash=true&doc=72. Copyright in the Public Domain.
2. Fig. 8.1: Alfred T. Palmer, "Women working at Douglas Aircraft," http://en.wikipedia.org/wiki/File:Women_working_at_Douglas_Aircraft.jpg. Copyright in the Public Domain.
3. Fig. 8.2: Ann Rosener, "A 'Wendy Welder' at work at a California shipyard (1943)," U.S. Office of War Information, http://www.loc.gov/pictures/item/oem2002008377/PP/. Copyright in the Public Domain.
4. Fig. 8.3: Ann Rosener, "African American worker Richmond Shipyards," U.S. Office of War Information, http://commons.wikimedia.org/wiki/File:African_American_worker_Richmond_Shipyards.jpg. Copyright in the Public Domain.
5. Fig. 8.4: Ann Rosener, " WWII daycare Richmond CA," U.S. Office of War Information, http://commons.wikimedia.org/wiki/File:WWII_daycare_Richmond_CA.jpg. Copyright in the Public Domain.
6. Fig. 8.5: John Ferrell, "Zoot Suites," https://commons.wikimedia.org/wiki/File:Zootsuit2.jpg. Copyright in the Public Domain.

7. Fig. 8.6: "Map of World War II Japanese American internment camps," U.S. National Parks Service, http://commons.wikimedia.org/wiki/File:Map_of_World_War_II_Japanese_American_internment_camps.jpg. Copyright in the Public Domain.
8. W.H. Anderson, "The Question of Japanese Americans," *Los Angeles Times*. Copyright in the Public Domain.
9. Franklin D. Roosevelt, "Executive Order 9066: Resulting in the Relocation of Japanese," http://www.ourdocuments.gov/doc.php?flash=true&doc=74&page=transcript. Copyright in the Public Domain.
10. Lieutenant General J. L. DeWitt, "Instructions to All Persons of Japanese Ancestry." Copyright in the Public Domain.
11. "What You and I Can Do About It," *Los Angeles Times*. Copyright in the Public Domain.
12. Fig. 8.7: Dorothea Lange, "Air raid shelter poster next to an evacuation order poster, San Francisco, 1942," U.S. Farm Security Administration, http://commons.wikimedia.org/wiki/File:San_Francisco,_California._On_a_brick_wall_beside_air_raid_shelter_poster,_exclusion_orders_were_po_._._._-_NARA_-_536018.jpg. Copyright in the Public Domain.
13. Fig. 8.8: Clem Albers, "Pomona Fairgrounds Assembly Center," War Relocation Authority, http://en.wikipedia.org/wiki/File:Pomona,_California._General_view_of_assembly_center_being_constructed_on_Pomona_Fair_Grounds_for_ev_._._._-_NARA_-_536837.jpg. Copyright in the Public Domain.
14. Fig. 8.9: Ansel Adams, "Ansel Adams - Manzanar," http://commons.wikimedia.org/wiki/File:Ansel_Adams_-_Manzanar_LC-DIG-ppprs-00276.jpg. Copyright in the Public Domain.
15. Fig. 8.10: Ansel Adams, "Ansel Adams Manzanar," http://commons.wikimedia.org/wiki/File:Ansel_Adams_Manzanar_-_Roy_Takeno_(Editor)_and_group_reading_Manzanar_pap_-_LOC_ppprs-00006.jpg. Copyright in the Public Domain.

09

Postwar California and the Problem of Growth

INTRODUCTION

After a brief respite immediately following the end of World War II, the California economy entered one of the longest periods of growth in history. The war years had stimulated the development of industries, and even more important, the federal government continued its spending in the state. As part of the Cold War defense buildup, it poured billions of dollars into private sector defense contracts, creating what President Eisenhower later called America's "military-industrial complex." California's universities also benefited from this spending, providing research experience and expertise to federal projects. In addition, the federal G.I. Bill funded education for returning veterans, resulting in the explosive growth of the state's educational institutions. One example of these connections between higher education and the defense industry are the Rocket Boys. These were young engineers (or "rocketeers" as they

FIGURE 9.1. Science and Technology in California. The "Rocket Boys" in the Arroyo Seco near Pasadena (1936). From left to right: Rudolph Schott, Apollo Milton Olin Smith, Frank Malina, Ed Forman, and Jack Parsons.

nicknamed themselves) encouraged by the California Institute of Technology professor Theodore von Karman. They performed their first successful rocket experiment in the nearby Arroyo Seco in Pasadena in November 1936 (Figure 9.1). The first buildings of what later became the Jet Propulsion Laboratory (JPL) were built near this site in 1940. In 1958, JPL became part of the nation's space agency NASA.

With the economy booming, Californians enjoyed unprecedented prosperity, attracting a wave of new migrants. The state added more than one million people every two years between 1951 and 1963. They spilled out into the growing suburbs, where developers rushed to meet the demand for housing and the new residents pursued the "California lifestyle" in their single-family homes. The federal government fueled this move to the suburbs by offering generous home loans to war veterans, and tax benefits for home ownership. Aggressive building of highway systems and the parallel rise in automobile ownership contributed to the development of suburban communities. But the conformity of the suburbs also had its critics. Malvina Reynolds (1900–1978) was a folk singer, songwriter, and political activist, born in San Francisco. She came up with the song "Little Boxes" in 1962 while driving by the housing developments around Daly City, built in the postwar years by developer Henry Doelger. The song satirizes the middle-class conformity associated with the postwar suburban development (see reading 52 "Little Boxes").

The rapid economic and population growth of the postwar period brought with it a host of issues and concerns that defied solutions at the individual or municipal level. Increasingly, Californians were looking to government to regulate and guide change. Education was one key battleground. In 1947 young Sylvia Mendez was turned away from a public school in Orange County because it was for "whites only." Her father responded by taking four Los Angeles-area school districts to court (see reading 53 "*Mendez v. Westminster*"). The US Appeals Court for the Ninth Circuit affirmed the lower court's ruling. Two months later, Governor Earl Warren signed a bill ending school segregation, making California the first state in the country to officially desegregate its public schools.

Republican governors Earl Warren and his successor Goodwin J. Knight both adopted liberal policies. They expanded governmental services; improved the state's infrastructures; and invested in health, welfare, and education. In 1958, Democrat Edmund G. "Pat" Brown swept into office with nearly 60 percent of the vote and impeccable liberal credentials. He expanded on existing social programs, financing them with tax increases. Brown also tackled the issue of the state's dwindling water resources and overcame opposition to the California Water Project to expand the state's water infrastructure (see reading 54 "Brown Vows to Resolve All Water Issues" and Figure 9.2). And he vigorously supported the Master Plan for Higher Education that reorganized the state's higher education system into three tiers (University of California, California State University, and the community colleges) to meet the demands of a growing college population. But these liberal policies always operated against fears of Communism (see reading 55 "State of California Loyalty Oath") and a backdrop of conservatism (see reading 56 "La Cañada Woman, Mother of 2, Heads Young Republicans in State"). The election of Brown specifically produced a conservative backlash.

The postwar years also witnessed the 1955 opening of Disneyland, an icon and a globally popular, idealized version of American popular culture (see reading 57 "Dream Comes True in Orange Grove"). Walt Disney himself arrived in Los Angeles in 1923 and elevated animated films to an art form. During the war years he kept his studio afloat by producing government propaganda and training films. A firm believer in new technologies, Disney forayed into television in 1950, and with his business partners launched Disneyland, Inc., to build an amusement park in Anaheim. Reflecting Disney's conservative political views, Disneyland is a representation of a mythical America, designed to provide an escape from the stresses of urban, industrial life. It is a place of consumption, reflective of the decade in which it was imagined. In addition to Disneyland, Hollywood and Southern California became iconic as the center of a surfer culture. Polynesians like Hawaii's Duke Paoa Kahanamoku helped introduce the sport to California in the 1920s (Figure 9.3). Military personnel who had spent time in the Pacific during the war helped popularize surfing in the 1950s and 1960s. Even Hollywood caught the wave. Annette Funicello (1942–2013) rose to prominence in the 1950s as one of the most popular Mouseketeers in the original Mickey Mouse Club. The Mickey Mouse Club was Disney's television variety show for children, an effort to reach out to young audiences at a time when television was becoming a presence in American popular culture—and the center of the suburban lifestyle. Funicello made a successful transition to a movie and singing career. Together with Frankie Avalon, she helped popularize the 1960s beach party film genre. From Muscle Beach in Venice to the surf in Santa Cruz, the promotion of California's beach lifestyle of sun and fun further reinforced popular stereotypes about California (Figure 9.4). For millions of tourists from around the globe, no trip to the state is complete without a visit to the beach. California has learned to capitalize on its unique appeal. The tourist industry now supports more than a million jobs in California. In 2015 alone, tourism generated more than five billion dollars in state tax receipts, making tourism one of the most vital and important sectors of California's economy.

SUBURBIA

READING 52, MALVINA REYNOLDS

"Little Boxes"

1962

Little boxes on the hillside,
Little boxes made of ticky tacky,
Little boxes on the hillside,
Little boxes all the same.
There's a green one and a pink one
And a blue one and a yellow one,
And they're all made out of ticky tacky
And they all look just the same.

And the people in the houses
All went to the university,
Where they were put in boxes
And they came out all the same,
And there's doctors and lawyers,
And business executives,
And they're all made out of ticky tacky
And they all look just the same.

And they all play on the golf course
And drink their martinis dry,
And they all have pretty children
And the children go to school,
And the children go to summer camp
And then to the university,
Where they are put in boxes
And they come out all the same.

And the boys go into business
And marry and raise a family
In boxes made of ticky tacky
And they all look just the same.
There's a green one and a pink one
And a blue one and a yellow one,
And they're all made out of ticky tacky
And they all look just the same.

RACE AND EDUCATION IN CALIFORNIA

READING 53

Mendez v. Westminster

1947

THAT ALL CHILDREN OR PERSONS OF MEXICAN OR LATIN descent or extraction, though Citizens of the United States of America...have been and are now excluded from attending, using, enjoying and receiving the benefits of the education, health and recreation facilities of certain schools within their respective Districts and Systems....

In the Westminister, Garden Grove and El Modeno school districts the respective boards of trustees had taken official action, declaring that there be no segregation of pupils on a racial basis but that non-English-speaking children...be required to attend schools designated by the boards separate and apart from English-speaking pupils; that such group should attend such schools until they had acquired some proficiency in the English language.

The petitioners contend that such official action evinces a covert attempt by the school authorities in such school districts to produce an arbitrary discrimination against school children of Mexican extraction or descent and that such illegal result has been established in such school districts respectively....

The ultimate question for decision may be thus stated: Does such official action of defendant district school agencies and the usages and practices pursued by the respective school authorities as shown by the evidence operate to deny or deprive the so-called non-English-speaking school children of Mexican ancestry or descent within such school districts of the equal protection of the laws?...

We think they are....

We think the pattern of public education promulgated in the Constitution of California and effectuated by provisions of the Education Code of the State prohibits segregation of the pupils of Mexican ancestry in the elementary schools from the rest of the school children.

...The common segregation attitudes and practices of the school authorities in the defendant school districts in Orange County pertain solely to children of Mexican ancestry and parentage. They are singled out as a class for segregation. Not only is such method of public school administration contrary to the general requirements of the school laws of the State, but we think it indicates an official school policy that is antagonistic in principle to...the Education Code of the State....

We perceive in the laws relating to the public educational system in the State of California a clear purpose to avoid and forbid distinctions among pupils based upon race or ancestry except in specific situations not pertinent to this action. Distinctions of that kind have recently been declared by the highest judicial authority of the United States "by their very nature odious to a free people whose institutions are founded upon the doctrine of equality." They are said to be "utterly inconsistent with American traditions and ideals."...

The evidence clearly shows that Spanish-speaking children are retarded in learning English by lack of exposure to its use because of segregation, and that commingling of the entire student body instills and develops a common cultural attitude among the school children which is imperative for the perpetuation of American institutions and ideals. It is also established by the record that the methods of segregation prevalent in the defendant school districts foster antagonisms in the children and suggest inferiority among them where none exists....

WATER AND GROWTH

FIGURE 9.2. California Water Project

READING 54

"Brown Vows to Resolve All Water Issues"

***Los Angeles Times*, September 23, 1959**

GOV. BROWN PROMISED THE PEOPLE OF CALIFORNIA today that he would resolve all the major policy problems on water before they vote on a $1.75 billion water-bond issue.

The governor spoke at ground-breaking ceremonies for Frenchman Reservoir near here and called it the "formal start of the moving of dirt" for California's gigantic water program.

He pointed out that in November of 1960 the people will vote on a bond issue to provide funds for transporting northern water to thirsty Southern California. It also will allow completion of four remaining reservoirs in the upper Feather River service area.

Reviews Benefits

He reviewed benefits to Northern California from the proposed bond issue. These include $130 million for local projects, North and South Bay aqueducts and an aqueduct serving the Southern San Joaquin Valley.

"We will have contract principles, we will have rates for water established before you are asked to vote on the bond issue in November of 1960 and as far in advance of that time as is humanly possible," Brown said.

The governor said preliminary work toward this end already is being done.

Studying Needs

"We are studying power needs and power output to determine the best manner in which power can be utilized for the greatest public good," he said.

On the problem so-called "unjust enrichment" of interests along the huge spiderweb of canals, criticized in legislative committees and by state AFL-CIO Brown reiterated a previous stand in saying that "no single individual or group of individuals will obtain more than his fair share of the benefits to be derived from the state's investment..."

COLD WAR POLITICS

READING 55

State of California Loyalty Oath

1957

CALIFORNIA CONSTITUTION
ARTICLE 20: MISCELLANEOUS SUBJECTS

SEC. 3. Members of the Legislature, and all public officers and employees, executive, legislative, and judicial, except such inferior officers and employees as may be by law exempted, shall, before they enter upon the duties of their respective offices, take and subscribe the following oath or affirmation:

"I, ______, do solemnly swear (or affirm) that I will support and defend the Constitution of the United States and the Constitution of the State of California against all enemies, foreign and domestic; that I will bear true faith and allegiance to the Constitution of the United States and the Constitution of the State of California; that I take this obligation freely, without any mental reservation or purpose of evasion; and that I will well and faithfully discharge the duties upon which I am about to enter.

"And I do further swear (or affirm) that I do not advocate, nor am I a member of any party or organization, political or otherwise, that now advocates the overthrow of the Government of the United States or of the State of California by force or violence or other unlawful means; that within the five years immediately preceding the taking of this oath (or affirmation) I have not been a member of any party or organization, political or otherwise, that advocated the overthrow of the Government of the United States or of the State of California by force or violence or other unlawful means except as follows:

____

(If no affiliations, write in the words "No Exceptions")

and that during such time as I hold the office of ______________I will not advocate nor become a member of any party or organization, political or otherwise, that advocates the overthrow of the Government of the United States or of the State of California by force or violence or other unlawful means."

And no other oath, declaration, or test, shall be required as a qualification for any public office or employment. "Public officer and employee" includes every officer and employee of the State, including the University of California, every county, city, city and county, district, and authority, including any department, division, bureau, board, commission, agency, or instrumentality of any of the foregoing.

READING 56

"La Canada Woman, Mother of 2, Heads Young Republicans in State"

***Los Angeles Times*, February 15, 1960**

MRS. VIRGINIA (GINGER) SAVELL, LA CANADA HOUSEwife, mother of two children and past president of Los Angeles County Young Republicans, was elected president of the California Young Republicans yesterday as the organization's three-day convention ended with adoption of a resolution favoring Richard Nixon for President.

Mrs. Savell won over Frank Creede Jr., who entered tardily from Fresno County but waged a vigorous campaign up to the balloting. She succeeds Alan H. Nichols of San Francisco. The new president was a delegate to the national YR biennial conventions in 1957 and last year was one of 10 Young Republicans chosen nationally to represent the United States in a NATO "youth-in-politics" project.

The election took place in the Statler Hilton at an action-packed session at which the delegates issued a "black paper" criticizing Democratic leadership and adopted numerous resolutions on major issues.

Besides Mrs. Savell, officers chosen were:

National committeeman, Pete Ashen, San Francisco
National committeewoman, Helen Johnson, Orange
Executive vice president, Russell Clarke, Mendocino
Secretary, Carol Brost, Santa Clara

Assistant secretary, Wilma Dickerhoff, Los Angeles
Treasurer, Richard Noble, San Mateo
Assistant treasurer, Joyce Weisz, Alameda
General counsel, Harry Keaton, Los Angeles
Sergeant at arms, Dan Ferniel, San Francisco
Chaplain, Jim Goodhue, Contra Costa

The "black paper" dealing with the Democratic Party made observations as follows:

> "Defense—While professing great military knowledge, the Democratic Party still cannot explain why they were not prepared in 1941 and in 1950 with an adequate military program to defend America.
>
> "Primaries—In all its wisdom, the California Democrat Councils has chided the GOP for having only a single major candidate for President...then they vote to restrict the California Democrats to sometime Presidential candidate Pat Brown.
>
> "CDC—Unwilling to accept the legal and constituted political organization as provided in the California Constitution, the CDC bypasses the California voter and runs the Democrat Party in the tradition of great machines like Tammany and Pendergast.
>
> "Issues—In hunting desperately for issues, the Democrats are willing to provide our enemies with secret military information and the resulting headlines give the Russians an American blueprint of defense in letters a foot high for the sake of a vote.
>
> "Leader-less—With wails of anguish over what they call 'lack of leadership,' neither the Democrat Party nor its 10 of 13 Presidential candidates are able to offer a single program to Americans in areas like civil rights, labor, defense."

Resolutions adopted included a statement "that the $1.75 billion bond issue for the State Water Plan should provide legislative directives that the water projects will pay for themselves by adequate charges to users of water and power and that Gov. Brown should call a special session of the legislature to enact such guarantees before the people vote on the bond issue next November."

Another resolution declared for abolishment of the Consumers' Counsel and Economic Development Agency, creations of the present administration.

Former Gov. Goodwin J. Knight had attacked the offices as unnecessary on the previous day.

The delegates held that "the right to freedom of expression is being undermined by the recent California court decision upholding the action of a union in expelling one of its members in reprisal for his support of a proposition." They resolved that the Young Republicans urge the legislature to enact laws that will permit union members to express their opinions without being subject to the threat of expulsion or forced resignation.

The delegates took note of abuses committed under welfare laws and resolved that their organization should urge the Legislature to study and pass necessary legislation to correct the situation. Another resolution favored exemption of public schools from payment of sales taxes. Still another urged Gov. Brown to call a special session to deal with the narcotic problem.

A resolution noted that the governor's budget for 1960-61 calls for $2,477,122,000, or $184,307,000 more than the 1959-60 budget and put the organization on record against the increase. The Legislature was asked to cut the budget wherever possible.

The delegates took a stand supporting the referee plan proposed for supervision of state and federal elections in which discrimination is charged.

In still another resolution the Young Republicans took note of President Eisenhower's pledge of 1952 to conduct the government on the basis of what is best for the American family, declared that the policy had been of great and lasting benefit and resolute to adopt the phrase "Republican – the Family Party" as a credo of political action.

A committee will choose the place for the next convention.

DISNEYLAND

READING 57

"Dream Comes True in Orange Grove: Disneyland to Open Tomorrow"

***Los Angeles Times*, July 17, 1955**

A DREAM COMES TRUE TOMORROW—DISNEYLAND OPENS.

It has been exactly a year and a day since ground was broken for this multimillion-dollar magic kingdom which Walt Disney has created on what used to be a 160-acre orange grove in Anaheim.

Undoubtedly destined to become one of Southern California's greatest attractions, Disneyland is also a prime proof that dreams do not come true all by themselves. For into this spectacular project has gone meticulous planning almost awesome in its details.

It seems somewhat incongruous that such a large and fabulous place should have an address, but its exact location is 1313 Harbor Blvd., Anaheim.

As practically everyone in the world already knows, Disneyland has five sections, all distinctly different and yet all cleverly blended—Adventureland, Frontierland, Fantasyland, Tommorowland and Main Street.

They are peopled by Davy Crocketts, Peter Pans, Snow Whites, Captain Hooks, Dumbos and other Disney characters, including, of course, Mickey Mouse.

Keynote of the park is delightful realism—on a five-eighths scale.

In Adventureland, there's a ride in an explorer's boat through a jungle filled with lifelike snapping crocodiles, chattering monkeys, and stalking lions and tigers. To make this section truly authentic, trees ranging in age from 30 to 50 years were imported from South Africa, South America, Australia, New Zealand, China and Japan.

In Frontierland is the Mark Twain, a 105-foot paddle-wheel riverboat which plies the park's picturesque Rivers of America section. Also in this section, of course, is an authentic frontier town—plus a stagecoach ride through the Painted Desert under full-scale Indian attack.

Entrance to Fantasyland is through Sleeping Beauty Castle. Inside is the Peter Pan Fly Through to take children on an aerial trip over London and the Thames. And it's lucky it's an aerial trip because, along the way, cannonading pirates fire table-tennis balls. Capt. Hook swings his vicious hook in frustration and there are all sorts of other narrow escapes.

Also in Fantasyland is the King Arthur Carousel which, with 78 horses—and some of them jumping horses at that—is reportedly the world's largest merry-go-round.

In Tomorrowland, naturally, is a rocket trip to the moon. While other sections of the park required much painstaking research into the past for authentic designs and materials, Tomorrowland presented an unusual situation. Designers created everything from spaceships to stools and chairs as they think everyday articles will look in the future.

On Main St. is located the Santa Fe & Disneyland Railroad Station, passenger terminal for the two 5/8-scale trains carrying as many as 300 passengers and which, operated like a regular railroad, travel the perimeter of the entire park.

Replica of an American town in the 1890-1910 era, Main St. also is the location of Disneyland tenants—restaurants and shops.

Unique Logistics

Here are the details of some of the meticulous planning that went into the project: It took three cities to supply the 100-year-old gas lamps that line Main St. and which will be set aglow each evening at dusk by a costumed lamplighter. Cresting and railing for some of the buildings came from old plantations in the South and some came from San Francisco, Oakland and Sacramento.

An old Los Angeles mansion, with its wood paneling, stained-glass windows and crystal chandelier, supplied much of the interior of the Delmonico-style restaurant and other portions of Main St. buildings.

Statistically speaking, 3,500,000 board feet of lumber went into construction of Disneyland. The park, including its huge parking lot, contains 3,000,000 square feet of paving. There were 350,000 cubic yards of dirt removed, a large part of it in excavations for the waterways and in building the 15-foot-high, artistically landscaped embankment that entirely surrounds the park. Approximately $500,000 worth of trees and shrubs were imported and transplanted.

During the year's construction, 800 workmen—most of them skilled craftsmen—were employed in the building of Disneyland but this number has been upped to 2500 (working in 10-hour shifts) as the opening date neared.

Permanent employees at Disneyland will number from 850 to 1000 and their positions will range from bus boys to riverboat captains, from cowboys to receptionists. Each employee has been hand-picked. And Disneyland officials are so determined to maintain a distinct atmosphere within the park that all employees have been required to attend orientation classes as part of a training course in Disneyland policies, to become acquainted with what they call "the Disneyland way of life."

POPULAR CULTURE IN POSTWAR CALIFORNIA

FIGURE 9.3. Duke Paoa Kahanamoku (c. 1920)

FIGURE 9.4. Actors Annette Funicello and Frankie Avalon (mid-1960s)

QUESTIONS FOR STUDY

1. What argument is Malvina Reynolds making about the impact of 1950s suburbia on the people living there? What do you think of that argument? Can you relate this argument to contemporary California?

2. What argument does the Mendez v. Westminster decision make about segregation of Mexican and Mexican American children from Anglo children in public schools? How does this decision compare to the more commonly-known 1954 U.S. Supreme Court decision in Brown v. Board of Education?
3. Why did the state of California implement a loyalty oath for state employees in 1952? Reading the text of the oath, are there any people you think might object to signing it? If so, who and why? The state still requires this oath today. In your opinion, is this a good idea or a bad one? Why?
4. What do the sources in this chapter tell us about the opportunities in postwar California? What limits were there to these opportunities? Why?

CREDITS

1. Fig. 9.1: "Science and Technology at Midcentury," NASA/Jet Propulsion Laboratory, http://www.jpl.nasa.gov/jplhistory/captions/rocketboys-t.php. Copyright in the Public Domain.
2. Malvina Reynolds, "Little Boxes." Copyright © 1962 by Schroder Music Company. Reprinted with permission.
3. "Mendez v. Westminster," http://www.digitalhistory.uh.edu/disp_textbook.cfm?smtID=3&psid=607. Copyright in the Public Domain.
4. Fig. 9.2: Copyright © Shannon1 (CC BY-SA 4.0) at http://commons.wikimedia.org/wiki/File:State_water_project.jpg.
5. "Brown Vows to Resolve All Water Issues," *Los Angeles Times*, pp. 7. Copyright © 1959 by United Press International (UPI). Reprinted with permission.
6. "Article 20," Constitution of the State of California. Copyright in the Public Domain.
7. "La Canada Woman, Mother of 2, Heads Young Republicans in State," *Los Angeles Times*. Copyright © 1960 by Los Angeles Times Syndicate. Reprinted with permission.
8. "Dream Comes True in Orange Grove: Disneyland, Multimillion Dollar Magic Kingdom, to Open Tomorrow," *Los Angeles Times*. Copyright in the Public Domain.
9. Fig. 9.3: "Anonymous Photograph of Duke Paoa Kahanamoku," http://commons.wikimedia.org/wiki/File:Anonymous_photograph_of_Duke_Paoa_Kahanamoku_with_his_surfboard.JPG. Copyright in the Public Domain.
10. Fig. 9.4: "Beach Party Annette Funicello Frankie Avalon Mid-1960s," http://commons.wikimedia.org/wiki/File:Beach_Party_Annette_Funicello_Frankie_Avalon_Mid-1960s.jpg. Copyright in the Public Domain.

10 Conflicted California

INTRODUCTION

The postwar era produced an unprecedented period of growth in California and the nation. This era emphasized the American values of freedom, democracy, individual rights, economic opportunity, equality, private property, and free enterprise. Yet, there were cracks in this American Dream, and the civil rights movement brought them to the surface. This movement for black equality in the South engendered a series of social movements that culminated in the decade of the 1960s. In California, student dissent against the conformist values of the postwar years began on the Berkeley campus as early as 1957, when the student government raised the issue of discrimination on campus. By 1960, students were protesting the House Un-American Activities Committee hearings at San Francisco City Hall, and were arrested. Four years later, after having volunteered as part of the Freedom Summer to register black voters in the American South,

Mario Savio and a group of his fellow students formed the Free Speech Movement (FSM) in opposition to a ban on political speech on campus. The FSM resulted in the arrest of hundreds of persons for occupying the administration building; the removal of the campus administration; and an expansion of student rights for political activity and debate on campus. It was the first of the 1960s student movements to make headlines all over the world (see reading 59 "Thirty Years Later"; Figure 10.2). The administration's view is represented in the excerpt from the memoir of Clark Kerr, who served as the president of the University of California during its years of turbulence (see reading 58 "Things Start to Fall Apart").

FIGURE 10.1. Ronald Reagan

This movement for free speech also helped launch the political career of Ronald Reagan. Reagan had arrived in Hollywood in 1937 to work in the film industry. During World War II, he served in the Army Air Force Motion Picture Unit in Culver City, making movies that cultivated a positive image of America in the war. At war's end he returned to Hollywood and became active in the Screen Actors Guild, serving as its president from 1947 to 1952, and again from 1959 to 1960. In 1952 Reagan became the host of General Electric': Theater, an experience he later credited for honing his oratorical skills (Figure 10.1). In the process, the registered Democrat grew into a recognized conservative spokesman and changed his party affiliation in 1964, when he spoke on behalf of conservative Republican presidential candidate Barry Goldwater in a stunning national debut. In his successful campaign for governor of California in 1966, his first elective office, he attacked the events on the Berkeley campus, cementing what would remain a turbulent relationship between Reagan and California's leading institution for public higher education. After his election, Reagan promptly fired the university president, Clark Kerr.

Despite California's reputation as a bastion of liberalism, racial equality remained elusive in the Golden State. One area of conflict was housing. In response to activists' calls for fair housing legislation, Assemblyman William Byron Rumford sponsored a sweeping bill that called for an end to racial discrimination in all public and private housing. When it finally passed in September 1963, the California Fair Housing Act, generally known as the Rumford Act, had been watered down by Republican legislators, exempting most forms of private and single housing. Yet, the California Real Estate Association immediately launched a repeal campaign, exploiting the growing hostility toward all liberal social programs and promoting "property owner rights." As a result, Proposition 14 passed in November 1964 with 2-to-1 majority to repeal the Act (see reading 60 "Byron Rumford Remembers Housing Discrimination in California" and Figure 10.3).

Although the California Supreme Court restored the Rumford Act in 1967, ruling Proposition 14 illegal, the damage had been done. The proposition was among the contributing factors to the growing isolation of impoverished minority communities across California. In the majority black Watts neighborhood of Los Angeles, the brutality of the mostly white police department served as the final catalyst for mounting anger. The Watts Riots in August 1965 raged for six days and resulted in more than $40 million dollars of property damage and thirty-four deaths. It was both the largest and costliest urban rebellion of the civil rights era. Throughout the events, public officials advanced the argument that the riot was the work of outside agitators. An official investigation, prompted by Governor Pat Brown, found that the riot was a result of the Watts community's longstanding grievances and growing discontentment with high unemployment rates, substandard housing, and inadequate schools (see reading 61 "The Crisis"). Despite the reported findings of the gubernatorial commission, city leaders and state officials failed to implement measures to improve the social and economic conditions of African Americans living in the Watts neighborhood.

Similar conditions in Oakland led to the founding of the Black Panther Party in the fall of 1966 (Figure 10.4a and Figure 10.4b). Their agenda of "black power," emphasizing black self-determination, found a receptive audience among many young activists. In addition to its radical, revolutionary rhetoric, the Panther Party operated a number of social programs in poor African American neighborhoods (see reading 62 "The Ten Point Plan"). Eldridge Cleaver (1935–1998) served as the group's Information Minister, or spokesperson (Figure 10.4a).

Cleaver had served prison sentences for drug-related crimes and assault, and while in prison, wrote powerful essays on race relations and revolutionary violence. His book Soul on Ice (1968) became the philosophical foundation of the movement for black power. The Black Panther Party membership reached its peak in 1970, with offices in sixty-eight cities and thousands of members.

Influenced by the activism of the decade, American Indians also responded to the pressures and challenges of urban relocation and poverty by turning to indigenous cultural pride and intertribal unity. The occupation of Alcatraz, outside of San Francisco, from November 1969 to June 1971, signaled the birth of the red power movement. Many activists recall the occupation as "symbolic in the rebirth of Indian people" and as vital in bringing their issues to the consciousness of the nation (see reading 63 "Petition to Support the Claim to Alcatraz Island" and Figure 10.5). Similarly, the Mexican American civil rights movement encompassed a broad cross section of issues—from restoration of land grants, to farm workers' rights, to enhanced education, and voting and political rights. These concerns coalesced with the growing antiwar sentiments in the Chicano Moratorium. On August 29, 1970, an activist group of Chicano students and the Brown Berets organized a rally protesting the war in Vietnam and pushing for social justice in the barrios. The event drew a crowd of approximately thirty thousand, of every age and background, to the streets of east Los Angeles. The peaceful event turned into a riot when Los Angeles police attacked the demonstrators with tear gas (Figure 10.6).

Paralleling these developments in the nation's urban areas, César Chávez launched an uprising in the fields to confront the poverty and the poor working conditions of the state's farm workers. In 1962, Chávez founded the National Farm Workers' Association, which later became the United Farm Workers. He was joined in this vital work by Dolores Huerta. It was the beginning of La Causa, a cause supported by organized labor, religious groups, minorities, and students. Chávez and the National Farm Workers Association first joined the Delano Grape Strike, initiated by Filipino farm workers in 1965 (see reading 64 "Prayer of the Farm Workers Struggle" and Figure 10.7). In 1968, Chávez launched a national boycott against all table grapes. The result was the greatest advance for farm labor in American history, when most of the remaining growers signed contracts with the union in July 1970. In 1975, Governor Pat Brown signed the Agricultural Labor Relations Act to ensure stable agricultural labor relations and a degree of justice for farm workers through due process. California also established the Agricultural Labor Relations Board to enforce the principle of good-faith bargaining. Yet, the conditions of this segment of the work force seem to have remained the much the same (see reading 65 "Agricultural Labor Relations Board Fact Sheet").

STUDENT ACTIVISM

READING 58, CLARK KERR

"Things Start to Fall Apart"

2003

BEGINNING IN THE LATE 1950S, ACTIVIST STUDENTS wanted to turn the Associated Students into a political organization speaking on behalf of all students on off-campus political issues. The Associated Students had been established by the university to serve many aspects of student life on campus. Membership was compulsory for all undergraduates and so were fees to support the organization. The official university position then was that the university should not and would not compel students to belong to and support financially a political action group.

The university had conceded in 1960 that the officers of the Associated Students could take positions as individuals on off-campus matters and identify themselves as officers but that they could not commit the entire student body to the positions they took individually or use compulsory fees to advance their views. Activist students, particularly via SLATE, argued that they were being kept in a "sandbox" playing with on-campus affairs when they wanted to declare policy on matters of national and worldwide concern on behalf of a compulsory membership.

In 1960, SLATE began a campaign against what it called the "Kerr directives." It claimed that historic rights had been taken away from students. I replied that no such rights had been seized from the students and challenged SLATE to identify them, which they never could do. I also said that if the students so wished, they could have back the policies that existed before the Kerr directives.

On December 12, 1961, SLATE agreed that "great liberalizations have been made in the university's policies" but that there were still issues of "what ought to be." There were indeed. We later removed the ban on Communist speakers.

But other attacks continued. SLATE published a criticism of my views by an employee of the Berkeley campus library, Hal Draper, called "The Mind of Clark Kerr." Draper was a member of the Independent Socialist Committee, an anti-Stalinist group of Trotskyite persuasion. He said, "The Independent

Socialist view is that students must not accept Kerr's vision of the university-factory, run by a Captain of the Bureaucracy as a parts-supply shop to the profit system and the Cold War complex. We do not think they will."

This quote is about my Godkin lectures at Harvard in 1963 on the uses of the university. I never did refer to the university as a "factory." My phrase was a "city of intellect." What I did do was quote Fritz Machlup, a leading economist, on how the "Knowledge Industry" represents a major segment of the American economy, what others later called the "Information Society." The Knowledge Industry included the newspaper press, television, book publishers, schools, and universities. Neither Machlup nor I ever said that the press or the media or book publishers or schools or the university itself was a "factory" (Draper and Mario Savio and SLATE and others used the term "factory"). Nor did I support the development of the "multiversity" in its entirety. In fact, I gave the first and perhaps the strongest statement about its pathologies, and at the Santa Cruz campus and elsewhere I tried to help correct some of them.

Let me acknowledge here that in preparations for the new policy statements on student political activism, there never was adequate consultation with students about the rules. Suddenly, in fall 1959, we issued a whole series of regulations. Mostly it was a compendium of regental and presidential past policies and practices to guide the chancellors in the exercise of their new authority over student life—really the Sproul directives as amended and assembled. Brought together, this large body of existing rules looked like, or could be made to look like, a new set of rules. It could be made to look both new and oppressive. And it also came at a time of rising student political unrest around the world. It was, however, mostly old or, where new, liberating.

The timing of the new set of rules was bad and so was the method of its introduction. These were contentious issues and I can see why the chancellors involved might have wished to avoid them, and they were busy with other things. I did not follow up adequately to see that the consultations I had requested were properly carried out. I had no student affairs staff since I was delegating the whole area to the campuses. This, too, turned out to be a great mistake. I should have had a student affairs officer working in the president's office.

And I was in too great a hurry to get decentralization under way. I was obsessed with it. I did not realize how controversial the new set of rules might be, since they were mostly a restatement of the status quo, and where they differed they only liberalized the rules.

The biggest mistake was in treating rules on student political activities as part of the decentralization process that was then my first priority. Instead, I should have made them a separate agenda item. Another mistake was in turning consultation with students over to the chancellors without monitoring them. Basic errors.

In any event, to my then knowledge, only one big issue remained open on the student front by fall 1964, and it was fading away: should a compulsory student organization act on behalf of all its members on off-campus political issues and collect compulsory dues for this activity?

I had thought that after the AAUP award in spring 1964 that the worst of political confrontations at Berkeley was over. But the worst was still to come.

Behind the struggles were two models of the university. One model may be identified as "classical": the university is a place for study and contemplation. The other is "modern": the university is a place for study and contemplation *and* for active participation. The latter model viewed the university as a proper arena for political participation as well as a quiet classroom for discussion. The goal of participation as set forth in the "modern" model won out at Berkeley and almost everywhere else.

A basic question was whether study and analysis or direct action would better advance the modern model. Of the two models—the analytical, as in the early work of the John R. Commons group at the University of Wisconsin, or the agitational, as at Berkeley in the 1960s—the latter prevailed. Instead of adding careful intellectual analysis to public debate, it added passion. No cordon sanitaire was possible under either modern model. It was impossible to hold back the determination of so many faculty members and students to take part directly in political events—and on campus.

The only way to clean up a mess like that would be to start all over again, if only we could, or to go through a series of complicated political battles, which we did.

READING 59. MARIO SAVIO

"Thirty Years Later: Reflections on the Free Speech Movement"

1995

FIGURE 10.2. Mario Savio at the steps of Sproul Hall at UC Berkeley (1966)

I'D LIKE TO SHARE WITH YOU SOME ideas about how my consciousness, my piece of collective consciousness and that of my friends, developed. We had our beginnings in the 1940s and 1950s. [I was born in] 1942. I was a war baby. But spiritually speaking, [our consciousness formed largely] in reaction to the 1950s. It was in reaction to the 1950s that we did the kinds of things that we did.

The fifties are bizarre, but they were the last normal decade, [when] everything was still just in place the way it ought to be. The man thought he was in charge, the woman let him think that while making certain decisions in the house (she took care of the kids, made sure they were all washed and went to school, everything went just right), and the only black man they knew was the one who came around collecting money for charity.

Well, I'll tell you how it got this way for me. I grew up as a Catholic. I was an altar boy. I was going to be a priest. Now obviously the eldest son in an Italian Catholic family, a person who would become a priest if anyone was going to be—and I was going to be that person. My two aunts are nuns. I came into it from liberation theology. I read things that probably most people in this room have not read. I read [Jacques] Maritain, I read [Emmanuel] Mounier, I read things put out by *Catholic Worker* people; I was very much immersed in that sort of thing. And that was how I came at it. By virtue of my Catholicism and the particular character it was taking, for me a major decision was whether to be a priest. Therefore I was not a careerist. I couldn't be a careerist. I had something more important to do. I was trying to save my soul. And I made pacts with myself repeatedly. "If you can just believe these things, then you will have to apply to become a Jesuit." That was the image I had—a romantic image. But the point is, I certainly could not become a careerist.

Now it turns out that from various other paths, many people I met at Berkeley were in the same situation. Not all Catholics—mostly not. But they, for one reason or another, were in some kind of peripheral relationship to the society, not really able to put career first but rather to put ideas first. And maybe one of the reasons it was possible was because they were prosperous times. It's harder to eschew an excessive concern with career when you want to make sure you have one, right? We knew, no problem, you can get student digs for thirty- five dollars. Astonishing. So one didn't worry about the material world. One could afford to be above the material world, and a lot of people at that time really were, and I think fortunately.

We also were the first generation to grow up under the threat of the bomb. That actually was special. We were the first generation to do that. They exploded them on the [TV] tube. See, they hadn't yet put them [under] the ground. Periodically there would be an explosion of the hydrogen bomb or the latest device there, chow, boom! Right on the news. And I remember even as a little child they had us ["take cover"] under desks. There were periodically drills in the schools as I was growing up in the fifties and you would go under desks.

So, in other words, the Commies, I knew, were bad. I later met some and discovered they were very warm human beings, but it took me a while. But the bomb, you knew that was bad, right? So that was part of the background.

And then, part of the background for me and, I think, for others was the Holocaust. I'm not Jewish but I saw those pictures. And those pictures were astonishing. Heaps of bodies. Mounds of bodies. Nothing affected my consciousness more than those pictures. And those pictures had on me the following impact, which other people maybe came to in a different way. They meant to me that *everything* needed to be questioned. Reality itself.

I mean how could it possibly [be]? But I knew it was real. And this affected me more than any other single thing. I started to get the idea that people weren't really coming completely clean about things. In other words, that there was almost a conspiracy not to tell the truth to oneself, even on a mass scale.

In the midst of all this, the Civil Rights Movement exploded. To me that was very important at that moment because I had had this confrontation with the ideas of the Holocaust. I was not a careerist. I was someone who took good and evil exceptionally seriously. And since I'm breaking away from the Church, I see the Civil Rights Movement in religious terms. [In the] Civil

Rights Movement there were all those ministers; it was just absolutely rife with ministers, bristling with ministers. And so, to me, this was an example of God working in the world. Allying myself in whatever way I could with that movement was an alternative to the Church because I couldn't actually believe those [biblical] stories. Not that things couldn't have happened that way, but there seemed to be lots of reasons to think maybe they hadn't happened that way. I couldn't bring myself to believe the religion I was born into on a factual basis. But the spirit of "do good" and "resist evil" was an important part of my religious upbringing. I saw [that] present in the Civil Rights Movement—and I wanted to ally myself with that.

I then went to Berkeley. I was a philosophy student, and this was the case of "philosophy student goes South." I'd been studying physics. I then realized that I had to take a little sojourn into philosophy because I had to finally make the decision—am I a Catholic or not?

People on the Berkeley campus got very involved in the Civil Rights Movement. And there was a local branch of it. The Bay Area civil rights movement was tremendously attractive to students and a minority of [them] took part. There were demonstrations all over the Bay Area, often the same faces, and they're faces now that I see elsewhere at demonstrations, same people, a little grayer. And, here's what's interesting: they were successful demonstrations, militant demonstrations that brought results. And that was very energizing to people, the fact that you could compel a store to hire people [of color] they weren't previously hiring. And there were consequences if they didn't do that.

I went to the demonstration, got arrested for the first time, and I remember we were all holding hands, locking arms and stuff like that.

I was, as a result of getting that leaflet, arrested. I'm in the holding pen when someone named John King, whom I've never met, says, "Oh, are you going to Mississippi?" Well, that summer was going to be Mississippi Freedom Summer. This, if the good guys win, is the seminal event of the twentieth century. When you get past the Second World War, this is it. This is what determines the rest of the history of the country in this century. This particular event, the Mississippi Freedom Summer. That created the cadre [of student activists] for the whole country. Fantastic event. That doesn't mean that you had to be there. You just had to know somebody who was there. It was electric.

So I went and I had my touch with reality. And my touch with reality was one particular moment that summer. All that effort to get one particular moment. I brought somebody to register to vote. You weren't supposed to say a word. This guy comes. The guy was about sixty, seventy years old. There's the sheriff's wife behind the counter. 'Doffs his hat and he just stands there. Silent. She goes about her business. Finally, finally, she comes over: "What do you want, boy?" Head down. "Wanna reddish." *"Boy,* what do you want?" "Wanna reddish." "Reddish, what's that boy?" Here—he's obviously older than she is. He's worked all his life—such silence, such dignity, such composure. And meanwhile I cannot say anything. We're not allowed to say a word—going to watch that's all. And this went on for a long time. "What do you want, boy?" "Wanna reddish, ma'am." They all said "reddish." The word *register* became a two-syllable word in Mississippi and that's what they said: "Wanna reddish. Wanna reddish." Finally she throws the thing at him, and now he has to interpret a section of the Mississippi constitution in order to qualify as a registered voter. And that was my moment of reality. And you don't need that many. I only needed that one.

Obviously I endangered people. When I went back to Berkeley, back to California, nice, sunny California—home of none of that, right? [And] lots of other people were in the same boat. I was then the incoming president of University Friends of SNCC, and when we came back to California, the [campus] administration sent out letters to all these various organizations saying "that strip of land," the very place where I'd gotten the first leaflet, "we have now discovered that this is University property," and so we're not allowed to have advocacy of anything on University property and therefore there will no longer be these card tables to distribute literature. No more distribution of leaflets, no more collecting of money, no more doing all of the things that had gotten me to go to the demonstration where I was first arrested and ultimately to Mississippi to endanger these people.

So here's how the FSM [arose] in the simplest [terms]: We insisted on a reason. They said the only reason is that this is University property. But, as I and others pointed out in the very first meeting, "That's not a reason. That's a fact."

Now that was, that was really decisive. They got spiked right there: "That's not a reason. That's a fact." How'd they get spiked? See this was the "end of ideology" era. And we just had turned the tables on them. They were attacking people who were taking moral action on the basis of "well, you're just emoting, just making value judgments." As if this were not a normal human thing to do. That the only real solid things were facts. So when you tell me that the reason you're doing this is because it's University property, then I'm at perfect liberty to say, "Choup! That's a fact. That's not a reason." And of course that's exactly right, it was just a fact. What made it just a fact? The fact that they had discretion. That is, we had learned our end-of-ideology lessons very well.

And in learning the lessons, we had honed a very, very sharp knife. And that knife was now turned at them. I hope this point is really clear because it is extremely important. Why is this business about end of ideology important here and relevant to this? What was this end of ideology about? It was about destroying socialism. Because what were the alternatives? The alternative was a perfectly "natural" commercial society in which everything happened according to the laws of nature's god, or whatever. There it is. You couldn't tamper with that. The alternative was tampering with the market, maybe even elements of a command economy. All of that was against nature, and based upon an ideology. We here, in the land of nature's god, we have no ideology. It's just according to the facts. This is the natural way to do things, right? Buying and selling is natural. The market price, that's the natural price. It's only you wicked people over here who tamper with the laws of nature's god, and you have ideologies behind you. Okay. Very well. But then if you say that you have a policy, and you have discretion to develop that policy in this particular way, then, and you have no reason for that, and you offer as your reason that it's University property, I have learned very well what answer you need. "That's not a reason. That's just a fact. And facts can't be argued into reasons. No way." And we told them those things. It's quite remarkable to realize now. Now we're past those debates; they're in the past. But it was super powerful at that time. We talked their language but not to their purpose.

We almost lost. This is important to understand. To people today [the FSM seems] successful. [But] we were almost unsuccessful. We worked our little hearts out—our little tushes—for a whole term. We worked like crazy to mobilize the students and to educate the faculty. Above all we had to educate the faculty. Students come and go. Faculty had position there, they had jobs, they had tenure in many cases. And if we could educate them, we could win. There was this meeting at the Greek Theatre. Clark Kerr had decided on the solution. He had his plan. His plan had nothing in it about free speech. No correspondence at all between his plan for solving the "campus chaos," which was all he was concerned about, [and the FSM's free speech position]. Nothing at all in his plan that was responsive to any of the things that we had said. So the Greek Theatre. Very, very, very nice. The symbolism was beautiful. They had this stage, they had these *baronial* chairs and sitting on them were the department heads. The chairs on the chairs and there they were like the barons. And so he made a speech. The speech was over. They turned off the microphone. I walked to the center of the stage to tell people, to announce simply that we're going to have a meeting down in [Sproul] Plaza. That was my intention. To discuss these issues. We were afraid of losing it at that very moment. And we could have. And fortunately, they had ready their cops, and they came and they pulled me down. Astonishing!

We lucked out time after time, and that was our final luck out. We had argued it all beautifully; we presented all of the facts, the arguments, the reasons and theories. We talked to everybody, and yet at the very last moment we could have lost the whole thing. But they saved us in that way just as earlier they had saved [us]; luck had saved us. During the original gathering, they [had] put a police car on the campus to arrest one of our people. You've really got to be bereft of all sense to do that! We could not anticipate that they would do such a thing, that they would arrest a former student on the campus with a police car, that they [would] drive right in the middle of the Plaza, kaplunk! That'd be bereft of all sense. They do this. Okay, great, that's a plus. Just falls into our laps. Here it is. Then what happens? The next day is "Parents Visiting the Campus Day." We were around that car for thirty-two hours, for God's sake. We could have been around that car for another seventy, and that would have really been very upsetting to the trustees and the people who contribute money, the rich alumni; the whole little ball of wax would have just melted, just like that. What were they going to do? They had police ringing the campus. They threatened to come in bludgeoning people. Well, there would have been blood on the pavement, and they wouldn't have gotten the blood off the pavement so easily. That was luck, sheer luck. We knew how to take advantage of luck, but it was luck. And then likewise at the very end. They come [to the Greek Theatre]; I go up to make an announcement, whew! [The] police [drag me] down. I'm in a different place. I'm talking to one of the cops in Italian at this point, true. So I'm really just now in a different world. That's what won it for us.

A couple of days later [December 8] there's the meeting of the Berkeley Academic Senate, and we have worked with these guys, trying to tell them about free speech. These are smart guys. To be on the Berkeley faculty you can't be that dumb. [Yet] it took us a very long time to explain to them the niceties of civil liberties issues where they could understand [them]. But we didn't know even then whether they would understand. And we had done our all. If we'd lost it at that point, it would have been gone. And they voted by about eight to one. In those days it wasn't a representative body [of delegates]; it was a one person-one vote senate and they had a real debate. We had opened up a space for the faculty to have a debate. And that's really a side of the FSM which isn't understood. We had to work like crazy, disrupting the University, taking over buildings, having sit-ins, marches, all this sort of thing to just open up a little space where people would have a real debate. That was America. This is a free country here, and [yet] you had to go crazy so we can have an actual, real debate that could really decide something. Astonishing! And they voted the right way. And we were outside. And [the faculty] came walking through, and I remember we were clapping and tears were just streaming down our faces because, if we had not won at that point, if they didn't get it at that point, I wouldn't be here right now.

HOUSING DISCRIMINATION

READING 60

William Byron Rumford Remembers Housing Discrimination in California

1971

Prof. Edward France:

With the passage of the Rumford Bill in 1963 the opposition had lost the battle but they refused to recognize that they'd lost the war, and so a movement began for the initiative which later became famous as Proposition 14 in 1964. If we assume that those in power take as positive approach toward civil rights legislation as they can, in many cases it hasn't proved effective. Why the great opposition to the action of the California government at that time? Why the attempt to undo what had been done?

Rumford:

Well, having spent considerable time in the California legislature dealing with the problem of civil rights and trying to rectify many of the wrongs that exist in the so-called legal process by the legislative method, I would like to think that the representatives who voted for the legislation expressed the opinion, the ideas, and concepts of the people they represented. But this is not wholly true. There is---and I don't think we can avoid it—a basic racism in the country which exists and is contrary to some of our basic concepts as expressed in the Constitution and the Bill of Rights and other documents. When we attempt to emphasize or to develop concepts or practices based upon the concepts in these documents you find there is a contradiction. Some of those people who express a strong position on the Constitution, the Bill of Rights and other documents, will be some of those who are prone to express themselves forcefully on discrimination and to try to justify this by twisting the concepts on the Constitution.

Proposition 14 was an attempt to spell out in the Constitution of the state of California the right on an individual who owned property, who had control of property, who leased it out, rented it out, or otherwise had control of it, to make a selection of the person who could rent or who could lease the property. The proposition stated that neither the state nor any subdivision nor agency thereof shall limit of abridge the right of any person to decline to sell, lease or rent his real property to such persons as he in his absolute discretion chooses.

FIGURE 10.3. Picketers in a Torrance Housing Tract (July 1963)

Now Proposition 14, of course, was fought throughout the state from every corner, from every little nook in the state of California. Newspapers took positions on it. Some of our outstanding newspapers were in opposition to it. The California Federation of Labor came out against it. The churches throughout the state as a group came out against it. Prominent citizens throughout the state came out against Proposition 14 and yet when the final vote was taken, Propositions 14 passed almost 2 to 1. This was a sad day in the state of California, but the propaganda that was used up and down the state was in effect, that a person could walk in and take your home, that the blacks were coming from all over the nation to occupy homes in the state of California. The whole proposition was built on fear and discrimination and racism; however, there were those who expressed themselves as being liberals and who felt that this proposition was necessary in order to protect their homes...

Rumford:

Numerous cases [challenging Prop. 14] were prevalent in the lower courts and the municipal court judges did pass on these cases. However, they did not attempt to embrace the constitutional question. So the cases were carried to the Supreme Court of the state of California on the basis of the constitutional implications. In 1966, in May I believe it was, the California State Supreme Court issued a decision which declared Proposition 14 unconstitutional. Now this was appealed on the part of the sponsors of proposition 14 and was taken to the United States Supreme Court.

Joyce A. Henderson:

Were these cases you speak of filed by citizens against real estate brokers?

Rumford:

Yes, I find it very difficult at this point to remember each and all of the cases; however, some are filed in Sacramento, some are filed in Southern California, and I think there's one in San Francisco. This will have to be researched. I regret I do not recall the specific names of the cases filed. In most cases, these were cases which were filed against real estate brokers for discriminating, and in some instances against apartment house owners.

I think it important here, aside from the legal battle that ensued, to explain the difference in the approach in the initiative and the referendum, because many people are unaware that there is in the state of California the referendum procedure which would have nullified my act without this initiative business. Now. There are two methods whereby the people can react against legislation. They can do as they did with respect to Proposition 14. They can instigate an initiative measure which means they themselves are going to develop legislation, put it on their ballot, and submit it to the people for their consideration. This is what they did on Proposition 14. This proposition was a Constitutional amendment which in effect would have nullified all housing acts and which would have also spelled out in the Constitution the right of an individual to discriminate against anybody he so desires. The other approach of course is the referendum. Now the referendum is often submitted when people who have been subjected to laws passed by the legislature want to reject these laws and all they do then is get sufficient number of signatures to put on the ballot. They could vote down the law that was adopted by the legislature and they would simply say that this law was hereby repealed.

Now this is the approach that the California Real Estate Association and the Apartment House Owners Association did not want to take. They were fooling the people into believing that they were adopting a referendum, when in fact they were adopting an initiative. A referendum, had it been adopted, would have repealed my legislation and there would have been no other recourse. We could not have gone to the courts on that because people have the right to undo anything the legislature does. So you see, the people were thinking that they were really repealing my law, when in fact they were establishing basic Constitutional law which would spell out the fact that you could discriminate legally. I wanted to make that clear because an awful lot of people are totally unfamiliar with the initiative and referendum and they often say that, "Well, this Proposition 14 will repeal the Rumford Law"—which it would not! Because the court said that Proposition 14 was unconstitutional, the Rumford Act is still on the books today! This would not have been so if they had gone the shorter route and the more clear-cut route of repealing the act rather than adopting an initiative. But the sponsors again—and I emphasize this—again the sponsors of Proposition 14 were determined to have a more vicious vehicle whereby they could discriminate against people and not necessarily repeal the Rumford Act.

On May the 29th, 1967, almost a year later, the United States Supreme Court on a five to four decision upheld the California State Supreme Court in declaring Proposition 14 unconstitutional.

France:

In May, 1967. Now it is some four years later, Mr. Rumford. If you had to do it again, would you do it again?

Rumford:

Oh, sure! I think that there is no substitute for right. Either we have a Constitution which protects all of its citizens or we do not; and if we do not, then we do not have a democratic society in this nation. I think that it is absolutely necessary that all people have the right to move about freely in this nation, to purchase and to sell. I do not think that there should be any restrictions whatsoever based upon race, color, creed, ancestry, or religion. I think our legislation attempted to do away with such restrictions.

RIOTS IN LOS ANGELES

READING 61, JOHN MCCONE ET AL.

"The Crisis"

1965

THE RIOTING IN LOS ANGELES IN THE LATE, HOT SUMmer of 1965 took six days to run its full grievous course. In hindsight, the tinder-igniting incident is seen to have been the arrest of a drunken Negro youth about whose dangerous driving another Negro had complained to the Caucasian motorcycle officer who made the arrest. The arrest occurred under rather ordinary circumstances, near but not in the district known as Watts, at seven o'clock on the evening of 11 August, a Wednesday. The crisis ended in the afternoon of 17 August, a Tuesday, on Governor Brown's order to lift the curfew which had been imposed the Saturday before in an extensive area just south of the heart of the City.

In the ugliest interval, which lasted from Thursday through Saturday, perhaps as many as 10,000 Negroes took to the streets in marauding bands. They looted stores, set fires, beat up white passersby whom they hauled from stopped cars, many of which were turned upside down and burned, exchanged shots with law enforcement officers, and stoned and shot at firemen. The rioters seemed to have been caught up in an insensate rage of destruction. By Friday, the disorder spread to adjoining areas, and ultimately an area covering 46.5 square miles had to be controlled with the aid of military authority before public order was restored.

The entire Negro population of Los Angeles County, about two thirds of whom live in this area, numbers more than 650,000. Observers estimate that only about two per cent were involved in the disorder. Nevertheless, this violent fraction, however minor, has given the face of community relations in Los Angeles a sinister cast.

When the spasm passed, thirty-four persons were dead, and the wounded and hurt numbered 1,032 more. Property damage was about $40,000,000. Arrested for one crime or another were 3,952 persons, women as well as men, including over 500 youths under eighteen. The lawlessness in this one segment of the metropolitan area had terrified the entire county and its 6,000,000 citizens.

Sowing the Wind

In the summer of 1964, Negro communities in seven eastern cities were stricken by riots.

Summary of the 1964 Riots					
City	Date	Killed	Injured	Arrests	Stores Damaged
New York City	July 18–23	1	144	519	541
Rochester	July 24–25	4	350	976	204
Jersey City	August 2–4	0	46	52	71
Paterson	August 11–13	0	8	65	20
Elizabeth	August 11–13	0	6	18	17
Chicago (Dixmoor)	August 16–17	0	57	80	2
Philadelphia	August 28–30	0	341	774	225

TABLE 10.1. Summary of the 1964 Riots

Although in each situation there were unique contributing circumstances not existing elsewhere, the fundamental causes were largely the same:

- Not enough jobs to go around, and within this scarcity not enough by a wide margin of a character which the untrained Negro could fill.
- Not enough schooling designed to meet the special needs of the disadvantaged Negro child, whose environment from infancy onward places him under a serious handicap.
- A resentment, even hatred, of the police, as the symbol of authority.

These riots were each a symptom of a sickness in the center of our cities. In almost every major city, Negroes pressing ever more densely into the central city and occupying areas from which Caucasians have moved in their flight to the suburbs have developed an isolated existence with a feeling of separation from the community as a whole.

Many have moved to the city only in the last generation and are totally unprepared to meet the conditions of modern city life. At the core of the cities where they cluster, law and order have only tenuous hold; the conditions of life itself are often marginal; idleness leads to despair and finally, mass violence supplies a momentary relief from the malaise.

Why Los Angeles?

In Los Angeles, before the summer's explosion, there was a tendency to believe, and with some reason, that the problems which caused the trouble elsewhere were not acute in this community. A "statistical portrait" drawn in 1964 by the Urban League which rated American cities in terms of ten basic aspects of Negro life - such as housing, employment, income - ranked Los Angeles first among the sixty-eight cities that were examined. ("There is no question about it, this is the best city in the world," a young Negro leader told us with respect to housing for Negroes.)

While the Negro districts of Los Angeles are not urban gems, neither are they slums. Watts, for example, is a community consisting mostly of one and two-story houses, a third of which are owned by the occupants. In the riot area, most streets are wide and usually quite clean; there are trees, parks, and playgrounds. A Negro in Los Angeles has long been able to sit where he wants in a bus or a movie house, to shop where he wishes, to vote, and to use public facilities without discrimination. The opportunity to succeed is probably unequaled in any other major American city.

Yet the riot did happen here, and there are special circumstances here which explain in part why it did. Perhaps the people of Los Angeles should have seen trouble gathering under the surface calm. In the last quarter century, the Negro population here has exploded. While the County's population has trebled, the Negro population has increased almost tenfold from 75,000 in 1940 to 650,000 in 1965.

Much of the increase came through migration from Southern states and many arrived with the anticipation that this dynamic city would somehow spell the end of life's endless problems. To those who have come with high hopes and great expectations and see the success of others so close at hand, failure brings a special measure of frustration and disillusionment. Moreover, the fundamental problems, which are the same here as in the cities which were racked by the 1964 riots, are intensified by what may well be the least adequate network of public transportation in any major city in America.

Looking back, we can also see that there was a series of aggravating events in the twelve months prior to the riots:

- Publicity given to the glowing promise of the Federal poverty program was paralleled by reports of controversy and bickering over the mechanism to handle the program here in Los Angeles, and when the projects did arrive, they did not live up to their press notices.
- Throughout the nation, unpunished violence and disobedience to law were widely reported, and almost daily there were exhortations, here and elsewhere, to take the most extreme and even illegal remedies to right a wide variety of wrongs, real and supposed.
- In addition, many Negroes here felt and were encouraged to feel that they had been affronted by the passage of Proposition 14 - an initiative measure passed by two-thirds of the voters in November 1964 which repealed the Rumford Fair Housing Act and unless modified by the voters or invalidated by the courts will bar any attempt by state or local governments to enact similar laws.

When the rioting came to Los Angeles, it was not a race riot in the usual sense. What happened was an explosion -- a formless, quite senseless, all but hopeless violent protest - engaged in by a few but bringing great distress to all.

Nor was the rioting exclusively a projection of the Negro problem. It is part of an American problem which involves Negroes but which equally concerns other disadvantaged groups. In this report, our major conclusions and recommendations regarding the Negro problem in Los Angeles apply with equal force to the Mexican-Americans, a community which is almost equal in size to the Negro community and whose circumstances are similarly disadvantageous and demand equally urgent treatment. That the Mexican-American community did not riot is to its credit; it should not be to its disadvantage.

The Dull Devastating Spiral of Failure

In examining the sickness in the center of our city, what has depressed and stunned us most is the dull, devastating spiral of failure that awaits the average disadvantaged child in the urban core. His home life all too often fails to give him the incentive and the elementary experience with words and ideas which prepares most children for school. Unprepared and unready, he may not learn to read or write at all; and because he shares his problem with 30 or more in the same classroom, even the efforts of the most dedicated teachers are unavailing. Age, not achievement, passes him on to higher grades, but in most cases he is unable to cope with courses in the upper grades because they demand basic skills which he does not possess. ("Try," a teacher said to us, "to teach history to a child who cannot read.")

Frustrated and disillusioned, the child becomes a discipline problem. Often he leaves school, sometimes before the end of junior high school. (About two-thirds of those who enter the three high schools in the center of the curfew area do not graduate.) He slips into the ranks of the permanent jobless, illiterate and untrained, unemployed and unemployable. All the talk about the millions which the government is spending to aid him raise his expectations but the benefits seldom reach him.

Reflecting this spiral of failure, unemployment in the disadvantaged areas runs two to three times the county average, and the employment available is too often intermittent. A family whose breadwinner is chronically out of work is almost invariably a disintegrating family. Crime rates soar and welfare rolls increase, even faster than the population.

This spiral of failure has a most damaging side effect. Because of the low standard of achievement in the schools in the urban core and adjacent areas, parents of the better students from advantages backgrounds remove them from these schools, either by changing the location of the family home or by sending the children to private school. In turn, the average achievement level of the schools in the disadvantaged area sinks lower and lower. The evidence is that this chain reaction is one of the principal f actors in maintaining de facto school segregation in the urban core and producing it in the adjacent areas where the Negro population is expanding. From our study, we are persuaded that there is a reasonable possibility that raising the achievement levels of the disadvantaged Negro child will materially lessen the tendency towards de facto segregation in education, and that this might possibly also make a substantial contribution to ending all de facto segregation.

All Segments of Society

Perhaps for the first time our report will bring into clear focus, for all the citizens to see, the economic and sociological conditions in our city that underlay the gathering anger which impelled the rioters to escalate the routine arrest of a drunken driver into six days of violence. Yet, however powerful their grievances, the rioters had no legal or moral justification for the wounds they inflicted. Many crimes, a great many felonies, were committed. Even more dismaying, as we studied the record, was the large number of brutal exhortations to violence which were uttered by some Negroes. Rather than making proposals, they laid down ultimatums with the alternative being violence. All this nullified the admirable efforts of hundreds, if not thousands, both Negro and white, to quiet the situation and restore order.

What can be done to prevent a recurrence of the nightmare of August? It stands to reason that what we and other cities have been doing, costly as it all has been, is not enough. Improving the conditions of Negro life will demand adjustments on a scale unknown to any great society. The programs that we are recommending will be expensive and burdensome. And the burden, along with the expense, will fall on all segments of our society - on the public and private sectors, on industry and labor, on company presidents and hourly employees, and most indispensably, upon the members and leaders of the Negro community. For unless the disadvantaged are resolved to help themselves, whatever else is done by others is bound to fail.

The consequences of inaction, indifference, and inadequacy, we can all be sure now, would be far costlier in the long run than the cost of correction. If the city were to elect to stand aside, the walls of segregation would rise ever higher. The disadvantaged community would become more and more estranged and the risk of violence would rise. The cost of police protection would increase, and yet would never be adequate. Unemployment would climb; welfare costs would mount apace. And the preachers of division and demagoguery would have a matchless opportunity to tear our nation asunder.

Of Fundamental and Durable Import

As a Commission, we are seriously concerned that the existing breach, if allowed to persist, could in time split our society irretrievably. So serious and so explosive is the situation that, unless it is checked, the August riots may seem by comparison to be only a curtain-raiser for what could blow up one day in the future.

Our recommendations will concern many areas where improvement can be made but three we consider to be of highest priority and greatest importance.

1. Because idleness brings a harvest of distressing problems, employment for those in the Negro community who are unemployed and able to work is a first priority. Our metropolitan area employs upwards of three millions of men and women in industry and in the service trades, and we f ace a shortage of skilled and semi-skilled workers as our economy expands. We recommend that our robust community take immediate steps to relieve the lack of job opportunity for Negroes by cooperative programs

for employment and training, participated in by the Negro community, by governmental agencies, by employers and by organized labor.

2. In education, we recommend a new and costly approach to educating the Negro child who has been deprived of the early training that customarily starts at infancy and who because of early deficiencies advances through school on a basis of age rather than scholastic attainment. What is clearly needed and what we recommend is an emergency program designed to raise the level of scholastic attainment of those who would otherwise fall behind. This requires pre-school education, intensive instruction in small classes, remedial courses and other special treatment. The cost will be great but until the level of scholastic achievement of the disadvantaged child is raised, we cannot expect to overcome the existing spiral of failure.

3. We recommend that law enforcement agencies place greater emphasis on their responsibilities for crime prevention as an essential element of the law enforcement task, and that they institute improved means for handling citizen complaints and community relationships.

The road to the improvement of the condition of the disadvantaged Negro which lies through education and employment is hard and long, but there is no shorter route. The avenue of violence and lawlessness leads to a dead end. To travel the long and difficult road will require courageous leadership and determined participation by all parts of our community, but no task in our times is more important. Of what shall it avail our nation if we can place a man on the moon but cannot cure the sickness in our cities?

MINORITY ACTIVISM

FIGURE 10.4A. Leroy Eldridge Cleaver

FIGURE 10.4B. Two Black Panther men standing on the steps of the Alameda County Court House during Huey P. Newton's trial for murder (July 14, 1968)

FIGURE 10.4C. Black Panther DC Rally Revolutionary People's Constitutional Convention (1970)

READING 62. THE BLACK PANTHER PARTY

"The Ten Point Plan"

1966

1. WE WANT FREEDOM. WE WANT POWER TO DETERMINE THE DESTINY OF OUR BLACK AND OPPRESSED COMMUNITIES.

We believe that Black and oppressed people will not be free until we are able to determine our destinies in our own communities ourselves, by fully controlling all the institutions which exist in our communities.

2. WE WANT FULL EMPLOYMENT FOR OUR PEOPLE.

We believe that the federal government is responsible and obligated to give every person employment or a guaranteed income. We believe that if the American businessmen will not give full employment, then the technology and means of production should be taken from the businessmen and placed in the community so that the people of the community can organize and employ all of its people and give a high standard of living.

3. WE WANT AN END TO THE ROBBERY BY THE CAPITALISTS OF OUR BLACK AND OPPRESSED COMMUNITIES.

We believe that this racist government has robbed us and now we are demanding the overdue debt of forty acres and two mules. Forty acres and two mules were promised 100 years ago as restitution for slave labor and mass murder of Black people. We will accept the payment in currency which will be distributed to our many communities. The American racist has taken part in the slaughter of our fifty million Black people. Therefore, we feel this is a modest demand that we make.

4. WE WANT DECENT HOUSING, FIT FOR THE SHELTER OF HUMAN BEINGS.

   We believe that if the landlords will not give decent housing to our Black and oppressed communities, then housing and the land should be made into cooperatives so that the people in our communities, with government aid, can build and make decent housing for the people.

5. WE WANT DECENT EDUCATION FOR OUR PEOPLE THAT EXPOSES THE TRUE NATURE OF THIS DECADENT AMERICAN SOCIETY. WE WANT EDUCATION THAT TEACHES US OUR TRUE HISTORY AND OUR ROLE IN THE PRESENT-DAY SOCIETY.

   We believe in an educational system that will give to our people a knowledge of the self. If you do not have knowledge of yourself and your position in the society and in the world, then you will have little chance to know anything else.

6. WE WANT COMPLETELY FREE HEALTH CARE FOR All BLACK AND OPPRESSED PEOPLE.

   We believe that the government must provide, free of charge, for the people, health facilities which will not only treat our illnesses, most of which have come about as a result of our oppression, but which will also develop preventive medical programs to guarantee our future survival. We believe that mass health education and research programs must be developed to give all Black and oppressed people access to advanced scientific and medical information, so we may provide our selves with proper medical attention and care.

7. WE WANT AN IMMEDIATE END TO POLICE BRUTALITY AND MURDER OF BLACK PEOPLE, OTHER PEOPLE OF COLOR, ALL OPPRESSED PEOPLE INSIDE THE UNITED STATES.

   We believe that the racist and fascist government of the United States uses its domestic enforcement agencies to carry out its program of oppression against black people, other people of color and poor people inside the united States. We believe it is our right, therefore, to defend ourselves against such armed forces and that all Black and oppressed people should be armed for self defense of our homes and communities against these fascist police forces.

8. WE WANT AN IMMEDIATE END TO ALL WARS OF AGGRESSION.
   We believe that the various conflicts which exist around the world stem directly from the aggressive desire of the United States ruling circle and government to force its domination upon the oppressed people of the world. We believe that if the United States government or its lackeys do not cease these aggressive wars it is the right of the people to defend themselves by any means necessary against their aggressors.

9. WE WANT FREEDOM FOR ALL BLACK AND OPPRESSED PEOPLE NOW HELD IN U. S. FEDERAL, STATE, COUNTY, CITY AND MILITARY PRISONS AND JAILS. WE WANT TRIALS BY A JURY OF PEERS FOR All PERSONS CHARGED WITH SO-CALLED CRIMES UNDER THE LAWS OF THIS COUNTRY.
   We believe that the many Black and poor oppressed people now held in United States prisons and jails have not received fair and impartial trials under a racist and fascist judicial system and should be free from incarceration. We believe in the ultimate elimination of all wretched, inhuman penal institutions, because the masses of men and women imprisoned inside the United States or by the United States military are the victims of oppressive conditions which are the real cause of their imprisonment. We believe that when persons are brought to trial they must be guaranteed, by the United States, juries of their peers, attorneys of their choice and freedom from imprisonment while awaiting trial.

10. WE WANT LAND, BREAD, HOUSING, EDUCATION, CLOTHING, JUSTICE, PEACE AND PEOPLE'S COMMUNITY CONTROL OF MODERN TECHNOLOGY.
    When, in the course of human events, it becomes necessary for one people to dissolve the political bonds which have connected them with another, and to assume, among the powers of the earth the separate and equal station to which the laws of nature and nature's God entitle them, a decent respect to the opinions of mankind requires that they should declare the causes which impel them to the separation.

We hold these truths to be self-evident, that all men are created equal; that they are endowed by their Creator with certain unalienable rights; that among these are life, liberty, and the pursuit of happiness. That to secure these rights, governments are instituted among men, deriving their just powers from the consent of the governed; that, whenever any form of government becomes destructive of these ends, it is the right of the people to alter or to abolish it, and to institute a new government, laying its foundation on such principles, and organizing its powers in such form as to them shall seem most likely to effect their safety and happiness. Prudence, indeed, will dictate that governments long established should not be changed for light and transient causes; and, accordingly, all experience hath shown that mankind are most disposed to suffer, while evils are sufferable, than to right themselves by abolishing the forms to which they are accustomed. But, when a long train of abuses and usurpation, pursuing invariably the same object, evinces a design to reduce them under absolute despotism, it is their right, it is their duty, to throw off such government, and to provide new guards for their future security.

READING 63

Indians of All Tribes, Petition to Support the Claim to Alcatraz Island

c. 1969

*FELLOW INDIANS, WE ARE APPEALING TO YOU FOR SUP*port in our efforts to regain Alcatraz Island in the middle of the San Francisco Bay.

Our fight with the whiteman's power structure demands a united front. There is no need to cite the past histories of differences caused largely by factionalism—what we must do now is demonstrate faith in our Indian brothers and demand this symbolic bit of reparation for the millions of acres of land stolen from Native Americans.

We fully realize the resistance we will meet from the white power structure in the form of law and order—that age old method used to suppress the oppressed. But in this case the law will have to change in order to preserve order.

White America's dealings with Indians must change: we must be allowed to negotiate, not beg!

Specifically, we are requesting you to fill these petitions with as many names as possible and send them back to the American Indian Center, 3189 16th Street, San Francisco 99103.

Other types of assistance can be in the form of letters to your congressman, the Secretary of the Interior, the Commissioner of Indian Affairs, etc.

Any checks or money orders should be made out to the American Indian Center Building Fund or Alcatraz Relief Fund. Bank addresses for funds is Bank of California, Mission Branch, 3060 16th St., San Francisco, Cal. 94103.

Signed,
INDIANS OF ALL TRIBES
San Francisco, California

FIGURE 10.5. Alcatraz Takeover

ANTI-WAR PROTESTS

FIGURE 10.6. National Chicano Moratorium (1970)

FARM WORKERS' STRUGGLE

READING 64, CÉSAR CHÁVEZ

Prayer of the Farm Workers' Struggle

Show me the suffering of the most miserable
So I will know my people's plight.

Free me to pray for others;
For you are present in every person
[...]

Grant me courage to serve others ;
So that I can work with other workers.

[...]

Help us love even those who hate us;
So we can change the world.

Enséñame el sufrimiento de los más desafortunados;
Así conoceré el dolor de mi pueblo.

Librame a orar por los demás;
Porque estás presente en cada persona.

Concédeme honoradez y paciencia;
Para que yo pueda trabajar junto con otros
trabajadores.

Ayúdanos a amar aún a los que nos odian;
Así podremos cambiar el mundo.

FIGURE 10.7. Dolores Huerta holding Huelga ("strike") sign during the first grape strike

READING 65

Agricultural Labor Relations Board Fact Sheet

Q: WHAT IS THE AGRICULTURAL LABOR RELATIONS ACT?

A: All agricultural employees in California, whether or not they are represented by a labor organization (union), have certain rights under the Agricultural Labor Relations Act (ALRA or Act). The purpose of the Act is to "ensure peace in the agricultural fields by guaranteeing justice for all agricultural workers and stability in labor relations." The ALRA became law in 1975. The Act describes and protects the rights of agricultural employees to make their own decisions about whether or not they want a union to negotiate with their employer about their wages, hours, and other working conditions. Where the employees, through a secret ballot election, have selected a union to represent them, the Act requires that the employer bargain in good faith with the union concerning wages, hours, and other working conditions. Additionally, even if no union is present, two or more workers may act together to ask their employer to change their wages, hours or other terms and conditions of their employment without fear of discharge or retaliation.

The Act makes it unlawful for an employer to fire, refuse to rehire, or discriminate in any other manner against an employee because he or she has supported a union, has participated in union activities, or has exercised any of the other rights protected by the Act.

Effective January 1, 2003, the Act provides for mandatory mediation in selected circumstances where the parties have been unable to reach a collective bargaining agreement.

Q: WHAT IS THE FUNCTION OF THE AGRICULTURAL LABOR RELATIONS BOARD AND THE GENERAL COUNSEL?

A: The Agricultural Labor Relations Board (ALRB) is the state agency established to enforce the Act. The members of the Board are appointed by the Governor and confirmed by the California State Senate. The Board interprets and enforces the Act by deciding the rights of parties to labor disputes. The General Counsel, who is also appointed by the Governor, is independent of the Board and has exclusive authority to investigate unfair labor practice charges and to determine if a complaint should issue. If a complaint issues, the General Counsel's staff presents the case before an administrative law judge, whose decision may be appealed to the Board.

Q: WHAT KINDS OF MATTERS DOES THE BOARD HANDLE?

A: The ALRB conducts elections where employees may choose or reject union representation. The Board also remedies unfair labor practices and, in that capacity, functions like a court.

The Board does *not* decide matters concerning worker's compensation, health and safety, unlawful race, sex, or age discrimination, safe housing, or violations of state or federal wage laws (minimum wage, overtime). Other state and federal agencies enforce the laws in those areas.

QUESTIONS FOR STUDY

1. What is the picture that emerges of the Free Speech Movement in these documents? Had you been a student at the time, how would you have responded to Savio? What would it take you, as a student today, to take up the banner of activism?
2. What caused the shift in black activism from civil disobedience to more confrontational tactics? How would you have reacted to the Black Panther Party at the time as a young black person? As a non-black person? In light of more recent events in American history, how do you interpret the Cone Commission report? How much have things changed?
3. How did Cesar Chavez's work with organizing farm workers impact the Mexican American community? What explains the continuing problems with farm labor?
4. What are the legacies of these 1960s protest movements today? How did they change California?

CREDITS

1. Fig. 10.1: Bettmann, Corbis, "Ronald Regan at General Electric Theater," AP Images, http://commons.wikimedia.org/wiki/File:Ronald_Reagan_and_General_Electric_Theater_1954-62.jpg. Copyright in the Public Domain.

2. Clark Kerr, "Things Start to Fall Apart," *The Gold and the Blue: A Personal Memoir of the University of California*, 1949-1967 (*Volume Two: Political Turmoil*), pp. 149-157. Copyright © 2003 by University of California Press. Reprinted with permission.
3. Fig. 10.2: Copyright © Nat Farbman, Time Life Pictures, Getty Images (CC BY-SA 3.0) at http://commons.wikimedia.org/wiki/File:MarioSavio.JPG.
4. Mario Savio, "Thirty Years Later: Reflections on the FSM," *The Free Speech Movement: Reflections on Berkeley in the 1960s*, ed. Robert Cohen and Reginald E. Zelnik, pp. 57-72. Copyright © 2002 by University of California Press. Reprinted with permission.
5. Fig. 10.3: "CORE Picketers in Torrance," Los Angeles Public Library, Order # 00047255. Copyright © 1963 by Los Angeles Public Library. Reprinted with permission.
6. *William Byron Rumford: Legislator for Fair Employment, Fair Housing and Public Health*, pp. 123-124, 126-128. Copyright © 1973 by The Regents of the University of California. Reprinted with permission.
7. John McCone et al., "The Crisis," *Violence in the City: An End or a Beginning?* Copyright in the Public Domain.
8. Fig. 10.4a: Marion S. Trikosko, "Leroy Eldridge Cleaver," https://commons.wikimedia.org/wiki/File:Eldridge_Cleaver_1968.jpg. Copyright in the Public Domain.
9. Fig. 10.4b: Lonnie Wilson, "Two Black Panther Men," http://www.museumca.org/picturethis/pictures/two-black-panther-men-standing-steps-alameda-county-court-house-during-huey-p-newtons-trial. Copyright © 1968 by Oakland Museum of California. Reprinted with permission.
10. Fig. 10.4c: "Black Panther DC Rally Revolutionary People's Constitutional Convention 1970," https://commons.wikimedia.org/wiki/File:Black_Panther_DC_Rally_Revolutionary_People%27s_Constitutional_Convention_1970.jpg. Copyright in the Public Domain.
11. Huey P. Newton, Bobby Seale and David Hilliard, "The Ten Point Program," The Black Panther Party for Self Defense. Copyright © 1972 by Dr. Huey P. Newton Foundation. Reprinted with permission.
12. Fig. 10.5: Vince Maggiora, "Alcatraz Takeover," http://www.sfgate.com/bayarea/article/Alcatraz-pays-tribute-to-Indian-occupation-4191169.php#photo-1893841. Copyright © 1969 by Hearst Communications Inc. Reprinted with permission.
13. "Support the Claim to Alcatraz Island." Copyright in the Public Domain.
14. Fig. 10.6: Sal Castro, "Moratorium March," Los Angeles Public Library, Order # 00048207. Copyright © 1970 by Los Angeles Public Library. Reprinted with permission.
15. Fig. 10.7: Harvey Richards, "Dolores Huerta (19 of 55)," *Farm Workers on Strike, 1959-1966.* Copyright © by Paul Richards. Reprinted with permission by Harvey Richards Media Archive.
16. Cesar Chavez, "Prayer of the Farm Workers' Struggle / Oracion del Campesino en la Lucha," http://www.ufw.org/. Copyright © by Cesar E. Chavez Foundation. Reprinted with permission.
17. Agricultural Labor Relations Board Fact Sheet, Agricultural Labor Relations Board. Copyright in the Public Domain.

14 New Economy, New Immigrants

INTRODUCTION

Following the tumultuous 1960s, California faced a set of new challenges as it moved into the next decade. In 1965, Congress rewrote the nation's immigration policy, reversing decades of systematic exclusion and restrictive immigration policies. The Immigration and Naturalization Act eliminated the quota system, emphasized family reunification, and reopened immigration from Asian countries (see "Immigration Act"). As a result, unprecedented numbers of immigrants from Asia, Mexico, Latin America, and other non-Western nations entered the United States. Additionally, most immigrants now first entered the country via the West Coast. Many settled in California, specifically. In the process, they dramatically and permanently reshaped the racial and ethnic composition of the state. By 2014, Latinos made up nearly 40 percent of the total state population, making them the largest single racial/ethnic group, and surpassing non-Hispanic whites at 38.8 percent. Asian and Pacific Islanders followed at 13 percent of the state's population. By the twenty-first century, Asia surpassed Latin America as the leading source of immigrants (Figure 11.1). Urban areas in Los Angeles County and Orange County transformed into thriving ethnic districts with their own enclave economies and residential communities.

The environmental effects of the growing population, combined with increasing residential and commercial development, also came to a head at this time. Smog—a combination of vehicle emissions, industrial fumes, and sunlight—first became a problem in the 1940s, and only worsened with the increase in automobiles and industrial development in California (Figure 11.3). After decades of living with declining air and water quality, Californians began to demand better protection of the state's natural resources. A catastrophic oil spill off the coast of Santa Barbara further fueled the push for new legislation on environmental issues. On January 29, 1969, a Union Oil Corporation platform, stationed six miles off the coast of Summerland, suffered a blowout. For eleven days, oil workers struggled to cap the rupture while two hundred thousand gallons of crude oil bubbled to the surface and spread into an eight-hundred-square-mile slick. Incoming tides brought the thick tar to the beaches, marring thirty-five miles of coastline (see reading 67 "Great Oil Spill in Santa Barbara"; Figures 11.4 and 11.5). Environmental activism gained widespread support: for example, in the two years following the oil spill, membership in the pro-environmental group the Sierra Club doubled. The Santa Barbara oil spill also inspired the first Earth Day, proposed by then-US senator from Wisconsin Gaylord Nelson. On April 22, 1970, twenty million Americans took to the streets to demonstrate for a healthy, sustainable environment in rallies across the nation. By the end of that year, the first Earth Day also led to the creation of the United States Environmental Protection Agency and the passage of the Clean Air, Clean Water, and Endangered Species Acts (Figure 11.2).

California also became a hub for new technologies in the postwar era. This culminated in the 1970s and 1980s when Silicon Valley, in the southern portion of the Bay Area, emerged as the center for the new technology industry. In 1939, Stanford alumni David Packard and William Hewlett established a little electronics company in a Palo Alto garage, later dubbed "the Birthplace of Silicon Valley." Stanford University established the Stanford Research Park in 1951, offering access to the university's facilities, faculty, and students. Over the following years, Stanford University became a source of innovation, producing advances in research and the formation of many companies that have made Silicon Valley one of the most innovative and productive high-tech regions in the world. Today, more than 150 companies on the leading edge of technology call the Park home (see reading 68 "Revolution in Silicon Valley").

While these new industries were creating great wealth, the state was struggling to provide for its rapidly growing population and to keep up with the demands for more roads, schools, police, and other public services. Even with the presence of Silicon Valley, the economy was struggling amidst the general stagnation of the 1970s. California responded by raising taxes in an effort to fill the gap. This, in turn, triggered a revolt from taxpayers that culminated in the passage of one of the most influential and controversial initiatives in the state's history, Proposition 13. On June 6, 1978, two-thirds of Californians voted to pass Proposition 13, also known as the People's Initiative to Limit Property Taxation. Proposition 13 mandated a property tax rate of 1 percent, required that properties be assessed at market value at the time of sale, and allowed assessments to rise by no more than 2 percent per year until the next sale (reading 69 "California Constitution, Article 13A"). The proposition certainly succeeded at its primary goal: cutting property tax rates. For ordinary households, that was good news. But Proposition 13 also applies to corporations, and as a result, corporations pay a lower share of property taxes than they used to.

Now called the "third rail" of California politics, Proposition 13 irrevocably changed the relationship between state and local government, and limited tax revenues in prosperous times. Property taxes are collected and spent locally, by cities, counties, and school districts. Because of Proposition 13, though, local jurisdictions cannot collect enough to fund their school districts. The state has to step in to provide support, leaving local governments more fully at the mercy of the state and its funding decisions. And, to compensate for lower property taxes, the state has become increasingly dependent on income and other taxes. Increasingly, Proposition 13 has been reassessed due to its long-term impacts on the state's finances, most recently during the governorship of Arnold Schwarzenegger (see reading 70 "Don't Be a 'Girlie Man'"). Yet, funding for state services, particularly education, continues to be sporadic.

NEW IMMIGRANTS

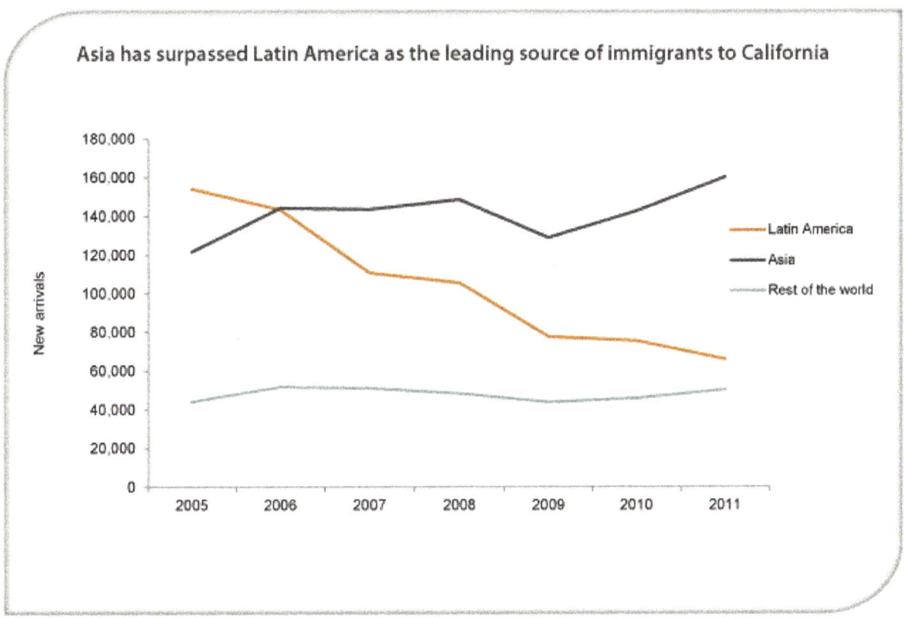

Source: American Community Survey.

Note: New arrivals are based on the place of residence one year prior to the survey.

From: Just the Facts: Immigrants in California, PPIC, 2013.

FIGURE 11.1. Asian and Latin American Immigrants in California

READING 66

Immigration Act

1965

PUBLIC LAW 89-236

AN ACT

To amend the immigration and Nationality Act, and for other purposes.

Be it enacted by the Senate and House of Representatives of the United States of America in Congress assembled, That section 201 of the Immigration and

Nationality Act (66 Stat. 175; 8 U.S.C. 1151) amendments, be amended to read as follows:

"Sec. 201, (a) Exclusive of special immigrants defined in section 101(a) (27), and of the immediate relatives of United States citizens specified in subsection (b) of this section, the number of aliens who may be issued immigrant visas or who may otherwise acquire the status of an alien lawfully admitted to the United States for permanent residence, or who may, pursuant to section 203(a) (7) enter conditionally, (i) shall not in any of the first three quarters of any fiscal year exceed a total of 45,000 and (ii) shall not in any fiscal year exceed a total of

"(b) The 'immediate relatives' referred to in subsection (a) of this section shall mean the children, spouses, and parents of a citizen of the United States: Provided, That in the case of parents, such citizen must be at least twenty-one years of age. The immediate relatives specified in this subsection who are otherwise qualified for admission as immigrants shall be admitted as such, without regard to the numerical limitations in this Act.

"(c) During the period from July 1, 1965, through June 30, 1968, the annual quota of any quota area shall be the same as that which existed for that area on June 30, 1965.

"(d) Quota numbers not issued or otherwise used during the previous fiscal year, as determined in accordance with subsection (c) hereof, shall be transferred to an immigration pool. The immigration pool shall be made available to immigrants otherwise admissible under the provisions of this Act who are unable to obtain prompt issuance of a preference visa due to oversubscription of their quotas, or subquotas as determined by the Secretary of State.

Sec. 2. Section 202 of the Immigration and Nationality Act (66 Stat. 175; 8 U.S.C. 1152) is amended to read as follows :

"(a) No person shall receive any preference or priority or be discriminated against in the issuance of an immigrant visa because of his race, sex, nationality, place of birth, or place of residence.

"(b) Each independent country, self-governing dominion, mandated territory, and territory under the international trusteeship system of the United Nations, other than the United States and its outlying possessions shall be treated as a separate foreign state for the purposes of the numerical limitation set forth in the proviso to sub section (a) of this section when approved by the Secretary of State.

ENVIRONMENTAL CHANGES

FIGURE 11.2. The Official Earth Day Flag

FIGURE 11.3. Low-Hanging Smog (1970)

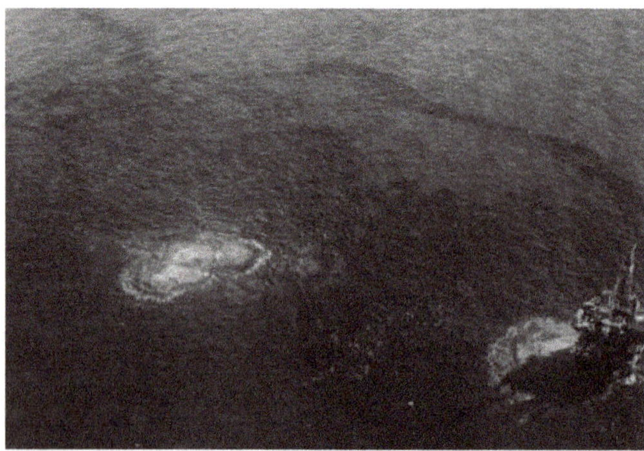

FIGURE 11.4. An aerial view of oil rising to the ocean surface during the Santa Barbara oil spill (1969)

FIGURE 11.5. Oil piled up at the seawall near the Santa Barbara Harbor

READING 67, LEE DYE

"Great Oil Spill in Santa Barbara"

***Los Angeles Times*, July 14, 1969**

ALMOST SIX MONTHS HAVE passed since the shores of Santa Barbara were blackened for the first time by crude oil from an offshore drilling platform.

The petroleum oozed to the surface on Jan. 28 from fissures beneath Union Oil Co.'s Platform A, 5.5 miles west of Santa Barbara, and drifted toward the coastline.

Overnight, Santa Barbara became a battlefield for conservationists. More than 100,000 signatures were collected on petitions calling for an end to offshore drilling. The cause was carried across the nation. Political leaders picked up the increasingly popular banner of conservation.

Total Result Still Unknown

Now, many months after the oil first gurgled to the surface, the controversy goes on and so does the drilling. The total result of the Santa Barbara oil spill may not be known for years but at this point these trends emerge:

- The pure conservationists, those who argue that all drilling in the Santa Barbara Channel must stop, will have to settle for negotiated peace. Unconditional surrender by the opposition seems out of the question and that is perhaps an indication of the trend in other conservation matters as well.
- The oil companies, it appears, will get their oil, but public pressure for oil field aesthetics and improved safety measures will force their production costs upward, and they will be subjected to more controls and closer scrutiny by government officials.

- The winners, and theirs is but a partial victory, are the new breed of conservationists who seek "resource management." Their aim is to get the oil out while protecting the environment and they expect to accomplish this by compromising in each direction.

'Valuable Resource'

California's director of finance, Caspar Weinberger, termed the oil fields a "very valuable resource" and indicated that as time goes on the temptation to relax the state's present ban on new drilling in the channel will be great.

"There is no feeling here that drilling should be resumed in the Santa Barbara Channel," Weinberger said, "but as the pressures for state dollars increase there will be strong desires that some of these royalties be realized."

Weinberger estimates that if the state were to prohibit drilling on the 45 active state leases in the channel it would cost California at least $166 million, plus the "astronomical" costs for legal claims which would undoubtedly be filed by the lessees.

The state has reaped a total of $270 million in revenues from offshore wells in Santa Barbara and Ventura County and expects to earn another $191 million.

Opponents of the drilling argue that such figures do not reflect the true picture because they fail to take into account the loss to the state in other areas, such as tourism, if the beaches become polluted.

Others argue that while the wells themselves may be offshore, supporting activities require space on the beach which might be put to better use.

Direct Effect

There is a direct effect upon the overlying area as oil is withdrawn from the earth and sometimes this cuts into the state's profits also.

During a recent meeting of the State Lands Commission, for example, a $250,000 expenditure for a study on subsidence in the Long Beach area was approved.

So much oil has been removed from fields there that parts of Long Beach are gradually sinking into the sea.

The commission also approved $70,000 for repairs to facilities in that area for damage resulting from the subsidence.

Huntington Beach has dropped 3 feet over many years due to the extraction of oil from beneath the city.

Does all this mean that the cause of conservation has been defeated?

"I don't feel the battle has been lost," Dep. Controller John P. Sheehan said. "But the pure conservationist has got to give a little."

It is a matter of options, Sheehan said. If the oil can be extracted without destroying the natural environment, then "the resource should be realized."

"But if it is going to deplete a better natural resource, then you're an idiot to continue the drilling. But you've got to be reasonable."

At the risk of being accused of seeing a silver lining around every dark cloud, some officials are saying the oil spill may have its redeeming qualities after all.

California now has an "Oil Spill Disaster Plan" and regulations have been tightened not only on drilling but on all offshore oil activities, including the transporting of petroleum aboard tankers.

The controversy has sharpened public attention on pollution. It also has redirected attention to the visual effects.

So although the conservationists have not lost entirely, and end to all offshore drilling is not in the cards.

But some observers are saying that the oil industry's profit margin as well as its image, has been diminished, and chances are it will tread more softly across the troubled face of nature.

Perhaps, as one official mused, the shock value of the Santa Barbara oil spill awakened the right people in the right places, just in time.

CHANGING ECONOMY

READING 68, VICTOR K. MCELHENY

"Revolution in Silicon Valley"

***New York Times*, 1976**

SANTA CLARA, CALIF.—THE LOW, RECTANGULAR FACTORies and laboratories proliferate on what used to be orchard land around here. It seems like an unlikely place to start a revolution.

Yet the engineers tucked away behind temporary partitions within these buildings are convinced they are revolutionaries and that their discoveries will affect the way Americans work, live and play within a decade.

Here in Silicon Valley, as the area is called, they design and produce the ever-tinier electronic systems called semiconductor memories and microprocessors. Already tens of millions of Americans are familiar with products using these miniature systems: the pocket calculator, the digital watch, and the electronic games played on home television screens.

Two things stand out among these products: they have swept through consumer markets like prairie fires with unit sales often doubling each year; and the price cuts are dramatic.

What new products will evolve over the next few years is not known. There could be wristwatch telephones. There could be computers on every desk, including school desks.

"This talk about the pervasiveness of advanced electronics, it's all an understatement. The technology is going to move faster than we can be sensible in applying it," says Robert H. F. Lloyd, a key group head of tile National Semiconductor Corporation, largest of the electronics companies clustered here.

"The basic thing that drives the technology is the desire to make money," he says. Developing products that sell by the millions, like the digital watch or the video games, is a key to making money.

These information-storing memories and information-processing microprocessors are becoming precipitously smaller and cheaper. This is why engineers here are convinced that computer functions will soon push their way virtually anywhere the consuming public finds them useful for leisure or business.

Dr. Robert N. Noyce, chairman of the Intel Corporation, thinks that the new technology will favor individually controlled, self-sufficient devices that plug in anywhere, meaning that microelectronics will tend to decentralize control in the society rather than concentrate it.

According to prophets of microelectronics such as Dr. Noyce and Dr. Gordon E. Moore, president of Intel, there is at least a decade ahead of an ever-denser packing of thousands of components onto ultra-pure silicon chips smaller than a fingernail.

Dr. Moore said recently that "integrated structures containing several million components can be expected within 10 years. These new devices will continue to reduce the cost of electronic functions and extend the utility of digital electronics more broadly throughout the society."

As the increasing component density continues to push down the prices, Dr. Noyce said in an interview, computers could turn up everywhere. Students who now use telephone lines to talk to a big computer could find self-sufficient computers "available at every desk."

Intel pioneered the semiconductor memories and microprocessors that are expected to account for perhaps 15 percent of the $5 billion in worldwide sales forecast this year for the semiconductor industry against $4 billion in total sales last year.

Industry leaders from Silicon Valley to Dallas, home of Texas Instruments, are convinced that component price-cutting, leading to more computer use, will continue.

One reason is the competition among half a dozen highly innovative companies, each struggling for "firsts" that leapfrog another company's leadership in a product. Any company that seizes a commanding market share in a new field is thus fortified for the roller-coaster ride that typically reduces costs by a factor of 10 every five or six years.

In 1960, a single transistor sold for $1. Today, a memory device with 6,000 transistors that stores 1,024 bits of information sells for the same price.

Microprocessors, containing both information-storage and information-processing on the same tiny chip, can do the work of room-sized computers of 30 years ago, and sell for a few dollars. Dr. Noyce has predicted a price of one thousandth of a cent per bit of memory by 1990.

There are two types of competition in this industry now. There is the competition among companies. There is also internal competition among technologies.

Each technology, with different advantages in speed, density, power-usage or manufacturing cost, tends to develop new wrinkles making it competitive where it was not competitive before.

Adding pressure to the competition among companies and technologies, the engineers here say, is a force that the semiconductor makers find more powerful than the sophisticated needs of the defense and space programs: the prospect of almost unlimited consumer markets and the profits those markets can bring.

These consumer markets are expected, by the companies here in Silicon Valley, to build the microprocessor industry from $150 million in sales this year to $600 million in 1980, and to push the semiconductor memory market from $350 million this year to $1.2 billion in 1980. Total volume of the semiconductor industry by then is expected to be $7 billion.

This kind of potential excites and worries semiconductor makers, unused to mass markets. They believe that their cost-cutting will open up more possibilities very soon. Their only problem is: which ones?

Mr. Lloyd of National Semiconductor dreamed out loud about one feasible television set-up in the not-too-distant future.

The user could sit on a couch with a hand-held device containing both a programmable pocket calculator and an electronic set-tuner.

He would point the device toward the screen, behind which would be an electronic module for translating the beamed instructions into visual displays.

Depending on the computer program he had fed into the pocket calculator, the user could rotate drawings of buildings for his architecture class, do his taxes or expense account—or just play a game for a breather.

Mr. Lloyd notes that television makers presently resist incorporating such electronics into the set because they don't think today's buyers will pay extra for the new feature. But the buyer of the 1.980's may not have to pay much of a premium.

In his office at Intel, Dr. Noyce looked out at streams of cars on a nearby freeway. How soon, he asked, would the growth of decentralized computers—and parallel cheapening of communications links—abolish much of the travel?

"Ninety-nine percent of the people in those cars are not transporting anything in bulk," Dr. Noyce said. "If the communications were rich enough, most of them could do their jobs at home."

Commanding positions in this field depend more on economics—lowering costs—than on any patent protection.

The ability to deposit vast arrays of devices onto tiny chips of silicon may be an industrial event similar to Andrew Carnegie's harnessing of cost-cutting in steel a century ago. Within 20 years, Carnegie pushed the price of steel down from three cents a pound to a penny, giving engineers the incentive to find uses for the metal.

Just a few years ago semiconductor makers were being forced to tailor their integrated circuits to each separate type of machine in which they would be installed.

But then all-purpose devices such as the semiconductor memory and the microprocessor, which could be readily programmed for each specific use, were developed, opening floodgates to mass production and mass use.

READING 69

California Constitution Article 13A

Tax limitation; 1978

*SECTION 1. (A) THE MAXIMUM AMOUNT OF ANY AD VA-*lorem tax on real property shall not exceed One percent (1%) of the full cash value of such property. The one percent (1%) tax to be collected by the counties and apportioned according to law to the districts within the counties. (b) The limitation provided for in subdivision (a) shall not apply to ad valorem taxes or special assessments to pay the interest and redemption charges on any of the following: (1) Indebtedness approved by the voters prior to July 1, 1978. (2) Bonded indebtedness for the acquisition or improvement of real property approved on or after July 1, 1978, by two-thirds of the votes cast by the voters voting on the proposition. (3) Bonded indebtedness incurred by a school district, community college district, or county office of education for the construction, reconstruction, rehabilitation, or replacement of school facilities, including the furnishing and equipping of school facilities, or the acquisition or lease of real property for school facilities, approved by 55 percent of the voters of the district or county, as appropriate, voting on the proposition on or after the effective date of the measure adding this paragraph. This paragraph shall apply only if the proposition approved by the voters and resulting in the bonded indebtedness includes all of the following accountability requirements: (A) A requirement that the proceeds from the sale of the bonds be used only for the purposes specified in Article XIII A, Section 1(b) (3), and not for any other purpose, including teacher and administrator salaries and other school operating expenses.

(B) A list of the specific school facilities projects to be funded and certification that the school district board, community college board, or county office of education has evaluated safety, class size reduction, and information technology needs in developing that list. (C) A requirement that the school district board, community college board, or county office of education conduct an annual, independent performance audit to ensure that the funds have been expended only on the specific projects listed. (D) A requirement that the school district board, community college board, or county office of education conduct an annual, independent financial audit of the proceeds from the sale of the bonds until all of those proceeds have been expended for the school facilities projects. (c) Notwithstanding any other provisions of law or of this Constitution, school districts, community college districts, and county offices of education may levy a 55 percent vote ad valorem tax pursuant to subdivision (b).

READING 70, LEE GREEN

"Don't Be a 'Girlie Man'"

***Los Angeles Times*, April 17, 2005**

AS LONG AS CALIFORNIA IS PROJECTING A POTENTIAL $10-billion deficit, governor, now is the right time to reconsider Prop. 13. Come on . . .

OK, you've been in office nearly a year and a half now, and we've yet to see any evidence that you're willing to curl, thrust, jerk, bench press or even touch one of the heaviest issues in California's political weight room. As Warren Buffett famously hinted during your campaign, it's time to do some heavy lifting, governor.

In fact, let's go back to that Buffett thing. Here's a man who knows finance better than Einstein knew physics, and who manages money better than

California does. Actually, everyone manages money better than California does, but Buffett has proved to be especially adept--so adept that you cast him as an economic advisor during your campaign. He had barely warmed his chair, though, when he did something frowned upon in politics: He spoke the truth.

Buffett's truth, you'll recall, concerned California's property tax-limiting Proposition 13, the most famous ballot initiative in American history. He casually mentioned that a system enabling today's homeowners to pay property taxes based on what their houses were worth when the Bee Gees topped the charts "makes no sense," particularly for a state barely clinging to solvency. In a blink he had done the unthinkable: tarnished the Holy Grail we call Proposition 13, the state constitutional amendment that California voters overwhelmingly approved in 1978.

What were we to make of such blasphemy? If you landed the governor gig, would you step out of character, wander off script and take a hard, open-minded look at Proposition 13 and all of its consequences? Your spokesmen immediately assured us that you would not. "Warren Buffett is speaking about his own philosophical position," one declared, suggesting that you weren't about to be swayed by opinions you didn't already hold. "Arnold Schwarzenegger has supported Prop. 13 for 25 years. He will be a fierce protector of Prop. 13."

"My position is rock solid in support of that initiative," you confirmed. More memorable, though, was your rebuff of Buffett, the world's second-richest Homo sapiens: "I told Warren if he mentions Prop. 13 one more time he has to do 500 sit-ups."

At this point you're probably wondering why I'm dredging all of this up again. After all, that was nearly two years ago.

Here's why: Buffett was right.

Forget politics for a moment and let's be honest. If Proposition 13 were one of your Hummers, you'd drive it straight to the shop for repairs because it's running rough and leaking oil. Worse, it's backfiring. Many of the best and the brightest in economics, law, public finance, public policy, planning and tax theory believe that Proposition 13--born out of homeowners' anger over rocketing property taxes and government indifference--has caused or contributed to some of the state's most pressing problems. Granted, it didn't unleash the economic Armageddon prophesied by its opponents, and we certainly can't hold it responsible for the state's current fiscal fiasco, which owes its existence to executive and legislative mismanagement several magnitudes greater than anything Proposition 13 could conjure. Still, the measure's untoward consequences--from the disempowerment of local government to the decimation of a once-proud educational system, unequal taxes on equal properties and yawning tax loopholes for business--demand a rigorous reexamination of Proposition 13 and its legacy. In tax lingo, a reassessment.

For a California governor to legitimately claim vision and leadership he must take Proposition 13 off the shelf and put it back on the table. A state with compounding problems and cascading fiscal shortfalls projected at as much as $10 billion a year can hardly afford to declare anything out of bounds. Not that you haven't proposed solutions. You want to eliminate state contributions to teacher retirement accounts and take more than $1 billion from funds earmarked for our sadly neglected transportation infrastructure. You even want to take billions more from a public school system already last or near last in the nation in per-student ratios of teachers, counselors, librarians, principals and administrative staff. The one thing you appear unwilling to mess with--or to even talk about messing with--is the most sacred cow in our pasture, good old Proposition 13.

QUESTIONS FOR STUDY

1. How did the arrival of new groups of immigrants from Asia and Latin America impact California? What challenges would these immigrants have faced? What challenges might California have faced in accommodating them? Why?
2. In the 1940s and 1950s smog was often viewed as simply a part of life in California. How would Californians' new awareness of environmental issues in the 1970s have changed how they thought about air pollution and environmental issues in general? What changes might have been implemented?
3. What has been the long-term impact of Silicon Valley on the state of California? How has it changed the role of the state in the nation and the world? Are there any drawbacks to the concentration of high-tech industries in California? If so, what are they?
4. Discuss the pros and cons of Proposition 13. What positive impact(s) did it have on the state? What were the negative impact(s)? Should it be reassessed? Why or why not?

CREDITS

1. Fig. 11.1: Hans Johnson and Marisol Cuellar Mejia, "Asian and Latin American Immigrants in California," http://www.ppic.org. Copyright in the Public Domain.
2. "Immigration Act of 1965," http://library.uwb.edu/guides/usimmigration/79%20stat%20911.pdf. Copyright in the Public Domain.
3. Fig. 11.2: "1969 Santa Barbara Oil Spill CA," U.S. Geological Survey, http://commons.wikimedia.org/wiki/File:1969_Santa_Barbara_Oil_Spill_CA.jpg. Copyright in the Public Domain.
4. Fig. 11.3: "Oil Spill Off Coast of Santa Barbara," U.S. Geological Survey, http://www.fnal.gov/pub/today/archive/archive_2009/today09-03-30.html. Copyright in the Public Domain.
5. Fig. 11.4: John McConnell, "Earth Day Flag," http://commons.wikimedia.org/wiki/File:Earth_Day_Flag.png. Copyright in the Public Domain.
6. Fig. 11.5: "Low Hanging Smog," U.S. Environmental Protection Agency, http://research.archives.gov/description/542683. Copyright in the Public Domain.
7. Lee Dye, "Great Oil Spill in Santa Barbara," *Los Angeles Times*. Copyright © 1969 by Los Angeles Times Syndicate. Reprinted with permission.
8. Victor K. McElheny, "Revolution in Silicon Valley," *The New York Times*. Copyright © 1976 by The New York Times Company. Reprinted with permission.
9. "Article 13A," California Constitution. Copyright in the Public Domain.
10. Lee Green, "Don't Be a Girlie Man," *Los Angeles Times*. Copyright © 2005 by Lee Green. Reprinted with permission.

12 California Enters the New Millennium

INTRODUCTION

As the twentieth century drew to a close, many Californians were wondering about the state's direction. The composition of the people who called California home had become increasingly diverse, and the growing immigrant and minority populations began to flex their political muscle in the 1980s and 1990s. In Los Angeles, for instance, the population growth in the 1990s derived almost entirely from immigration. Over 40 percent of its residents were born outside the United States; Mexico, Central America, and East Asian countries all contributed heavily to the city's workforce (Figure 12.1). At the same time, the economic difficulties that plagued Southern California for much of the 1990s separated the population by race and income. White residents continued their flight out of Los Angeles County. Median household income in Los Angeles also fell at a faster rate than in any other city between 1990 and 2000.

FIGURE 12.1. Los Angeles County Racial and Ethnic Breakdown, 1960-2000

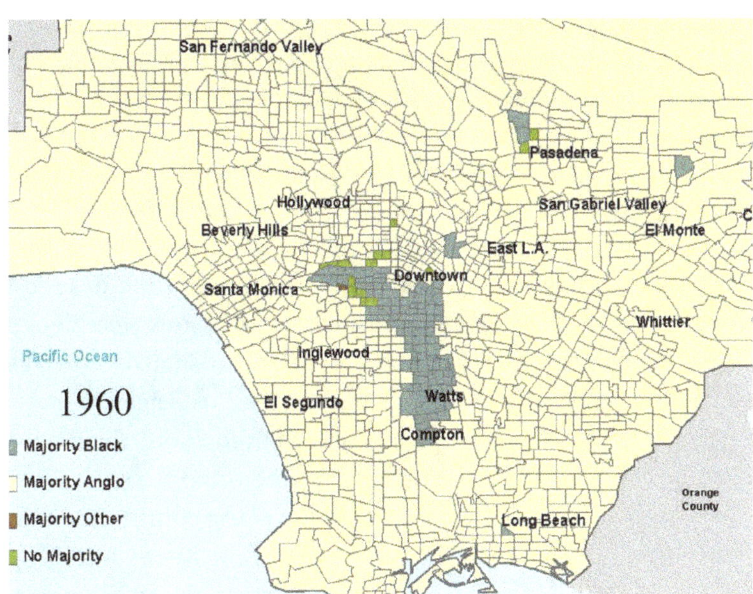

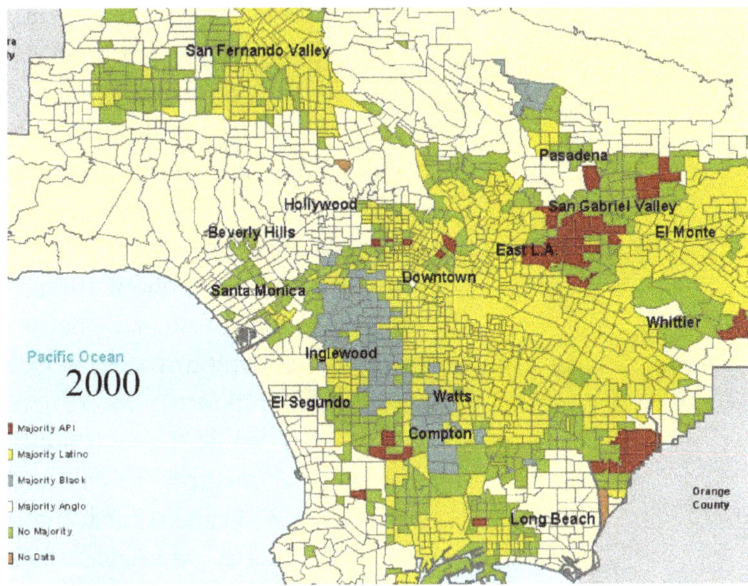

Furthermore, annual household incomes for African Americans and Latinos lagged significantly behind those of white households.

These changing demographics posed significant challenges to local law enforcement and highlighted the need for diversification and cultural awareness. The issue was most acute in Los Angeles, where the Los Angeles Police Department (LAPD) had for decades been accused of using racial profiling and excessive force against Latino/a and African American communities. Things came to a head with the beating of African American Rodney King at the hands of four LAPD officers on March 3, 1991. The videotape of this incident quickly spread via electronic media, bringing to the forefront concerns about racism and police brutality within the LAPD. In April 1991, Los Angeles Mayor Tom Bradley, the city's first African American mayor elected to that office in 1973 and ultimately serving five terms, formed an independent commission to investigate the accusations of excessive use of force specifically in minority communities. The Christopher Commission, as it was informally called, issued its findings in a 228-page report in the summer of 1991 (see reading 71 "Report of the Independent Commission of the Los Angeles Police Department").

After seven weeks of hearing testimony, on April 29, 1992, a jury with no African Americans on it acquitted the four officers involved in the beating of Rodney King, touching off a storm of anger in the city. Mayor Bradley immediately called for calm, admitting that "today the system failed us." Nonetheless, Los Angeles erupted in the deadliest riots of the century. Both the National Guard and federal troops were deployed to calm down the city. The six days of the Los Angeles Riots (also known as the Rodney King Riots, the Los Angeles Uprising, and the Los Angeles Urban Uprising) claimed the lives of fifty-three people and injured more than two thousand. Property damages from fires and looting amounted to one billion dollars (Figure 12.2). By the twenty-first century, some of the communities damaged in the riots had recovered; others had not. Meanwhile, the relationship between law enforcement and minority communities across the state remains tense, as illustrated in the spread of the 2013 Black Lives Matter movement.

Immigration also continued to be a contentious issue throughout the state, with focus on the growing numbers of undocumented, also called illegal, immigrants. The best estimates suggest that in 2013 California was home to about 2.67 million undocumented immigrants, making up approximately 6 percent of the state's population (Figure 12.3). They worked disproportionately in the farming, construction, production, services, and transportation industries, making up about 10 percent of the workforce. Debates over these immigrants culminated in the battle over Proposition 187, also called the SOS (Save Our State) initiative, in 1994 (see reading 72 "Closing the Door on Illegal Immigrants"). California voters approved the proposition by a wide margin (59% to 41%). While the courts ultimately threw it out because it infringed on the federal government's authority over matters related to immigration, Proposition 187 brought forth the issue of undocumented immigration that continued to dominate discussions about immigration in the new century.

By the mid-1990s, the Internet started to catch on commercially and had an estimated eighteen million users. This rise in usage created a new, untapped, and international, market—and a boon for Silicon Valley. Investors attracted to this "new economy" wanted big ideas, not solid marketing plans, and new Internet companies exploded on the stock market. The result was the so-called Dotcom Crash of 2001, as many of these new companies reported huge losses and some folded outright within months of their initial public offering (IPO). When the bubble burst, Silicon Valley lost 200,000 jobs overnight, dragging the national economy in a recession (Figure 12.4). Since then, the revolution in mobile and cloud-based services has created another rise in this sector of the economy, opening wide the window of new technology IPOs.

Environmental concerns in recent decades have increasingly focused on global warming. Scientists predict more variability in California's climate, with more intense storms, longer dry periods, and less snowpack. The state needs to figure out how to protect its coastline, maintain the agricultural industry, apportion dwindling water resources, and encourage "smart development." The passage of Assembly Bill 32, the California Global Warming Solutions Act of 2006, marked a watershed moment in California's history. By requiring a sharp reduction of greenhouse gas emissions, California set the stage for transitioning to a sustainable, low-carbon future. AB 32 is the first program in the country to take a comprehensive, long-term approach to addressing climate change, in a way that aims to improve the environment and natural resources while maintaining a robust economy (see reading 73 "California Global Warming Solutions Act").

The last decades of the twentieth century also witnessed the re-emergence of California's indigenous population. At the forefront were debates over gaming, as several Native groups experimented with boosting tribal revenue by offering bingo and card games on reservations (Figure 12.5). The State of California opposed these experiments on the grounds that they violated existing state laws prohibiting gambling. The Cabazon and Morongo Bands of Mission Indians, living on reservation lands near Palm Springs, challenged the State of California in court. The result was *California v. Cabazon Band of Mission Indians* (1987; see reading 74), the first step in legalizing gaming operations on Indian reservations nationwide. In 1988 the United States Congress passed the Indian Gaming Regulatory Act (IGRA), maintaining tribal sovereignty to create casinos. However, the states and the gaming tribes must enter tribal–state compacts, and the federal government maintains the power to ultimately regulate gaming (see reading 75 "Rincon Band Becomes First California Tribe to Renegotiate Tribal-State Gaming Compact with Federal Courts"). Casinos have allowed many California tribes to bring much-needed revenue to improve conditions in reservation communities, while creating a host of new challenges. The issue of Indian gaming remains controversial and many question how long it can feasibly grow.

California had also been a trailblazer in gay civil rights, dating back to 1950, when Harry Hay founded the Mattachine Society in Los Angeles. The first gay rights organization in the nation, the Mattachine Society attempted to change public perception of homosexuality and to eliminate discrimination and prejudice. Meanwhile, the Daughters of Bilitis in San Francisco became the first lesbian rights organization in the United States in 1955. In 1977, Harvey Milk won a seat on the San Francisco Board of Supervisors and introduced a gay rights ordinance. He also led a successful campaign against Proposition 6, an initiative forbidding homosexual teachers. By the twenty-first century, the issue of same-sex marriage had moved to the forefront of national debate. In California, Proposition 22 (2000) forbade recognition or licensing of same-sex marriages in the state. When San Francisco Mayor Gavin Newsom directed the licensing of same-sex marriage marriages on the basis of the state's equal protection clause in 2004, the stage was set for a battle. The California Supreme Court protected same-sex marriage as a constitutional right in a May 2008 ruling. However, opponents succeeded in placing Proposition 8 on the November ballot. Following an acrimonious campaign, Californians approved Proposition 8 (52.25% voting yes), creating an amendment to the constitution that defined only marriage between a man and a woman as valid in the state. Protests and litigation followed, dividing the state in very real ways (Figures 12.6 and 12.7). In June of 2015, the United States Supreme Court ruled 5 to 4 that same-sex marriage is a constitutional right, ending a decades-long battle and signaling a major victory for gay rights.

It is evident that California remains a diverse and complex state. Its past demonstrates, and the documents in this reader tell us, that California has the power, for good or for ill, to set national and international trends. Among the world's largest economies, the state undoubtedly will confront new global challenges in the 21st century. How we rise (or fail to rise) to meet these challenges will have repercussions not just for Californians but for individuals far beyond the borders of the Golden State.

URBAN UNREST

READING 71

Report of the Independent Commission of the Los Angeles Police Department

1991

The Problem of Excessive Force

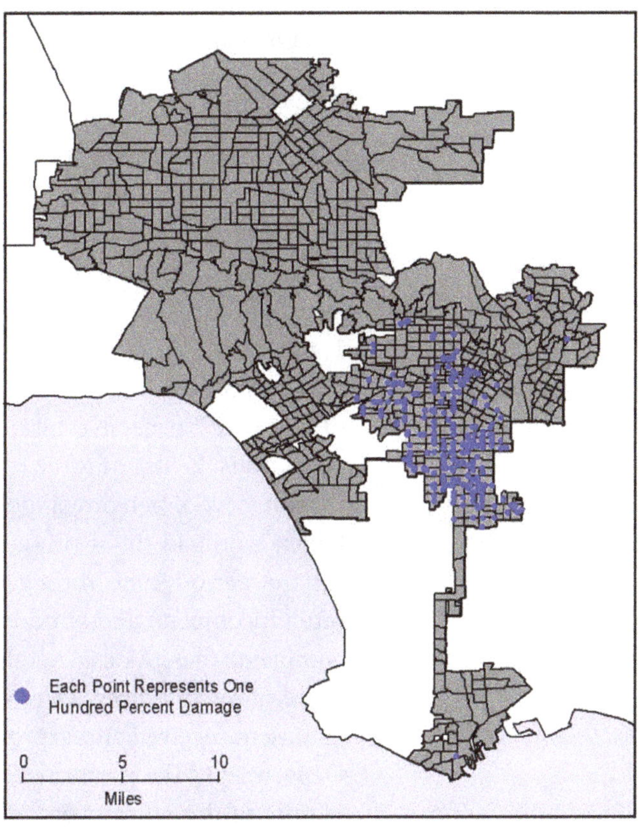

FIGURE 12.2. Percent of structural damage from the Los Angeles Riots (1992)

LAPD OFFICERS EXERCISING physical force must comply with the Department's Use of Force Policy and Guidelines, as well as California law. Both the LAPD Policy and the Penal Code require that force be reasonable; the Policy also requires that force be necessary. An officer may resort to force only where he or she faces a credible threat, and then may use only the minimum amount necessary to control the suspect.

The Commission has found that there is a significant number of LAPD officers who repetitively misuse force and persistently ignore the written policies and guidelines of the Department regarding force. The evidence obtained by the Commission shows that this group has received inadequate supervisory and management attention.

The Commission's extensive computerized analysis of the data provided by the Department (personnel complaints, use of force reports, and reports of officer-involved shootings) shows that a significant group of problem officers poses a much higher risk of excessive force than other officers:

- Of approximately 1,800 officers against whom an allegation of excessive force or improper tactics was made from 1986 to 1990, more than 1,400 had

only one or two allegations. But 183 officers had four or more allegations, 44 had six or more, 16 had eight or more, and one had 16 such allegations.
- Of nearly 6,000 officers identified as involved in use of force reports from January 1987 to March 1991, more than 4,000 had fewer than five reports each. But 63 officers had 20 or more reports each. The top 5% of the officers (ranked by number of reports) accounted for more than 20% of all reports

Blending the data disclosed even more troubling patterns. For example, in the years covered, one officer had 13 allegations of excessive force and improper tactics, 5 other complaint allegations, 28 use of force reports, and 1 shooting. Another had 6 excessive force/improper tactics allegations, 19 other complaint allegations, 10 use of force reports, and 3 shootings. A third officer had 7 excessive force/improper tactic allegations, 7 other complaint allegations, 27 use of force reports, and 1 shooting.

A review of personnel files of the 44 officers identified from the LAPD database who had six or more allegations of excessive force or improper tactics for the period 1986 through 1990 disclosed that the picture conveyed was often incomplete and at odds with contemporaneous comments appearing in complaint files. As a general matter, the performance evaluation reports for those problem officers were very positive, documenting every complimentary comment received and expressing optimism about the officer's progress in the Department. The performance evaluations generally did not give an accurate picture of the officers' disciplinary history, failing to record "sustained" complaints or to discuss their significance, and failing to assess the officer's judgment and contacts with the public in light of disturbing patterns of complaints.

While the precise size and identity of the problem group of officers cannot be specified without significant further investigation, its existence must be recognized and addressed. The LAPD has a number of tools to promote and enforce its policy that only reasonable and necessary force be used by officers. There are rewards and incentives such as promotions and pay upgrades. The discipline system exists to impose sanctions for misconduct. Officers can be reassigned. Supervisors can monitor and counsel officers under their command. Officers can be trained at the Police Academy and, more importantly, in the field, in the proper use of force.

The Commission believes that the Department has not made sufficient efforts to use those tools effectively to address the significant number of officers who appear to be using force excessively and improperly. The leadership of the LAPD must send a much clearer and more effective message that excessive force will not be tolerated and that officers and their supervisors will be evaluated to an important extent by how well they abide by and advance the Department's policy regarding use of force.

Racism and Bias

The problem of excessive force is aggravated by racism and bias within the LAPD. That nexus is sharply illustrated by the results of a survey recently taken by the LAPD of the attitudes of its sworn officers. The survey of 960 officers found that approximately one-quarter (24.5%) of 650 officers responding agreed that "racial bias (prejudice) on the part of officers toward minority citizens currently exists and contributes to a negative interaction between police and community." More than one-quarter (27.6%) agreed that "an officer's prejudice towards the suspect's race may lead to the use of excessive force."

The LAPD has made substantial progress in hiring minorities and women since the 1981 consent decree settling discrimination lawsuits against the Department. That effort should continue, including efforts to recruit Asians and other minorities who are not covered by the consent decree. The Department's statistics show, however, that the vast majority of minority officers are concentrated in the entry level police officer ranks in the Department. More than 80% of African-American, Latino and Asian officers hold the rank of Police Officer l-lll. Many minority officers cite white dominance of managerial positions within the LAPD as one reason for the Department's continued tolerance of racially motivated language and behavior.

The Commission heard substantial evidence that female officers utilize a style of policing that minimizes the use of excessive force. Data examined by the Commission indicate that LAPD female officers are involved in use of excessive force at rates substantially below those of male officers. Those statistics, as confirmed by both academic studies and anecdotal evidence, also indicate that women officers perform at least as well as their male counterparts when measured by traditional standards.

The Commission believes that the Chief of Police must seek tangible ways, for example, through the use of the discipline system, to establish the principle that racism and bias based on ethnicity, gender, or sexual orientation will not be tolerated within the Department. Racism and bias cannot be eliminated without active leadership from the top. Minority and female officers must be given full and equal opportunity to assume leadership positions in the LAPD. They must be assigned on a fully nondiscriminatory basis to the more desirable, "coveted" positions and promoted on the same nondiscriminatory basis to supervisory and managerial positions.

Community Policing

The LAPD has an organizational culture that emphasizes crime control over crime prevention and that isolates the police from the communities and the people they serve. With the full support of many, the LAPD insists on aggressive detection of major crimes and a rapid, seven-minute response time to calls for service. Patrol officers are evaluated by statistical measures (for example, the number of calls handled and arrests made) and are rewarded for being "hardnosed." This style of policing produces results, but it does so at the risk of creating a siege mentality that alienates the officer from the community.

Witness after witness testified to unnecessarily aggressive confrontations between U\PD officers and citizens, particularly members of minority communities.

A model of community policing has gained increased acceptance in other parts of the country during the past 10 years. The community policing model places service to the public and prevention of crime as the primary role of police in society and emphasizes problem solving, with active citizen involvement in defining those matters that are important to the community, rather than arrest statistics. Officers at the patrol level are required to spend less time in their cars communicating with other officers and more time on the street communicating with citizens. Proponents of this style of policing insist that addressing the causes of crime makes police officers more effective crime- fighters, and at the same time enhances the quality of life in the neighborhood.

The LAPD made early efforts to incorporate community policing principles and has continued to experiment with those concepts. For example, the LAPD's nationally recognized DARE program has been viewed by officers and the public alike as a major achievement. The LAPD remains committed, however, to its traditional style of law enforcement with an emphasis on crime control and arrests. LAPD officers are encouraged to command and to confront, not to communicate. Community policing concepts, if successfully implemented, offer the prospect of effective crime prevention and substantially improved community relations. Although community-based policing is not a panacea for the problem of crime in society, the U\PD should carefully implement this model on a City-wide basis. This will require a fundamental change in values. The Department must recognize the merits of community involvement in matters that affect local neighborhoods, develop programs to gain an adequate understanding of what is important to particular communities, and learn to manage departmental affairs in ways that are consistent with the community views expressed. Above all, the Department must understand that it is accountable to all segments of the community.

ILLEGAL IMMIGRATION

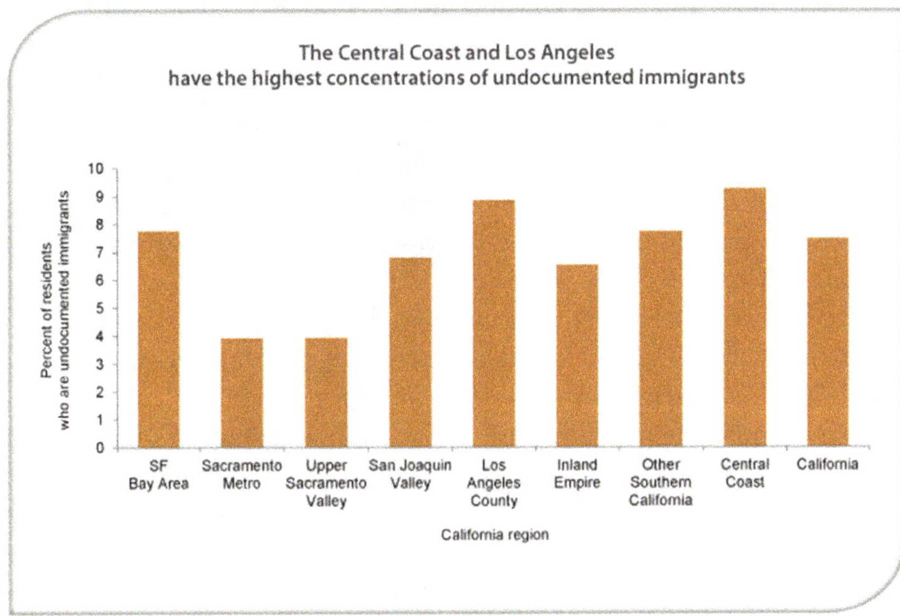

Sources: Lee, Hill, and McConville, "Access to the Health Care Safety Net in California" (PPIC, 2012); Hill and Johnson, "Unauthorized Immigrants in California: Estimates for Counties" (PPIC, 2011). Data from 2009.

From: Just the Facts: Undocumented Immigrants, PPIC, 2013.

FIGURE 12.3. Undocumented Immigrants in Los Angeles County (2012)

READING 72, PAMELA BURDMAN

"Closing the Door on Illegal Immigrants"

***San Francisco Chronicle*, October 23, 1994**

VOTERS, POLICYMAKERS AROUND THE COUNTRY WILL BE watching next month when Californians vote on a sweeping measure to cut off state-funded services for illegal immigrants.

Illegal immigration has become a hot-button issue, and nowhere is the temperature higher than in California. The state is host to about half of the nation's undocumented population, and continuing economic woes are contributing to fear and bitterness among voters.

Against that backdrop, Proposition 187 has been favored by wide margins in polls.

But the measure is so controversial that virtually every powerful lobby group in the state opposes it: Teachers, doctors, religious leaders, senior citizens, environmental groups, organized labor, immigrants' rights advocates and even some law enforcement officials have joined in the campaign to defeat 187. They worry that the proposed law would lead to scapegoating and cost the state billions of dollars—while doing nothing to stop illegal immigration.

"That's really our challenge, to change the message between now and November from being a referendum about illegal immigration, which we would lose, to something that is really about Proposition 187," said Ignatius Bau, an immigrant-rights advocate in San Francisco and an organizer for Californians United Against 187.

The ballot measure is endorsed by Governor Pete Wilson and the state Republican party and a grass-roots network of immigration-control groups. Backers predict that the measure will win handily, much like Proposition 13—a tax reform law opposed by every influential organization and politician in the state—did in 1978.

"The key to winning is the people of California," said Ron Prince, chairman of the pro-187 Save Our State Committee. "They know about this problem, and they know that there is no other solution being offered."

Proposition 187 would bar illegal immigrants from attending public schools and receiving nonemergency health care and other social services. It also would require schools, hospitals and law enforcement agencies to report suspected illegal immigrants to state and federal authorities. If voters approve the measure, it will undoubtedly face a series of legal and bureaucratic challenges. Exclusion of illegal immigrants from public schools, for example, is prohibited under a 1982 U.S. Supreme Court ruling. Authors admit that the proposed law was designed in the hope overturning that decision.

The measure could also put in jeopardy about $15 billion in federal funding to the state, because asking schools and hospitals to report the immigration status of the people they serve directly conflicts with federal law.

Proposition 187 is the product of a zealous anti-immigration movement that has galvanized a spectrum of voters—law-and-order activists, fiscal conservatives, xenophobes and even some legal immigrants—who resent those who break laws to come to this country. Their campaign began in the spring, with proponents complaining of an "invasion" of illegal immigrants taking advantage of state handouts at taxpayers' expense and destroying Californians' way of life.

Frustrated that the federal government has not done enough to control borders, they believe they have devised a way for the state to have its way on immigration policy.

"Once this passes, the message will be heard loud and clear, not only in Sacramento, but in Washington," said Rick Oltman, chairman of the San Rafael-based Yes on 187/Save Our State Committee. He dismisses the claim that the federal government would withdraw funding to the state. "If this passes, we're going to get more money for California, because Bill Clinton needs California to win in 1996," Oltman said.

When backers began gathering signatures to put Proposition 187 on the ballot, their most vocal opponents were immigrant-rights advocates, who traditionally have opposed attempts to curb immigration. They denounced the measure as blatant immigrant-bashing. But soon after the initiative qualified for the November ballot, a coalition of more mainstream opponents began signing on. They enlisted Woodward and McDowell, an expensive consulting firm with a winning formula for anti-initiative campaigns. Their typical strategy is to make people suspicious of the measure by picking out weaknesses in its language.

This time their attack is multipronged. Doctors say that withholding medical care will leave diseases untreated, posing a serious public-health threat. Teachers warn that keeping children out of school will create an illiterate, unskilled and crime-prone underclass. Senior citizens fear the state will lose $15 billion in federal money for Medi-Cal and other health programs.

"When this began, the public probably perceived that everybody was on the side of Yes on 187, and that the only people who opposed it were Latinos and some other ethnic groups and some liberal groups," said Karen Kapler, campaign manager for Taxpayers Against 187. "What we've been able to show people is that that's not the case, that in fact the world is opposing it—the entire education community, the medical community, the law-enforcement community. The 'no' side is where mainstream Californians are headed."

What Proposition 187 Would

SUMMARY

Supporters say Proposition 187 will stop the "incredible flow" of illegal immigrants that is throwing California into "social and economic bankruptcy."

Opponents say it could threaten public health and safety, create a police state mentality, and potentially cost California billions of dollars in federal funding.

Here is a summary of the ballot measure, together with pro and con arguments on its main points and the legal challenges the initiative faces if it passes in November:

SCHOOLS

Proposition 187 would exclude undocumented immigrants from enrolling in public schools or universities.

PRO: Those who violate immigration laws, including children, should not benefit from taxpayer-funded education, particularly when the state's resources are dwindling.

CON: Undocumented children would most likely remain in the state, becoming an unskilled and uneducated underclass that could be drawn to crime.

HURDLE: Would force a court challenge, because of conflict with 1982 Supreme Court ruling

HEALTH CARE

Under Proposition 187, undocumented immigrants would be barred from receiving care at medical facilities that receive public funds. Emergency and maternity care would continue, but prenatal and preventive care would not be available.

PRO: With health care funds for citizens already in jeopardy illegal immigrants should not receive a free ride.

CON: Allowing infectious diseases to go untreated would endanger public health and raise long-term costs.

HURDLE: The initiative could be challenged because its wording suggests that people willing to pay for medical treatment would first have to prove their legal presence in the country. It also suggests that nonemergency health care would be withheld from undocumented inmates in state prisons and county jails.

REPORTING

Schools, hospitals, and social service agencies would be required to report suspected illegal immigrants—including the parents of children who are citizens—to state and federal officials.

PRO: Cooperation of public officials is essential for immigration laws to be effectively enforced.

CON: Besides being costly to implement, this provision would impose a "police state mentality'" in hospitals and schools, leading to discrimination against people with accents or dark skin.
HURDLE: The law may violate federal regulations requiring that student and patient files be kept confidential, putting up to $15 billion in federal funds at risk. Educators and doctors might be reluctant to enforce the reporting provisions.

ALSO...

The initiative would cut off social service programs—possibly including foster care, family planning, disability insurance, and services provided by some nonprofit agencies—for illegal immigrants. It would also make manufacture, sale, and use of phony immigration documents, already a federal crime, a felony under state law.

WHO'S FOR PROPOSITION 187?

Pete Wilson
California Republican Party
United Organizations of Taxpayers, Inc.
United We Stand America of California (Ross Perot supporters)
San Fernando Valley Chambers of Commerce
Representative Dana Rohrabacher, R-Huntington Beach
Federation for American Immigration Reform
California Coalition for Immigration Reform
Americans Against Illegal Immigration
Stop the Out-of-Control Problems of Immigration Today

WHO'S AGAINST PROPOSITION 187?

California Teachers Association
California Medical Association
Congress of California Seniors
League of Women Voters
Mexican American Legal Defense and Education Foundation
California Labor Federation, AFL-CIO
Sierra Club
Catholic Charities
American Jewish Congress
Los Angeles County Sheriff Sherman Block

CONFRONTING A NEW CENTURY

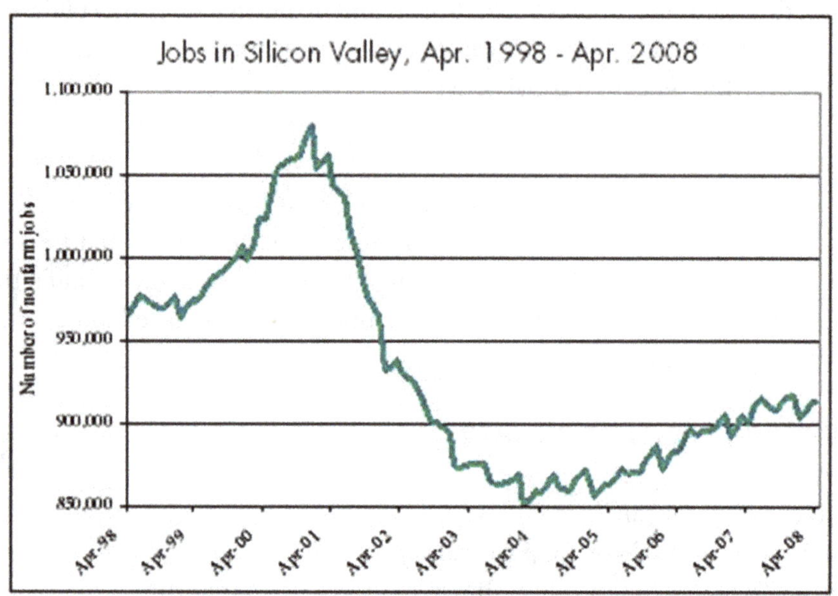

FIGURE 12.4. The "Great Recession" Hits Silicon Valley (2008)

READING 73

California Global Warming Solutions Act

2006

Assembly Bill 32 Overview

The passage of AB 32, the California Global Warming Solutions Act of 2006, marked a watershed moment in California's history. By requiring in law a sharp reduction of greenhouse gas (GHG) emissions, California set the stage for its transition to a sustainable, low-carbon future. AB 32 was the first program in the country to take a comprehensive, long-term approach to addressing climate change, and does so in a way that aims to improve the environment and natural resources while maintaining a robust economy.

What Does AB 32 Do?

AB 32 requires California to reduce its GHG emissions to 1990 levels by 2020 — a reduction of approximately 15 percent below emissions expected under a "business as usual" scenario.

Pursuant to AB 32, ARB must adopt regulations to achieve the maximum technologically feasible and cost-effective GHG emission reductions. The full implementation of AB 32 will help mitigate risks associated with climate change, while improving energy efficiency, expanding the use of renewable energy resources, cleaner transportation, and reducing waste.

Why is AB 32 Needed?

According to leading climate scientists from around the world, anthropogenic climate change (that caused by humans) is a significant and growing problem that must be addressed in order to avoid the worst effects. Climate change is the result of various GHGs that are emitted into the atmosphere, such as carbon dioxide (CO2) and methane (CH4), which have a heat forcing effect on the atmosphere. Sharp rises of GHGs over the last century and a half have led to higher overall worldwide temperatures, reduced snowpack in the higher elevations, greater fluctuations of temperature and precipitation, global sea level rise and more frequent and severe extreme weather events, including hurricanes, heatwaves and droughts.

AB 32 describes the problem for California:

> The Legislature finds and declares all of the following: (a) Global warming poses a serious threat to the economic well-being, public health, natural resources, and the environment of California. The potential adverse impacts of global warming include the exacerbation of air quality problems, a reduction in the quality and supply of water to the state from the Sierra snowpack, a rise in sea levels resulting in the displacement of thousands of coastal businesses and residences, damage to marine ecosystems and the natural environment, and an increase in the incidences of infectious diseases, asthma, and other human health-related problems.

> (b) Global warming will have detrimental effects on some of California's largest industries, including agriculture, wine, tourism, skiing, recreational and commercial fishing, and forestry. It will also increase the strain on electricity supplies necessary to meet the demand for summer air-conditioning in the hottest parts of the state.

Separate from AB 32, the State of California is also making efforts to adapt to a changing climate. The State's climate change adaptation efforts are being led by the Natural Resources Agency.

What Gases or Compounds are Covered Under AB 32?

AB 32 includes the major GHGs and groups of GHGs that are being emitted into the atmosphere. These gases include:

1. Carbon dioxide (CO2)
2. Methane (CH4)
3. Nitrous oxide (N2O)
4. 4.Hydrofluorocarbons (HFCs)
5. Perfluorocarbons (PFCs)
6. Sulfur hexafluoride (SF6)7. Nitrogen trifluoride* (NF3)

*Nitrogen trifluoride was not listed initially in AB 32 but was subsequently added to the list via legislation.

Other compounds, including some aerosols, can also have a strong heat forcing effect on the atmosphere. This includes black carbon, comprised of microscopic particles which are emitted from incomplete combustion of biomass and fossil fuels. Reducing black carbon and other so-called short-lived climate pollutants (methane, tropospheric ozone and some hydrofluorocarbons) will help us slow the acceleration of climate change sooner than by reducing emissions of other GHGs alone. It will also improve public health, and will be an important element of California's climate change program strategy.

ARB annually updates a statewide GHG inventory. The inventory includes estimates of GHGs emitted to the atmosphere by human activities in California.

How Will AB 32 Goals be Met?

AB 32 requires ARB to develop a Scoping Plan which lays out California's strategy for meeting the goals. The Scoping Plan must be updated every five years. In December 2008, the Board approved the initial Scoping Plan, which included a suite of measures to sharply cut GHG emissions. In May 2014, ARB approved the First Update to the Climate Change Scoping Plan (Update), which builds upon the initial Scoping Plan with new strategies and recommendations. The Update highlights California's progress toward meeting the near-term 2020 GHG emission reduction goals, highlights the latest climate change science and provides direction on how to achieve long-term emission reduction goal described in Executive Order S-3-05.

Reductions in GHG emissions will come from virtually all sectors of the economy and will be accomplished from a combination of policies, planning, direct regulations, market approaches, incentives and voluntary efforts. These efforts target GHG emission reductions from cars and trucks, electricity production, fuels, and other sources. The status of these efforts can be found in Appendix B of the Update.

Who is Implementing AB 32?

AB 32 directs the California Air Resources Board (ARB) to be the lead agency to implement the law. The Climate Action Team, made up of relevant state agencies, is charged with helping direct state efforts on the reduction of GHG emissions and engaging state agencies.

The Climate Action Team includes:

- California Environmental Protection Agency
- Governor's Office of Planning and Research
- California Air Resources Board
- Business, Consumer Services, and Housing Agency
- Government Operations Agency
- California Natural Resources Agency
- California Department of Public Health
- Office of Emergency Services
- California Transportation Agency
- California Energy Commission
- California Public Utilities Commission
- California Department of Food and Agriculture
- Department of Forestry and Fire Protection
- Department of Fish and Wildlife
- Department of Transportation
- Department of Water Resources
- Department of Resources Recycling and Recovery
- State Water Resources Control Board

INDIAN GAMING

FIGURE 12.5. Morongo Casino

READING 74

Excerpt from *California v. Cabazon Band of Mission Indians*

1987

JUSTICE WHITE DELIVERED THE opinion of the Court.

The Cabazon and Morongo Bands of Mission Indians, federally recognized Indian Tribes, occupy reservations in Riverside County, California. Each Band, pursuant to an ordinance approved by the Secretary of the Interior, conducts bingo games on its reservation. The Cabazon Band has also opened a card club at which draw poker and other card games are played. The games are open to the public and are played predominantly by non-Indians coming onto the reservations. The games are a major source of employment for tribal members, and the profits are the Tribes' sole source of income. The State of California seeks to apply to the two Tribes Cal.Penal Code Ann. § 326.5 (West Supp.1987). That statute does not entirely prohibit the playing of bingo but permits it when the games are operated and staffed by members of designated charitable organizations who may not be paid for their services. Profits must be kept in special accounts and used only for charitable purposes; prizes may not exceed $250 per game. Asserting that the bingo games on the two reservations violated each of these restrictions, California insisted that the Tribes comply with state law. Riverside County also sought to apply its local Ordinance No. 558, regulating bingo, as well as its Ordinance No. 331, prohibiting the playing of draw poker and the other card games.

The Tribes sued the county in Federal District Court seeking a declaratory judgment that the county had no authority to apply its ordinances inside the reservations and an injunction against their enforcement. The State intervened, the facts were stipulated, and the District Court granted the Tribes' motion for summary judgment, holding that neither the State nor the county had any authority to enforce its gambling laws within the reservations. The Court of Appeals for the Ninth Circuit affirmed, 783 F.2d 900 (1986), the State and the county appealed, and we postponed jurisdiction to the hearing on the merits.

In Pub.L. 280, Congress expressly granted six States, including California, jurisdiction over specified areas of Indian country within the States and provided for the assumption of jurisdiction by other States. In § 2, California was granted broad criminal jurisdiction over offenses committed by or against Indians within all Indian country within the State. Section 4's grant of civil jurisdiction was more limited. ..... Congress' primary concern in enacting Pub.L. 280 was combating lawlessness on reservations. The Act plainly was not intended to effect total assimilation of Indian tribes into mainstream American society. ..Accordingly, when a State seeks to enforce a law within an Indian reservation under the authority of Pub.L. 280, it must be determined whether the law is criminal in nature, and thus fully applicable to the reservation under § 2, or civil in nature, and applicable only as it may be relevant to private civil litigation in state court....

We are persuaded that the prohibitory/regulatory distinction is consistent with Bryan's construction of Pub.L. 280. It is not a bright-line rule, however; and as the Ninth Circuit itself observed, an argument of some weight may be made that the bingo statute is prohibitory rather than regulatory. But in the present case, the court reexamined the state law and reaffirmed its holding in Barona, and we are reluctant to disagree with that court's view of the nature and intent of the state law at issue here.

There is surely a fair basis for its conclusion. California does not prohibit all forms of gambling. California itself operates a state lottery, ...and daily encourages its citizens to participate in this state-run gambling. California also permits parimutuel horse-race betting. ....Although certain enumerated gambling games are prohibited, games not enumerated, including the card games played in the Cabazon card club, are permissible. The Tribes assert that more than 400 card rooms similar to the Cabazon card club flourish in California, and the State does not dispute this fact. Also, as the Court of Appeals noted, bingo is legally sponsored by many different organizations and is widely played in California. There is no effort to forbid the playing of bingo by any member of the public over the age of 18. Indeed, the permitted bingo games must be open to the general public. Nor is there any limit on the number of games which eligible organizations may operate, the receipts which they may obtain from the games, the number of games which a participant may play, or the amount of money which a participant may spend, either per game or in total. In light of the fact that California permits a substantial amount of gambling activity, including bingo, and actually promotes gambling through its state lottery, we must conclude that California regulates rather than prohibits gambling in general and bingo in particular.

California argues, however, that high stakes, unregulated bingo, the conduct which attracts organized crime, is a misdemeanor in California and may be prohibited on Indian reservations. But that an otherwise regulatory law is enforceable by criminal as well as civil means does not necessarily convert it into a criminal law within the meaning of Pub.L. 280. .... Accordingly, we conclude that Pub.L. 280 does not authorize California to enforce Cal.Penal Code Ann. § 326.5 (West Supp.1987) within the Cabazon and Morongo Reservations.

California and Riverside County also argue that the Organized Crime Control Act (OCCA) authorizes the application of their gambling laws to the tribal bingo enterprises. The OCCA makes certain violations of state and local gambling laws violations of federal law. ... There is nothing in OCCA indicating that the States are to have any part in enforcing federal criminal laws or are authorized to make arrests on Indian reservations that in the absence of OCCA they could not effect. We are not informed of any federal efforts to employ OCCA to prosecute the playing of bingo on Indian reservations, although there are more than 100 such enterprises currently in operation, many of which have been in existence for several years, for the most part with the encouragement of the Federal Government. Whether or not, then, the Sixth Circuit is right and the Ninth Circuit wrong about the coverage of OCCA, a matter that we do not decide, there is no warrant for California to make arrests on reservations and thus, through OCCA, enforce its gambling laws against Indian tribes.

II

This case also involves a state burden on tribal Indians in the context of their dealings with non-Indians since the question is whether the State may prevent the Tribes from making available high stakes bingo games to non-Indians coming from outside the reservations. Decision in this case turns on whether state authority is pre-empted by the operation of federal law; and "state jurisdiction is pre-empted . . . if it interferes or is incompatible with federal and tribal interests reflected in federal law, unless the state interests at stake are sufficient to justify the assertion of state authority." ... The inquiry is to proceed in light of traditional notions of Indian sovereignty and the congressional goal of Indian self-government, including its "overriding goal" of encouraging tribal self-sufficiency and economic development.....

These are important federal interests. They were reaffirmed by the President's 1983 Statement on Indian Policy. More specifically, the Department of the Interior, which has the primary responsibility for carrying out the Federal Government's trust obligations....These policies and actions, which demonstrate the Government's approval and active promotion of tribal bingo enterprises, are of particular relevance in this case. The Cabazon and Morongo Reservations contain no natural resources which can be exploited. The tribal games at present provide the sole source of revenues for the operation of the tribal governments and the provision of tribal services. They are also the major sources of employment on the reservations. Self-determination and economic development are not within reach if the Tribes cannot raise revenues and provide employment for their members. The Tribes' interests obviously parallel the federal interests......

The sole interest asserted by the State to justify the imposition of its bingo laws on the Tribes is in preventing the infiltration of the tribal games by organized crime. To the extent that the State seeks to prevent any and all bingo games from being played on tribal lands while permitting regulated, off-reservation games, this asserted interest is irrelevant and the state and county laws are pre-empted. .... Even to the extent that the State and county seek to regulate short of prohibition, the laws are pre-empted. The State insists that the high stakes offered at tribal games are attractive to organized crime, whereas the controlled games authorized under California law are not. This is surely a legitimate concern, but we are unconvinced that it is sufficient to escape the pre-emptive force of federal and tribal interests apparent in this case. California does not allege any present criminal involvement in the Cabazon and Morongo enterprises, and the Ninth Circuit discerned none. ... An official of the Department of Justice has expressed some concern about tribal bingo operations, but far from any action being taken evidencing this concern—and surely the Federal Government has the authority to forbid Indian gambling enterprises—the prevailing federal policy continues to support these tribal enterprises, including those of the Tribes involved in this case.

We conclude that the State's interest in preventing the infiltration of the tribal bingo enterprises by organized crime does not justify state regulation of the tribal bingo enterprises in light of the compelling federal and tribal interests supporting them. State regulation would impermissibly infringe on tribal government, and this conclusion applies equally to the county's attempted regulation of the Cabazon card club. We therefore affirm the judgment of the Court of Appeals and remand the case for further proceedings consistent with this opinion.

It is so ordered.

READING 75

"Rincon Band Becomes First California Tribe to Renegotiate Tribal-State Gaming Compact with Federal Courts"

***Indian Country Today*, 2013**

AFTER SEVEN YEARS OF LITIGATION AND NEGOTIATIONS, the Rincon Band of Luiseno Indians has renegotiated its 1999 tribal-state gaming compact. The tribe took an unorthodox route to gain approval, setting a legal and political precedent by obtaining the first California agreement negotiated through the federal courts.

Kevin Washburn, assistant secretary of Indian Affairs, approved the secretarial procedures on February 8.

With the Rincon victory in the courts, the state was forced to end a number of illegal practices related to negotiating tribal state casino compacts and directed by the Southern District Federal Court to meet with the Rincon Band to negotiate a compact that complied with federal law.

The Rincon Band and California Governor Edmund G. Brown began negotiations in earnest over a year ago, after the U.S. Supreme Court refused to hear the state's appeal of the 2004 Rincon vs. Schwarzenegger lawsuit. The parties reached agreement on the vast majority of issues within the limited time frame set by law and the court. However, some issues remained unresolved at the expiration of the court-ordered deadlines.

On April 11, 2012, both sides submitted final offers to a mediator for baseball arbitration. On June 13, 2012, the court-appointed mediator, the Hon. Edward Panelli, former State Supreme Court Justice, selected the tribe's version as most consistent with the findings of the court and forwarded it to Interior for review. Gov. Brown had a 60-day window to approve the Rincon offer, or do nothing, leaving the final approval to the federal government in the form of secretarial compact procedures issued by the Interior.

When Rincon sued Gov. Arnold Schwarzenegger for "illegal taxation" and "bad faith" in renegotiations for a gaming compact, seeking to add 900 new machines to the tribe's gaming enterprise, Harrah's Rincon Casino and Resort, few expected the band to win—especially since California tribes had been unable to get the federal government to step in and force the state to comply with the rules of tribal state gaming compact negotiations, specifically bad faith remedies, beginning in 1990, when tribes were desperate to make gaming legal by negotiating a compact with a recalcitrant Gov. Pete Wilson. However, after seven years of litigation going from the federal District Court, twice to the 9th Circuit Court of Appeals, and a failed attempt by the state to involve the U.S. Supreme Court, the Rincon Band prevailed. The federal court stepped in, imposing oversight of compact negotiations between the state and the tribe, making it the first time in California legal remedies that an impasse in negotiations between a tribe and the state under the federal Indian Gaming Regulatory Act (IGRA) was triggered.

In the past, states took advantage of the desperation of tribal governments to acquire casino gaming as a means to climb out of poverty by blackmailing them with revenue sharing demands that literally wiped out the economic incentive and cash flow needed to ensure success of the enterprise.

To Rincon Chairman Bo Mazzetti, the frustrations, time and cost of the lawsuit were a price that had to be paid to protect tribal sovereignty and the expectation in federal law that tribes are equals in compact negotiations.

"The federal definition of the goal of Indian gaming is to generate revenues to fund tribal government responsibilities and obligations to provide jobs, health care, social and safety services for tribal members, not to pad or fix a state's budget," said Mazzetti.

"Someone had to make the state own up to the fact its negotiations with tribes were illegal. It was obvious Gov. Schwarzenegger was not interested in recognizing tribal sovereignty, or voluntarily abiding by laws governing tribal state compact negotiations," he added.

The lawsuit and resulting Rincon compact changed the scope and context of tribal state negotiations in California. Specifically, the state cannot demand revenue sharing as a condition for concluding a compact. Federal law is clear that states cannot use the compact process to impose taxes on tribal gaming revenues.

Also, if a tribe is willing to share gaming revenue with the state, the state must offer the tribe something of meaningful value that the tribe desires, above and beyond the state's legal obligations under IGRA. In other words, there has to be an exchange of mutual benefits.

In California, this means tribal exclusivity for "Class Three Games" can no longer be used by the state to leverage revenue sharing of 50 to 100 percent of casino profits. The courts held that exclusivity is granted by the voters and institutionalized in the state constitution; therefore, the governor is not in a position to offer it up, or take it away at the negotiation table.

At all times during the negotiations, Rincon was willing to pay for state regulatory costs and mitigate off-reservation impacts, but the Schwarzenegger administration overreached and demanded a severe tax on gross revenue to be paid into the state's General Fund, the press release states.

"Schwarzenegger's greed really made the case for us," noted Mazzetti. "Removing the economic incentives by demanding such a large share of future tribal revenue was not only illegal, it was economically counter intuitive. Tribal gaming is a positive example of California Indians pulling ourselves up by our own bootstraps, and generating benefits that go beyond the tribal community. For example, in 2010, our casino enterprise was responsible for 2,100 good, tax paying jobs; $20 million in state and local tax revenues; and another $276 million in purchases of goods and services invested in the regional economy."

The new Rincon compact eliminates the Schwarzenegger regulatory demands that went beyond gaming, broaching a tribe's governmental authority. Among them is the practice of obligating a tribe to agree to local contributions in significant revenue sharing dollar amounts to mitigate impacts prior to finalization of the compact and governor's signature.

Prior to the Rincon case, a governor could hold a tribe's economic growth ransom against one-sided demands by the state. IGRA remedies are intended to ensure compact negotiations are between equals, and the power of the state is not used to deny gaming to the tribes.

"We didn't take on this case for Rincon alone; we did it for all the tribes. And our goal to bring compacting back to the legitimacy of its legislative roots was applauded by the Department of Interior.

"The Rincon case and tribal compact offer proof that tribes have the law on our side and we can fight unfair and illegal practices by state governors," said Mazzetti, explaining that "our main objectives in negotiations with the Brown administration was to produce a prototype of fair negotiations envisioned by federal law. This included removing the illegal and politically inspired regulatory and revenue sharing requirements of the Schwarzenegger administration."

"Recalcitrant states had turned IGRA on its head, extorting tribes at the negotiation table to divert critically needed tribal governmental revenue, intended to fund tribal services and programs, to the state. These are funds tribes need to diversify their economies and take them out of the dire poverty that preceded Indian gaming. These states did not offer their revenues to assist when the tribes had nothing, but are the first with their hands out when the tribes begin to see some financial opportunity," said Scott Crowell, lead legal counsel throughout the litigation.

"Rincon fought hard, because, we believed winning this case enables other tribes to negotiate compacts that are fair to all parties and restore IGRA, as Congress intended; and also to educate people that the purpose of Indian gaming is first and foremost to promote tribal self-sufficiency and strong tribal government."

There were disappointments, and, as Chairman Mazzetti acknowledged, "unfinished business" on the way to finalizing the compact. One victim was the shared benefit fund with San Diego County.

In an attempt to establish an alternate, ongoing vehicle to fund community mitigation impacts directly through the county, rather than funneling the money through the state, or the faltering state-controlled Special Distribution Fund, as presently practiced, the band worked with San Diego County in an attempt to establish a shared benefit fund.

"Rincon was seeking a more fiscally responsible way of funding and prioritizing community mitigation projects by partnering with San Diego County to share in funding regional needs like traffic and transportation, police and fire services—all appropriately related to casino impacts. These programs, even though off the reservation, make sense because they benefit the tribal community and its economic ventures, as well as the larger non-Indian community," said Crowell.

The fund would have resulted in a percentage of revenues from Rincon's gaming profits to flow annually over the 25-year-life of the compact.

Unfortunately, according to Mazzetti, due to timelines established by IGRA and imposed by the federal court there was not enough time for the state, county and tribal negotiators to overcome the obstacles needed to secure a benefit from the state, warranting a legal exchange of revenues from the tribe.

"Sitting down with the county, we were able to explore many solid and reasonable cooperative approaches to addressing mutual community needs, and the San Diego County Rincon Benefit Sharing plan was a big one," noted Mazzetti.

"In the process, we started cutting through bureaucratic barriers in the state and the county to meaningful cooperation and benefit sharing. I am hopeful we will continue to work on issues such as formulas for sharing taxes on tobacco and fuel products sold on Indian lands. This is complicated and politically sensitive stuff. However, if we can move forward on agreements we discussed with the Brown administration, Rincon could reciprocate by adopting a local benefit sharing plan."

Critical new terms of the compact include:

Provides for an increase to 2,250 machines. (Current compact limit is 2,000 machines.)

Extends term of compact through 2037. (Current compact is set to expire in 2020.)

Provides for payment of proportionate share of state's costs to regulate gaming directly to state. Nearly $ 1 million per year is anticipated to be paid by Rincon under this provision. (Currently state regulatory costs are appropriated by the legislature out of the special distribution fund.)

Preserves existing obligations to revenue sharing trust fund. (Rincon currently pays in excess of $ 3million per year into fund, the proceeds of which are distributed to non-gaming tribes.) Under the new compact, RSTF would receive an additional $1 million, with the total exceeding $4 million if the band operates at 2,250 machine capacity.

The compact retains the regulatory scheme of 1999 compacts. (Rincon rejected the Schwarzenegger compact model as overly intrusive into tribal self-governance.)

Unresolved issues that the band and state commit to pursue outside of compact litigation:

Rincon/San Diego County Shared Benefits Funds: Rincon and country agreed upon preliminary statement of terms in September 2011 and will continue discussions.

Tribal/state compact(s) resolving issues of taxation: Substantial discussions occurred regarding unresolved issues of state-imposed taxes of gasoline, tobacco products and other on-reservation sales. Those discussions set a foundation for negotiating government-to-government tax compacts.

BATTLE OVER GAY MARRIAGE

FIGURE 12.6. Rally for Proposition 8 in Fresno

FIGURE 12.7. A crowd of people gather in front of the California Supreme Court headquarters in San Francisco

QUESTIONS FOR STUDY

1. What were the conclusions of the independent Commission of the Los Angeles Police Department about the LAPD's use of force? According to the commission, how is excessive force related to issues of racism and bias? How might such issues be addressed in the future?
2. Why do you think a majority of voters in 1994 voted in favor of Proposition 187? How might the fight over this initiative have reflected larger conflicts within the state of California? How does this issue compare to earlier, as well as more recent, debates about immigration to California?
3. Think about the California Global Warming Solutions Act. What is going to be required of Californians going forward to meet the goals it sets? Do you foresee this having any impact on your day-to-day life? Why or why not?
4. Why have many tribes in California embraced gaming? Do you regard this as a positive or a negative development for the Native peoples of California? Why?
5. California has always been regarded as a trendsetter. Ideas, innovations, and images from and of California have been known to have impacts well beyond the state's borders. Do you think now, in the early 21st Century, California still holds that place in the national and international imagination? Why or why not?

CREDITS

1. Fig. 12.1a: "LA County Racial/Ethnic Breakdown, 1960 map," http://uselectionatlas.org/FORUM/index.php?topic=169073.msg3617544#msg3617544. Copyright in the Public Domain.
2. Fig. 12.1b: "LA County Racial/Ethnic Breakdown, 2000 map," http://uselectionatlas.org/FORUM/index.php?topic=169073.msg3617544#msg3617545. Copyright in the Public Domain.
3. Fig. 12.2: Paul Watts, "Percent of Structural Damage Map," http://etd.lsu.edu/docs/available/etd-1111103-101742/unrestricted/Watts_thesis.pdf. Copyright in the Public Domain.

4. Report of the Independent Commission on the Los Angeles Police Department, pp. viii-xv. Copyright © 1991 by Independent Commission on the Los Angeles Police Department.
5. Fig. 12.3: "Just the Facts: Undocumented Immigrants," http://www.ppic.org. Copyright © 2013 by Public Policy Institute of California.
6. Pamela Burdman, "Closing the Door on Illegal Immigrants," *San Francisco Chronicle.* Copyright © 1994 by Hearst Communications Inc. Reprinted with permission.
7. Fig. 12.4: "Silicon Valley Jobs, 1998-2008," http://www.wpusa.org/blog/2008_05_01_archive.html. Copyright in the Public Domain.
8. "California Global Warming Solutions Act of 2006," http://www.arb.ca.gov/cc/ab32/ab32.htm. Copyright in the Public Domain.
9. Fig. 12.4a: "Satellite Image of California," http://www.arb.ca.gov/cc/ab32/ab32.htm. Copyright in the Public Domain.
10. Fig. 12.4b: "Climate Change Scoping Plan," http://www.arb.ca.gov/cc/ab32/ab32.htm. Copyright in the Public Domain.
11. Fig. 12.5: Takwish, "Morongo Casino, Riverside County, CA," http://commons.wikimedia.org/wiki/File:MorongoCasino1.JPG. Copyright in the Public Domain.
12. *California v. Cabazon Band of Mission Indians.* Copyright in the Public Domain.
13. ICTMN Staff, "Rincon Band Becomes First California Tribe To Renegotiate Tribal-State Gaming Compact With Federal Courts," Indian Country Today Media Network.com. Copyright © 2013 by Indian Country Today Media Network, LLC. Reprinted with permission.
14. Fig. 12.7: Copyright © Jamison Wieser (CC BY-SA 2.0) at https://commons.wikimedia.org/wiki/File:Supreme_Court_Prop8.jpg.
15. Fig. 12.6: Copyright © 1Flatworld (Richard Johnstone) (CC BY-SA 2.0) at https://commons.wikimedia.org/wiki/File:Fresno_-_Prop_8_Rally.jpg.

CPSIA information can be obtained
at www.ICGtesting.com
Printed in the USA
LVHW061428130820
663089LV00004B/97

9 781634 879699